CHANDIGARH
rethink

Publishers of Architecture, Art, and Design
Gordon Goff: Publisher

www.oroeditions.com
info@oroeditions.com

Published by ORO Editions

Text: Manu P. Sobti, Vinayak Bharne, Sangeeta Bagga-Mehta, Arijit Sen, Dongsei Kim & Arpan Johari
Book Design: Manu P. Sobti & Kinghi Thao
Edited: Manu P. Sobti
Project Manager: Jake Anderson

10 9 8 7 6 5 4 3 2 1 First Editions

Library of Congress data available upon request.

ISBN: 978-1-939621-36-8

Color Separations and Printing: ORO Group Ltd.
Printed in China.

International Distribution: www.oroeditions.com/distribution

ORO Editions makes a continuous effort to minimize the overall carbon footprint of its publications. As part of this goal, ORO Editions, in association with Global ReLeaf, arranges to plant trees to replace those used in the manufacturing of the paper produced for its books. Global ReLeaf is an international campaign run by American Forests, one of the world's oldest nonprofit conservation organizations. Global ReLeaf is American Forests' education and action program that helps individuals, organizations, agencies, and corporations improve the local and global environment by planting and caring for trees.

CHANDIGARH
rethink

Transforming Ruralities & Edge(ness) in Global Urbanities

edited by

MANU P. SOBTI

Cities grow outward swallowing up agrarian land and locating undesirable elements in the midst: Delhi's 'thick' northwestern edge on the GT Karnal Road near Bhalswa is characterized by the Bhalswa garbage dumping site, which was commissioned in 1994, and should ideally have been shut down in 2006. Around 2,700 metric tons of Delhi's garbage is still estimated to find its way to the landfill every day. The Municipal Corporation of Delhi (MCD), which manages the dumping site, admits to having exceeded the ground's capacity, but say they have no alternative. Bhalswa, one of three large garbage landfills, stands on previously agricultural land, and meets none of the scientific requirements for a landfill. There is no leachate treatment facility, so byproducts released during the decomposition seep (especially during the annual monsoon) to contaminate the groundwater, the nearby Bhalswa lake and the Yamuna River.

TO NEZAR —

AW SALUTES + REGARDS —
Mann

CONTENTS

On a cold, foggy winter morning in early-January of 2008, I arrived at New Delhi's IGI Airport with my first batch of 16 students from the University of Wisconsin-Milwaukee's School of Architecture & Urban Planning (SARUP). As we negotiated our way through the older avatar of the now-swanky terminal building, I quickly realized that arriving in a familiar setting on ones own is much removed from arrival with 'new' visitors who much depend on your interpretive stories, among other things. On this particular occasion, and in the days following, the detailed logistics of our travel and accommodations gave way to my own self-reflection on why we were in India and how I could effectively enable a 'self-conscious', critical reading of India's urbanities among my eager students.

While I had planned precisely such a trip for several years (even through my years as a graduate student), and carefully choreographed how and where we would go, my arrival in New Delhi this time around perplexed me about which side I was actually looking at India from - was I within or without? It would make all the difference to how I viewed India through new eyes, while reconstructing an image of place, culture, and event for myself and for others. Over this 2008 visit, in our three weeks of our travels, we focused mainly on the city of Ahmedabad, besides short side trips to New Delhi, Chandigarh, and Agra. In conversations with the students, even I re-learned to appreciate my immersive historical and cultural narrative on the Indian subcontinent. In the weeks following, the most critical objective became providing my students with a first-hand exposure to the processes of globalization and its dramatic impact on the making (and un-making) of physical and cultural environments. This was perhaps the only way even I could fathom the multitude of changes that India's new-found economic liberalization had emblazoned across her spectacular landscapes.

Over the next few years (2008-2015), I was able to direct six additional and successful iterations of this unique Indian journey, among my many journeys eastwards across Asia. However, beyond the obvious changes to our itineraries, perhaps my own rather unexpected discovery was that of the myriad of urban agencies and embedded actors who casually and deliberately left their marks on the rapidly expanding towns and cities. These urban places were big and small, countless morphing from their existence as petty towns to larger settlements, and all visibly embodying conflict, contestation, adjustment, and reconciliation between the past and present, their architects (or self-professed designers) continually seeking to render these battles in the forms of buildings, spaces, and places. This recognition of a multi-layered cultural phenomenon where the elephant and skyscraper seamlessly co-existed, with its complex nuances determining architecture and cities, with aesthetics emerging as a possibility versus a necessity, was seen as most instructive for students beginning to identify a design language of their own. Apparently, urban places were most substantially made via 'no-architectural' processes, with 'formal' legislation only making minimal impact. So while the more monumental, public works often met the eye in public space, their manner of usurpation by the public was beyond the gamut of any existing formal examination. I also discovered the 'rural' connections to urbanity, not as the 'expected' anti-thesis to urbanity, but as a series of formal and spatial strategies with strong validity much at par with the urban context.

While in India, I had the opportunity to formulate workshops with local schools of architecture and design, especially in Ahmedabad and Chandigarh, where we actually emerged as regular visitors, well-noticed by the friendly paparazzi and local students who generously collaborated on these workshops. While these travels dramatically changed my own insights into the India that I had grown up in, these sojourns have also jogged the global awareness of the one hundred or so students who participated on my multiple India Winterims over the years. This self-conscious, if not uncomfortable 'reading' of an India characterized by her 'changing globalities', has also transmitted to the six or fewer degrees of separation that served as the extended community around my students. About a dozen of my former Winterim participants visited India at least once, if not twice, following their travels as part of my group. A handful also teamed up with student and faculty collaborators at architecture schools across India, their visits resulting in directed/guided studies upon their return to the United States.

Three among my directed visits to India resulted in urban design studios at sites centered in Ahmedabad (2009) and Chandigarh (2010 & 2015). This volume references these three studios within the scope of my own research writings on Indian urbanities and rural change alongside invited contributions from a group of specialist scholars. Within this broad overview, it concentrates on the third - the SARUP Urban Edge Award Studio, which was conducted in Chandigarh and Milwaukee over Spring 2015, as one among a series of orchestrated, public events. The others included two international seminars and two mini seminars held at Milwaukee, and an exhibition-symposium that shared completed studio work in Chandigarh. In summary, the Urban Edge Award Studio brought together a total of 12 invited speakers alongside a multitude of participants both in the United States (at Milwaukee) and India (at Chandigarh).

Needless to say, this continued focus on the trials and tribulations of modernity in India, and its vicarious extrapolations to other regions of the Global South, would have only been possible given my utter fascination for what constitutes the intrinsic grammar of the Indian city. On how the past, present, and future of the city may (or may not) be reconciled, and the growing acceptance that architecture may only then be a means to an end, versus the end in itself. This book is an example of this fascination with urbanity and how it may be elaborated and mapped, via active participation and fieldwork. The 'activism' suggested in this volume via the studio 'interventions', is also one suggesting change and self reflection, and of looking beyond simplistic descriptions.

Manu P. Sobti   Milwaukee WI   May 27th 2016

Acknowledgements

This volume would have been impossible without the generous support of the following individuals in the United States, India, and Australia:

- Sangeeta Bagga-Mehta for remaining a wonderful and most able collaborator through the years of my India trips
- Vinayak Bharne, Sangeeta Bagga-Mehta, Ameen Farooq, Dongsei Kim, Antonio Furgiule & Arijit Sen for their participation in the 1st Urban Edge 'Sustainability' Symposium held in Milwaukee (April 2015)
- Manzoor Ahtesham, Peter Scriver , Luis Feduchi, Antonio Furgiule & Arijit Sen for their scholarly contributions to the 2nd Urban Edge 'Redux" Symposium held in Milwaukee (Oct. 2015)
- Anoma Pieris & Avigail Sachs for their presentations at the Urban Edge "Oppositions & Positions" Mini-Symposium held in Milwaukee (Oct. 2015)
- Dominique Waag, Sean Anderson & Arpan Johari for leading and directing public discussion and debate at the Urban Edge "Chandigarh" Seminar and Public Exhibition held at Chandigarh (Sept. 2015)
- Kinghi Thao for his exemplary skills, precision and commitment throughout the publication process
- Kate Malaia, Sahar Hosseini, Nader Sayadi, Leila Saboori & Dilrabo Toshaeva for their contributions during the 'Urban Edge 2015' Events (Fall & Spring Semesters)
- Gordon Goff & Jake Anderson at ORO Editions for their guidance and support towards project inception and completion
- Anurag Aggarwal IAS Home Secretary & Secretary of Culture for his support in Chandigarh
- Bhavana Garg IAS Commissioner Municipal Corporation for her generous support towards the Urban Edge Chandigarh Exhibition and Symposium in Oct. 2015
- Kavita Singh Director Tourism Chandigarh Administration for her generous support towards the Urban Edge Chandigarh Exhibition and Symposium in Oct. 2015
- Saravjit Singh IAS Finance Secretary UT for his support and guidance in Chandigarh
- P. S. Grewal Director Projects - Orbit Apartment Construction Pvt. Ltd. for his active participation on the Urban Edge Design Reviews 2014-15
- Vikas Gupta COO North - Emaar MGF Land Ltd. for his active participation on the Urban Edge Design Reviews 2015
- Dominique Waag (Director, Alliance Francaise-Chandigarh) for his generous support towards organizing the Urban Edge Exhibition at the Alliance Francaise-Chandigarh in Oct. 2015
- SARUP students Richard O. VanDerWal, Andreya S. Veintimilla, Nicholas Bree, Sisco S. Hollard, Michael J. Freund, James D. Ford, Chao Thao, Jessica R. Yester, Christopher W. Doerner, Anna Czajkowska-Szot, Hyrom Leon-Quartiez Stokes, Dominic M. Quinan for their very active participation in the Urban Edge Studio over Spring 2015 and travelling to India
- Drishti Sidhu, Kashish Singla, Vikram Singh Virk, Nikhil Pratap Singh, Geet Khurana, Anandita and Saniya Arif for their generous collaboration from the Chandigarh side during our annual India Winterim visits 2013-15
- Beeba Sobti for her contacts and organization in New Delhi, and Aparna Datey for her editorial support
- Dean Bob Greenstreet at the School of Architecture, University of Wisconsin-Milwaukee for delegating the Urban Edge Award Studio 2015 to my charge
- Dean and Head of School Sandra Kaji-O'Grady, Antony Moulis and Brit Winnen at the School of Architecture, University of Queensland-Brisbane towards suppporting this publication via a subvention

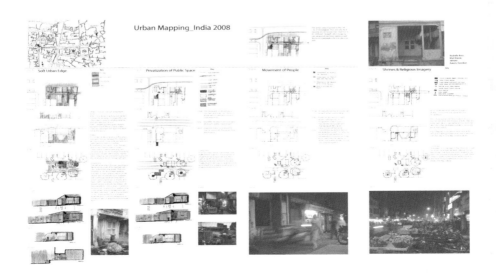

फाउन्ड्री नगर
FOUNDRY NAGAR
← 1 Km.

View of the in-between city of transit, trucking, people, and dust - the last stop before Foundry Nagar (colony) at Agra. Such 'non-places' exist on the outskirts of countless Indian towns, and serve as vantage points that connect to the nearby agricultural centers and villages. These non-places are places of temporal human choreographies, not necessarily buildings. The de-ruralization of landscapes on the urban fringes can create such non-places therby transforming the cultural meaning of place.

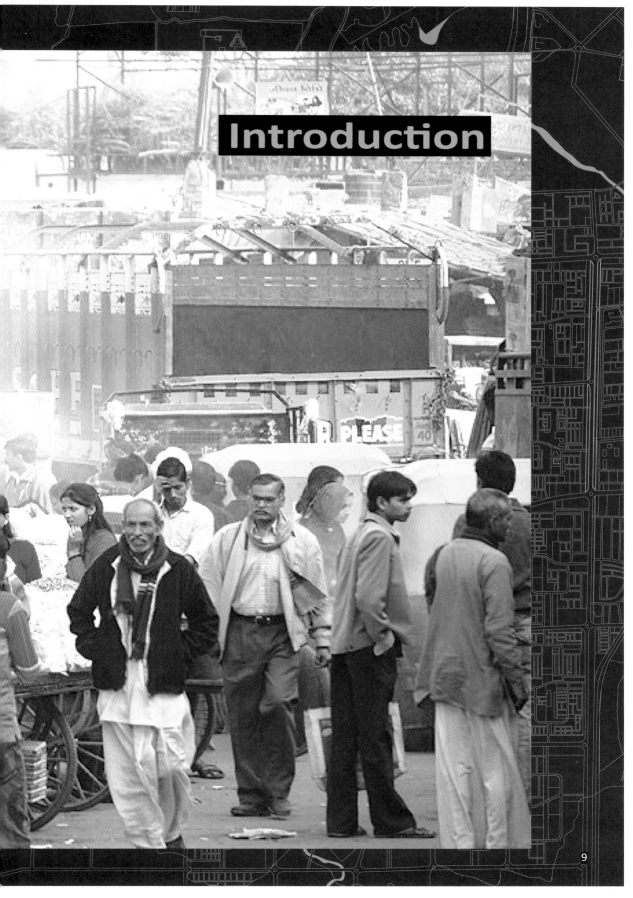

Introduction

Image 1:

The settlement of Kansal (Punjab) seen from the Chandigarh Secretariat Rooftop: The thick cover of trees around the Capitol Complex gives way to the densely built up fabric of Kansal village. Prior to expansion, Kansal was characterized by one distinct street that organized the layout of the village; Corbusier's plan conceptually linked the city to the foothills via this connection. Agricultural land lay to its east. Today, much of the agricultural plots are built up or else undergoing change.

Transforming Ruralities & Edge(ness)
in Global Urbanities

MANU P. SOBTI

ABSTRACT

Within the broad purview of postcolonial urbanities undergoing global change, scholars have often examined the mercurial changes wrought on the urban artifact owing to contingencies and conditions germinating from within. Little attention has been invested towards comprehending the transformations of the landscape matrix that traditionally held, and continues to hold, this perplexing field of urbanities. In suggesting the interrogation of the ex-urban landscape matrix as a point of departure, this introductory essay introduces the scenario of a rapidly de-ruralizing landscape between and along the very edges of globalizing cities in the Indian context. It questions if these edges are urban or rural, and evaluates the somewhat un-questioned validity of viewing these edges from within versus without. In setting out a frame of reference, it also views the urban edge as a physical boundary and border, a metaphoric concept, and as a design methodology, employing it as a limiting and delimiting component within the changing urbanities of the city. In the face of these imminent changes, what shall be the character of India's global cities in the future decades? Would they be sites of conflict or polycentric zones of tolerated contestations, similar to inhospitable border zones? How would proximal ruralities effect and be affected by globalizing urbanities? What impact shall the accelerated transformation of this predominantly rural urban hinterland matrix have on the political economies of proximal cities and urban centers?

Smart Cities

In 2015, within the purview of its continuing nationalistic development narratives, the Indian parliament approved its first-ever "Smart Cities Mission" - an urban renewal and retrofitting program whose specific objectives targeted the staged development of some 100 cities across the country.[1] Today, about a year since the program's inception, this ambitious mission continues with the Union Ministry of Urban Development directive underscoring emerging smart cities as those that would be "citizen-friendly and sustainable ... " as they serve to become the potential and real satellite cores of larger urban centers while transitioning into modernized extensions of existing, mid-sized towns.[2] Besides renewal and retrofitting, there also remains a demonstrated interest in the Green-City and Pan-City developments,[3] clearly showing that the Indian bureaucracy is not just interested in smart growth within pre-existing conditions, but also in achieving these goals via ex-novo developments on 'fresh' sites.

India's critical need to accommodate its urban migrants has always occupied the public debate, but this move to recognize the urgency of this task via a specific mission remains unprecedented. However, beyond the carefully staged and manicured images of these smart urbanities that now proliferate freely on the Internet and public media, this penchant for urban 'smart-ness' also opens a plethora of compelling questions. For one, what qualitative (and not necessarily, quantitative) benchmarks would allow for initiatives such as these to be evaluated

1

... dor, where Bus Rapid Transit corridors as well as suburban train networks are linked with pedestrian and cycle lanes. Furthermore, there are pods to carry people directly from point to point, with no stop at intervening stations.

on availability of public transport as well as the condition of traffic on routes.

■ Digital parking meters send information to mobile phones when a space opens up.

Seven smart cities are being developed by states with foreign assistance as part of the Delhi-Mumbai Industrial Corridor (DMIC); work has already begun.

Seven smart cities each will be built in Rajasthan, Gujarat, Karnataka and Kerala

THE PRIME MINISTER'S DREAM PROJECT

Coimbatore, Bangalore, Mangalore, Jamshedpur, Mumbai and Chennai have launched initiatives for deployment of advanced communications systems, Metro

■ The Narendra Modi government plans to

2

India's 2015 urban count

Data: Census of India 2011

41 Cities with populations of 1m to 2m

13 Cities with populations of 2m to 5m

9 Cities with populations of 5m and over

3

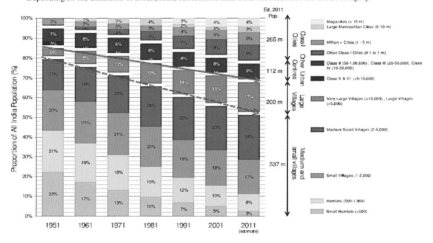

Depending on the definition of urban, more settlements shift from the rural into the urban category.

4

	1894	2013	2014
Social Impact Assessment (SIA)	No provision	SIA is a must for every acquisition	Not required if for security, defense, rural infra, industrial corridors and social infra
Consent from affected people	No provision	Consent of 80 % of displaced people required in case of acquisition for private companies and public-private partnerships.	Not required if for security, defense, rural infra, industrial corridors and social infra
Multi crop land	No provision	Only in extreme circumstances, where multi-cropped land has to be acquired at any cost, only 5% of the total multi-cropped land in the district can be acquired and not more. Otherwise, multi-cropped land should not be acquired.	multi-crop irrigated land can also be acquired if for security, defense, rural infra, industrial corridors and social infra

Image 2:

1) Indian Prime Minister Narendra Modi's "Smart Cities" Mission
2) India's 2015 Urban Population and its impact on metros across the country's landscape
3) The changing nature of villages and towns across India, and their growth (or decline)
4) The shifting provisions of the Land Acquisition Bill
5) India's 'vilage count' and resident population in these environments.
6) Website of the Smart Cities Mission (accessed May 25th 2016)

SOBTI

in the decades to follow? How smart would urban smart-ness really need to be, in order for cities (and growing towns) to actually qualify towards inclusion in this specific category?[4] Given that India's Union Ministry of Urban Development website ambitiously proclaims that "the growth story of India shall be written on the canvas of planned urban development ... " [notice the implied usage of the future tense], what 'objective' criteria (if any) would allow for any (and all) future 'correctives' to be developed and incorporated within existing urban legislative code? More importantly, what exactly would these smart urbanities replace or supplant, and via what kind of choreographed processes? Besides, serving as the energetic 'drivers of economic growth', how would these smart cities undermine the many un-smart echoes of urbanism that currently prevail across the Indian landscape? Of the hodge-podge, palimpsests of cities, these would clearly include the burgeoning and biggest urbanities of the Indian subcontinent - New and Old Delhi, Kolkata, Mumbai Chennai, and many more. Would the multiple and intertwined issues residing in the frequently abysmal, piece-meal and post-independence quality of urban life in these centers, be then viewed as a 'replace-worthy' collateral, fit to be replaced by the behemoth of accelerated developments offered by these smart visions? (Image 2)

Provocation

> *The city historically constructed is no longer lived and no longer understood practically. It is only an object of cultural consumption for tourists, for aestheticism, avid for spectacles and the picturesque. Even for those who seek to understand it with warmth, it is gone. Yet, the urban remains in a state of dispersed and alienated actuality, as kernel and virtuality. What the eyes and analysis perceive on the ground can at best pass for the shadow of the future object in the light of a rising sun. It is impossible to envisage the reconstitution of the old city, only the construction of a new one on new foundations, on another scale and in other conditions, in another society. The prescription is: there cannot be a going back (towards the traditional city), nor a headlong flight, towards a colossal and shapeless agglomeration. In other words, for what concerns the city the object of science is not given. The past, the present, the possible cannot be separated. What is being studied is a virtual object, with thought studies, which calls for new approaches.*

> - Henry Lefebvre (1968)

Cities and urban places, and in this case, those specifically vested with smart qualities, have always gained vantage. Within the Indian context specifically, there is also the growing assumption that cities and 'larger' urban places would be (and should be) the logical culmination of the nation's developmental processes. This

5

6

position perpetuates the misconception that villages and rural settlements are a traditional, relatively less-advanced way of life. In effect, only cities and their changing spatial patterns have attracted public and scholarly attention (and invariably, governmental funding), not the host of villages in their close proximities. Quite frequently, 'nested villages' within the urban fabrics of India's countless cities, remain relegated to being identified as 'undesirable habitats'; and are described in the somewhat pejorative vein. If we have indeed 'lost' our connection with the traditional city in the Lefebvren sense, should this extend to villages? In reaction, could these villages instead stay as ideal rural habitats - as smart environments in their own right, which adapt to changing context?

SOBTI

Image 3:

Delhi's smart urbanism consuming the city's urban peripheries: Housing complexes and encroachments (Fauji Colony & Jharoda Majra) bordering the Bhalswa garbage dumping site (left of picture) seen from the GT Karnal Road. The canal (nullah) carries water to the Yamuna River further to the south (right of picture), while children play on the canal banks. A nearby 'golf course' in the proximity of the Bhalswa lake (not in picture, further to right of frame) remains deliberately unaware of its surroundings.

If villages are viewed as the antithesis of the city, and undesirable habitats characterized by change, even lesser attention has been invested in comprehending the transforming 'landscape matrix' that traditionally held and continues to hold this perplexing field of Indian urbanities. How would these landscapes change when India's smart cities arrive - what functions would they absorb? Where would their 'displaced' populations move? How would land use rapidly change? In interrogating the ex-urban, landscape matrix as a point of departure, I therefore suggest, both as an introduction and as provocation, that it is would be more expedient to examine the rapidly de-ruralizing landscape between and along the very edges of globalizing (and smart) cities, versus the cities themselves. I question if these urban (or rural) edges are indeed urban or rural, and explore the un-questioned validity of viewing these edges from within versus without.

SOBTI

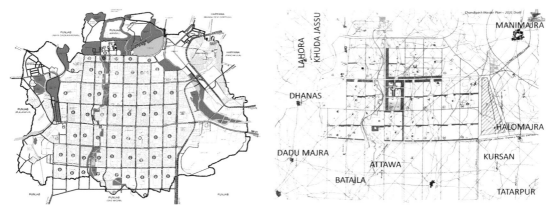

Image 5:

Top (left and right)- The current-day villages of Chandigarh, within and outside the city. The 23 villages are categorized as Sectoral and Non-Sectoral Villages, based on their locations. All are changing rapidly owing to their proximities to multiple urban magnets, including Chandigarh. As per the Department of Rural Development Panchayat (Union Territory of Chandigarh), most of these villages have grown well beyond their traditional boundaries with significant increases in resident populations from a few decades ago. The diagrams arranged below demonstrate this dramatic growth:

- Development outside the Abadi area of villages falling 'within' the Sectoral grid - Village Kajheri (a), Village Palsora (b), Village Badheri (d top), Village Buterlia (d bottom), Village Attawa (c) & Village Burail (e).

- Development outside the Abadi of villages 'outside' the Sectoral grid - Village Khuda Ali Sher (f), Village Dhghas (g), Village Behlana (h), Village Kaimbwala (i), Village Sarangpur (j), Village Makhanmajra (k), Village Dadumajra (m), Village Raipur Kalan (n), Village Hallomajra (p), Village Kishangarh (o), Village Maloya (q), Village Daria (l), Village Raipur Khurd (n)

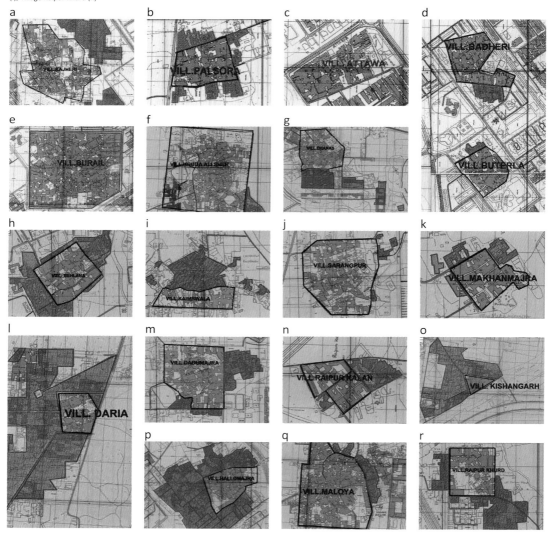

age 6:

e two 'action' areas of the SARUP Urban Edge Studio 2015, at BADHERI (top, Views 1- 8) &
NSAL (bottom, Views 1-7):

DHERI
e village of Badheri began as a minor destination along the local, inter-city road that
isted prior to Chandigarh's layout; the site is still indicated by its 'reconstructed' temple,
w decorated with images combining place histories and new identities (View 1). Views 3,
& 5 show aggressive fabric densification now ongoing in the Badheri village, characterized
cantilevered upper levels and vertical extensions. Most constructions are considered
authorized, but then Badheri does not fall under the city code. Views 2 & 7 show the
ll-existing, open spaces within the village of Badheri and their popular usage by local
habitants (see also plan of Badheri, Image 10). View 8 shows the narrow by-lanes of
dheri forming shaded and intimate street canyons (see also the top view of such a canyon
eated by cantilevered upper floors of Badheri homes, Image 14).

NSAL
e Kansal village (in current day Punjab) frames the Capitol Complex and its views of the
ivalik foothills. The now-overgrown village begins at the state line (boundary) created by
e road framing the Capitol Complex and remains separated from the city by a distinct ha-
wall created by a brick culvert (View 3). This two-lane roadway (View 1) has just started
receive substantial traffic in the last decade, given its recent role as a major linkage
nnecting Khuda Ali Sher, Kansal, and Kaimbwala villages, and is the site of several new
undary walls and decorated entry gates, all anticipating new construction projects. Many
nong these developments also pre-empt a significant real-estate speculation along this
adway, given its vantage to Chandigarh (Views 2 & 6). This humble roadway is therefore a
ritable cross section between two disparate worlds - the world of the planned city to the
uth and southwest (Views 3 & 4) with fleeting views of the Capitol over the tree canopy;
d the agricultural community that lies to the north and northeast (Views 5 & 7).

SOBTI

Image 7:

Views of the Jamuna Expressway Project, stretching 165 kms. and connecting the cities of Delhi and Agra. The Yamuna Expressway is a 6-lane (extendable to 8 lane) access controlled expressway, and is planned to have five LFDs (Land of concessionaire) with facilities for four toll plazas, and six interchanges along its entire length. The acquisition of land for the construction of this highway was a major experiment for India's future. land based projects.

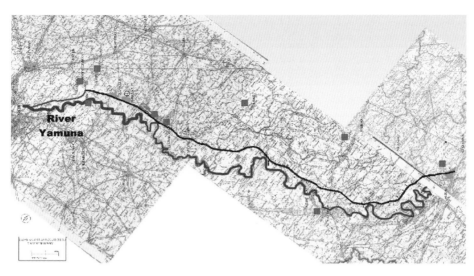

It is on these lines that the term *urban edge* emerged during the course of the Chandigarh Design Studios at SARUP. Examined by my fellow contributors in this volume broadly - the urban edge denotes a physical condition, a metaphoric concept, and a design methodology following upon these observations. The edge creates (and un-creates) boundaries, forms limiting conditions, expands and shrinks the city, while inducing building morphologies, instigating place definitions, and formulating new meanings. The edge can reside on the map and inside the mind; it is a barrier yet a catalyst of change, and a zone that remains in constant flux, reacting to conditions within and outside. In the context of the city, the urban edge manifests itself in countless ways, acquiring the ability to be adept at reacting to outside forces. On a horizon of thought about one's future, ambitions, and place within societal time and place, the edge is a temporal space between dreams and reality. In investigations of the edge, one cannot be indifferent, comfortable, or complacent. Variation is critical in this impermanent space between where we are and where we wish to go. When envisioning the edge in this manner, it is the physical place of transition, like a membrane through which the here and there interact - flexible and forever engaged. The edge condition represents the innovative systems developed by those who inhabit the spaces of transition, and in this lays the opportunities to embrace that innovation.

In my specific focus on edges as positioned within the rapid transformations of urban centers and rural landscapes in the Indian context, I suggest that physical changes manifest in the *de-ruralizing edges* around India's cities also create land conflict as the valuation of available land shifts mode from agrarian to urban, from fertility to location. More importantly, physical changes to both land and landscape, while evidently re-drawing plots and property borders, also instrumentalize radical shifts to the societal structures based on this changing land identity, its possession and possessors. In effect, and obviously exaggerated by the social frameworks and caste-based forms of agrarian land control still extant within many parts of India, the peculiar ramifications of globalization that these de-ruralizing landscapes at the edges face are therefore quite removed from the normative ones that generally pervade most urban discussions (Image 7).

Within the Indian subcontinent, it is critical to recognize that modernity and its mechanisms have catalyzed rapid urbanization not always within existing urbanities, but instead *in-between* urbanities and *outside* city centers. This is especially true along highway linkages that now haphazardly connect the many points in a previously agrarian, hinterland matrix. This would also be the scenario that India's other (and equally nationalistic) 'Rivers-Interlinking' project would potentially create. In inter-connecting river to river, riverine to city, and riparian to ordinary landscape, any remaining proximal and distal site and land-based indigeneities would eventually disappear, making way for a generic, acultural landscape. It is therefore worth considering that both the Smart Cities mission and the Rivers-Interlinking Project would radically alter the 'cultural' connection of millions of rural Indians to their land. Meanwhile, the Government of India's recent, and much touted Land Acquisition Amendment Bill opportunistically seizes up the described windows of imminent change that would arrive not just on the rural outskirts of cities, but also within village habitats and agricultural landscape.[5] It also progresses without serious consideration on the consequences of potential conflict and its impact on globalizing villages and towns in the vicinities of these de-ruralizing sites. Indian agriculture, despite all the homage that is paid by city dwellers and politicians to farmers and their purported sacrifices to plough the land, is mostly land aspiring to eventually become real estate. At least, this is what the land sales at Sanand-Gujarat (2008-13) would have us believe. For what other reason would an entire agrarian community willingly give up its landed heritage, and be relegated to a social group with resources but no access to tradition. Not that Sanand and India's development are unimportant, but that large-scale developments (Sanand and Singur) were obviously quite feasible on fallow lands where agriculture was not an established practice. Yet, it was Sanand's proximity to Ahmedabad that made it an urban satellite ripe for change.

Hopefully, and if Sanand's energy is any indicator, these shall be valuable lessons for the future. In fact, farming is today the least productive industry in India, and farmers are among its most impoverished laborers, even though the sheer size of India and the fact that more than 60% of its land is used for farming would ensure that it is a statistical giant in agriculture. In the face of these imminent changes, what would then be the character of India's global cities and irreversibly changed villages in the decades to follow? The emphasis here, on the loss of the rural environment and its embedded lessons in 'sustainable practices', is not so much about decreased agricultural productivity, or the lack of arable land (as is often projected in the social media). Rather, it is about the irretrievable loss of a way of life, where social lives can no longer remain closely connected to the 'legacy of land' and its spatial memories. In other words, Lefebvre's claim that the "urban remains in a state of dispersed and alienated actuality … " is here equally valid for the rural environment.

Situation

Within this broad umbrella of urban (and rural) concerns, SARUP's Urban Design Studios were conducted in Ahmedabad (2009) and Chandigarh (2010 & 2015). All three projects invoked the image of the changing Indian city that faces challenges both from within and outside its normative spatial geographies. The Ahmedabad-Madhavpura Studio (2009) examined activist engagements towards the expansion of a community marketplace located just outside the historic Delhi Gate of Ahmedabad's walled city. This northern, urban edge was a site on the verge of change, its functional 'vernacular' buildings preserving the last vestiges of a medieval public space of commerce and exchange. In reaction, the studio's multiple built interventions and proposed networks were small and large, skeletal and complete, singular and coupled, as these imagined the possibilities of continuing the social choreographies inherent to this edge. Pragmatism, participation, and adaptive reuse were suggested as strategies, contrary to familiar nostalgia and preservation. After all, a modified edge would at least strongly preserve its spatial identities, if none of the spaces and structures themselves survived. Building upon this 'accretive' understanding of the city, the 2010 Chandigarh Studio proposed an 'additive' vision for Chandigarh's existing City Center located in Sector 17. It advanced upon the prevalent assumption (well-documented in his sketch books) that Le Corbusier intended to highlight the northwestern corner (quadrant) of City Center Sector 17 Market with an emblematic, 11-story commercial tower. This tower would have accommodated public amenities, such as the Post & Telegraph offices occupying the ground level, while the upper levels would presumably be given out to commercial establishments. While this scheme was never realized for a variety of reasons, the studio questioned the importance of the site's potential location, scale, presence, and language in the urban fabric of an otherwise largely 'horizontal' city. It reflected on the addition of another 'verticality' in the City Center that would effectively 'compete' with the monumentality of Corbusier's Capitol Complex further to the northwest.

Following upon these described initiatives, SARUP's Urban Edge Award in 2015 was conceived as a bigger conversation on Indian urbanities, in particular provocations with expanding city edges and their rural environs. Supported by related seminars over Spring and Fall 2015, the Urban Edge Award Studio reexamined the concept of an urban edge within the *tabula rasa* of Chandigarh. Conceived by Corbusier as the culmination of his urban ideas in combination with the ideals of the CIAM and the City Beautiful Movement, Chandigarh's visceral urbanity, spatial and formal ordering, and the almost deliberate 'unfinished-ness', were among its many provocative qualities. With these in background, the studio deliberately moved away from the built legacy of Chandigarh, to instead engage with the narrative of 'un-built' action areas within this legislated canvas. Corbusier, in preparing the urban scheme of Chandigarh, had stopped short of determining a strategy to deal with the multiple villages that appeared on the site of the future city. His plan for the city (and its later elaborations by Pierre Jeanerret, Maxwell Fry, and Jane Drew),

Image 8:

(Top) a and b - showing agricultural land on the outskirts of Delhi being rapidly encroached upon by housing developments. This proximity of fields and buildings while surreal, is understandably tragic - it gives the village no option but to transform irreversibly.

(Bottom) c - View showing developer-promised vignettes of 'housing estates' located on the banks of a seasonal water canal. Many such canals and tracts of land were 'opened up' and made available following the land acquisition process (such as at Sanand). While developments, such as those exhibited here are desirable, at least in part, given India's divisive societal framework, accessibility would only be possible for certain economic classes.

Image 9:

The villages of
Kansal (top)
and Badheri
(botton) seen
highlighted on
an aerial plans of
Chandigarh.

actually appears to have included some of these villages within the urban sectors, allowing for their formative features (generally water bodies - ponds and reservoirs) to survive and continue a traditional way of life. Still more rural settlements survived outside the city proper, growing into larger townships and urban satellites in the following decades past the foundations of the city. The Urban Edge Studio stepped vicariously into Corb's shoes in reviving the urban perspective on where these rural settlements should turn as the urban hinterland around the city shrinks at an alarming rate (Image 13 - Ahmedabad Studio).

Chandigarh, as a city, embodied the realized dream of an egalitarian master plan. It was a materialization and exaggeration of the metaphoric edge. The juxtapositioning of the artifact of the city with the urbanism that flows through and around, provides a provocative context for examination. An artifact is a treasured object kept safe in an effort to remember, preserve the past, preserve a history, and preserve an idea. Yet urbanism is also a living organism; it must necessarily morph in order to survive. At Chandigarh, living urbanism occurs at the city edges where the very sites of change reside. This is not to suggest that one urban condition is better

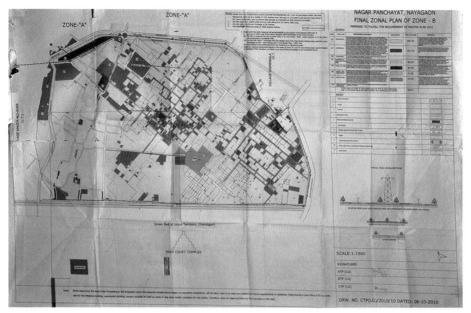

Image 10:

Kansal (top) and Badheri (bottom) seen in more detail vis a vis their limits, boundaries and fabric morphologies.

or to superimpose one on the other, but rather to envision the edge as a starting point where transformations could begin and extend outwards from.

The action areas at Chandigarh of particular interest to the Studio's edge investigations were situated along two instances within the fabric, where economic and formal change was imminent, yet which had remained as anomalies within the original plan. The first was the village of Kansal located just outside the city proper, northwest of the Capitol Complex and expanding into the agricultural hinterland at the base of the Shivalik Hills. Not quite a suburb, and still on its journey towards becoming a town, Kansal struggles with a future comprising of rapidly transforming building typologies that react to the ambitions of the neighboring Punjab. As the crow flies, Kansal is today the unsightly middle ground framing Corbusier's self-conscious vignette of the mountains. The second action area was the urban village of Badheri, now embedded within the urban fabric of Chandigarh and engulfed by its sectoral expansion. As a micro setting of distinct vernacular character, Badheri is effectively land-locked by its peripheral building blocks, and has reacted aggressively to its formal containment by growing inwards and vertically.

Both Kansal and Badheri prosper distinctly removed from Chandigarh, yet have symbiotic relationships with the city that adjoins them. At Kansal, the rural infill of the future was interpreted as one 'living' to become an inseparable component of local history. In its expansion and contraction, it become a literal endoskeleton and exoskeleton within a rapidly de-ruralizing terrain. While its future architecture would desperately serve to fulfill needs and transformations, it would also serve as an advocate for preserving the ecologies of the agricultural hinterland that once comprised these city peripheries. Badheri, in contrast, provided a context for investigating informalism through a transformative lens. It set up an argument for examining the choreographies of the urban migrants who arrive in the city, as these landscapes of the in-between gradually innovate and incorporate new building typologies.

Image 11:

View of Capitol Complex (Assembly Building), seen from Kansal's primary street, and looking across an unflattering garbage dump in the foreground and a cremation ground in the background. This sharp contrast of scales is unique to Chandigarh, given that there are no intermediate buildings to connect the monumentality of the Capitol Complex with the intimacy of Kansal's urban fabric.

Both these rural pockets have survived over the many decades since Chandigarh's legislated inception. At Kansal, this has largely occurred owing to the relative immunity of the rural (and quasi-rural) fabric from the legislations of Corb's proximal urbanity. This immunity has also thrived on the relative indifference of the city, which has rarely, if ever, expressed more than a passing interest in the fate of this and similar rural developments on the urban periphery. In contrast, at Badheri, the survival of the urban fabric is owing to the peculiar insularity of its rural environment within the urban plan of surrounding Chandigarh. While Badheri's deep nesting within this plan has meant its survival (at least for now), this has also co-existed with what may be best described as strangulation. Given these vivid descriptions, what changes would future decades thereby impart to Kansal and Badheri? If the 'edge' in both cases is indeed about 'contact' and 'built engagement', to what extent would the two action areas at Kansal and Badheri either become part of adjoining Chandigarh or else continue to survive as independent entities with a different built character and language? What manner of edges would their fabric transformations generate and by incorporating what kinds of legislative processes?

SOBTI

Image 12:

The settlement of Kansal (Punjab) seen from the Chandigarh Secretariat Rooftop: Within the media, the villages of Chandigarh (including Kansal - falling within Punjab) are seen as dismal in contrast to the city's well-planned 56 sectors. In response, the Chandigarh Administration has stressed on planned development of rural areas in its Master Plan 2031. Within this plan, however, little consideration has been given to how villages on the city's immediate edges, such as Kaimbwala and Khuda Ali Sher would continue to retain their rural character. Kansal's case is even more obscure, given that its legislation is controlled by the state of Punjab (versus Haryana, as for most of the others).

Image 13:

SARUP Ahmedabad - Madhavpura Urban Design Studio (2009), showing the city of Ahmedabad (top left), site with defined urban space created in the vicinity of the Delhi Darwaza. Middle and bottom images are design proposals to introduce a new morphology within this marketplace

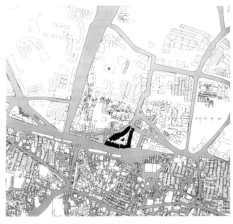

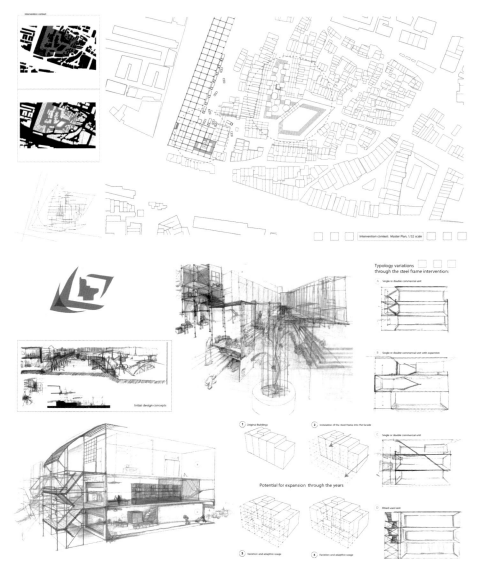

Emerging from a site visit to Chandigarh over January 2015 with SARUP students, collaborative workshops organized with enthusiastic students from the Chandigarh College of Architecture working with Sangeeta Bagga-Mehta, and passionate class discussions held following our return to Milwaukee, the Urban Edge Prize Studio enumerated several analytical frameworks. These included developing strategies of landscape and hinterland, re-visiting and re-imagining local histories, exploring the visions of sustainability in the broadest sense (and beyond the oversimplified notions of 'smart' cities), examining innovative building typologies as catalysts for urban growth, and developing the necessary stories of resilience and change. This range of edge stories and strategies, narrated via the Urban Edge Award Studio at Kansal and Badheri, appear to have continued well beyond Chandigarh, to the many large and small urban centers within the Indian subcontinent and also globally. These were the stories of urban making and un-making, and the city's unique ability to grapple with multiple histories, while her fabric continually re-invents itself. On similar lines, even the concept of the edge (or edge-ness) was effectively expanded across multiple scales - from the neighborhood and sector nested within the confines of the city, to the beginnings or liminal terrains of hinterland, and finally to the borders or boundaries of regions and territories. Would then these so-called edges be the sites of conflict or polycentric zones of tolerated contestations? How would proximal ruralities effect and be affected by globalizing urbanities? What impact would the accelerated transformations of this predominantly rural urban hinterland matrix have on the political economies of proximal cities and urban centers? These are among the plethora of thorny questions raised and examined in our continuing explorations on conflict or polycentric zones of tolerated contestations emerging within the studio and collated in this edited volume (Image 5, 6).

Given the similarities between the two cases, the studio also critically differentiated between the strategies employed. Kansal's relative immunity from the legislations of Chandigarh, while reflecting legislative indifference, was also owing to the easy (and popular) availability of a residential building typology that had survived well in this now-overgrown village. This building typology remains the local rural, courtyard dwelling alongside its modified phenotypes. Used and re-used multiple times, in predominantly functional (versus architectural) ways, this has constituted a local building grammar, that some would define as encroachment and others invention. In any case, this typology has also served as a repository for new constructions, both residential and beyond. In the absence of a legislated plan, it is this quasi-rural proliferation that creates the main street of Kansal and nodes of this overgrown village. Meanwhile, Kansal's building plots, and especially their configurations, proportions and orientations, were found to be intrinsically related to the pre-existing agricultural land sub-divisions. Several of these sub-divisions have continued to survive to the east of Kansal, etched in the historical imagery collated from Google maps, though these images also reveal rapid change over the past decade. If Kansal has remained pre-dominantly rural in its intrinsic character even while the village has expanded beyond its expected boundaries, Badheri by contrast, has seized the character of an urban village. In fact, Badheri's peculiar insularity within Chandigarh's fabric may have actually exaggerated this explosive urban growth. At Badheri, the absence of a legislative mechanism, allowed for intense densification and vertical expansion, via building typologies that had remained nascent in Chandigarh's sectors, but were recklessly employed in the other urban satellites around Chandigarh. This differentiation of growth mechanisms at Kansal and Badheri served as important tools to the participants of the Urban Edge Award Studio.

As among the key architects of modern India and her first Prime Minister, Jawaharlal Nehru had imagined cities such as Chandigarh to be constructed as the symbols of India's future, so much so that these would be "an expression of the nation's faith in the future." Within our modern day parlance, this so-called "faith in the future" bcould be interpreted as ownership, among other things, as inclusive (or public) 'rights' or access to urban space as urban citizens. It is of serious concern that this

Image 15:

Badheri's cantile-
vered balconies
are effective
social devices
and enhance
the real estate
value of these
properties.

right to one's city continues to remain conspicuously absent from the urban plan of Chandigarh today. While Chandigarh's spatial image connects it to the grand legacy of modern architecture, it continues to derive most of its apparent 'uncluttered-ness' (in contrast to other Indian cities of comparable size) by strategically negating easy access to the only overtly 'public space' in the city - the Capitol Plaza with its monumental buildings framed by the mountains. While Corbusier appears to have made accommodations for use of the Plaza as a public space (as archival photographs would suggest), any additional accommodations were conspicuously absent even in earlier plans for the city. These continue to remain woefully unaddressed even within Chandigarh's 2031 Master Plan. In the recent past, efforts have been made by the general public to 'recapture' the public space around the Open Hand Monument at Chandigarh. This has, however, had little more than a statistical impact, since while the barbed wires and protective fences around the plaza were indeed removed, their removal was predicated more by 'bureaucratic necessity' to make Chandigarh appear accessible to the UNESCO World Heritage Nomination Committee (2015), versus the general public. In its vein of 'aesthetic harmony', Chandigarh devotes more than 2,000 acres of land solely for parks, but does little to ameliorate the needs of incoming urban migrants who continue to arrive into the city, thereafter adapting to the ideosyncrasies of Kansal and Badheri.

One could, therefore, potentially ascribe Chandigarh's relative inflexibility to recognize real urban problems to its 'signature' ensemble and the related issues of preservation that this ensemble faces. Yet, as analysts mention, Chandigarh also remains but a sterile and heavily subsidized city that encourages neither public entrepreneurship nor tax-generating jobs. In sharp contrast (and given its unplanned mode), even the other 'accidential' urban anomoly on the north Indian plains remains surprisingly functional. While Gurgaon emerged from a set of humble villages bordering Delhi (as in its apt name), and whereas it remains much unlike what Nehru would have ever envisioned, erratic, unplanned, sporadic, and utterly lacking in its infrastructure (as Delhi residents incessantly complain and contrast), this new face of cities in 21st century India, is the place were 'dream houses' continue to be sold, and migrants pass through and settle. Of course, Gurgaon does not even claim to 'solve' urban problems, such as migrations and poverty, or even urban legislation. Nevertheless, it does own up to committing itself towards the function that cities are really meant for - accommodating incoming migrants.

Image 16:

Badheri's Sector 41 D - Main Market street elevation, showing the rapidly changing urban fabric on the sector peripheries. Beyond this first layer of fabric, the interior of Badheri is largely organic-accretive. Urban expansions and developments in such a scenario must therefore take into account the constitutive nature of the fabric.

In turning back to Kansal and Badheri action areas as they continue to grow on the shadowy edges of Chandigarh, there are only two tenable options that emerge for their urban futures. The first is their possible transformation towards becoming urban places, while moving away from the signature ensemble qualities of Chandigarh. In other words, celebrating the architecture of transition, of means and not ends, not of the past but of the future. This would make either Kansal or Badheri (or both), the commercial hot-spots in town, which they already are to an extent. Except that the rules of Chandigarh's urbanity would be surreptitiously subverted. The alternative option is for both Kansal and Badheri to aggressively transform into strong ecological models - the likes that shall carve out strong ruralities that are closely 're-connected' to the land that they emerged from in historical time, and well before the foundations of Chandigarh. These so-called 'ecological ruralities' would capture whatever little survives of the village and its rural landscape, re-packaging these places into smart villages alongside the overgrown urban follies that surround Chandigarh today.

SOBTI

Endnotes

1. See *http://smartcities.gov.in/*
2. See *http://moud.gov.in/*
3. See *http://smartcities.gov.in/writereaddata/Strategy.pdf*
4. Twenty Indian urban centers, including Bhubneshwar, Pune, Jaipur, Surat, Kochi, Ahmedabad, Jabalpur, Vishakhapatnam, Solapur, Davanagare, Indore, NDMC, Coimbatore, Kakinada, Belagari, Udaipur, Guwahati, Chennai, Ludhiana, and Bhopal are already included on the list of Smart Cities (as of March 28th 2016), see *http://smartcities.gov.in/Cities_Profile.aspx*. By all accounts, most of the list comprises of pre-existing cities. However, no details have been provided on how 'smart legislation' interacts with existing urban practices. It is expected that this list of cities shall grow in the future. Additionally, smart cities have been defined as cities with the following 'core infrastructural elements': adequate water supply, assured electricity supply, sanitation, including solid waste management, efficient urban mobility and public transport, affordable housing, especially for the poor, robust IT connectivity and digitalization, good governance, especially e-Governance and citizen participation, sustainable environment, safety and security of citizens - particularly women, children and the elderly - and health and education.
5. For current updates on the Land Acquisition Amendment Bill and its progress until 2015 and beyond, see http://www.prsindia.org/pages/land-acquisition-debate-139/. The current Bill is based on a version from 1894 (Land Acquisition Act, 1894).

References

Auge, Marc. *Non-Places - An Introduction to Supermodernity*. London: Verso, 1995.
Avermaete, Tom & Casciato, Maristella. *Casablanca Chandigarh: A Report on Modernization*. Zurich: Park Books 2014.
Gill, Sucha Singh (ed.). *Land Reforms in India*, Vol. 6; Intervention for Agrarian Capitalist Transformation in Punjab and Haryana. New Delhi/Thousand Oaks/London: Sage Publications, 2001.
Kalia, Ravi. *Chandigarh: The Making of an Indian City*. Oxford University Press, 2000.
Kroll, Clemens & Lederer, Arno. *Chandigarh: Living with Le Corbusier*. Berlin: Jovis, 2011.
Le Corbusier & Jeanneret, Pierre. *Le Corbusier & Pierre Jeanneret: Chandigarh, India*. Paris/London: Edition Galerie Patrick Seguin - Bilingual edition, 2014.
Prakash, Vikramaditya. *Chandigarh's Le Corbusier: The Struggle for Modernity in Postcolonial India* (Studies in Modernity and National Identity). University of Washington Press; 2002.
Sharma, Kavita et al. *Chandigarh Lifescape: Brief History of A Planned City*. Chandigarh: Chandigarh Administration, 1999.
Soja, Edward W. *Postmodern Geographies: The Reassertion of Space in Critical Social Theory*. London: Verso, 1994.
Takhar, Jaspreet. *Celebrating Chandigarh*. Mapin Publishing, 2007

Image 17:

View from the Chandigarh Secretariat building looking southeastwards towards the city. In many ways, Corbusier's monumental Capitol Complex represents the 'middle ground' between a legislated city and a largely autonomous village environment. How these effectively combine and reconcile in the future remains to be seen.

Elaboration

Re-reading Our Recent Past: Notes on Chandigarh and New Gourna

VINAYAK BHARNE

ABSTRACT

This essay focuses on two iconic architectural works that dominate the ongoing intellectual discourse on conserving our recent past – the City of Chandigarh in India designed by Le Corbusier, and the Village of New Gourna in Egypt designed by Hassan Fathy. By examining the differential between their originating visions and their legacies that were shaped over more than five decades through many unforeseen circumstances and unaccounted consequences, this article provokes deeper reflections on our modern heritage and on the forces and entities that should decide its future.

In the ongoing dialogue on conserving our recent past, two iconic places, designed by two brilliant architects in two different parts of the world at almost the same time, have come to the forefront – the city of Chandigarh designed by Le Corbusier in India, and the Village of New Gourna designed by Hassan Fathy in Egypt. Even though the original intentions shaping these two places were blatantly different, their evolving destinies are raising complex questions on the outlook and praxis of conserving modern landmarks, particularly beyond the West, forming a compelling narrative on the larger rubric of heritage, modernity, and Modern architecture. This article does not delve into the histories of these two places, as much as examines the differential between their originating visions and legacies - legacies that were shaped over more than five decades through many consequences and circumstances, largely unforeseen and unaccounted for. By highlighting this differential, the intention is to provoke deeper reflections on how we might reread our recent heritage, on who should define it, on whom it should it be conserved for, on who should play a role in these endeavors, and how and by what means they should be accomplished.

Chandigarh and New Gourna – A Historical Overview

When Le Corbusier landed in India for the first time in February 1951 on the invitation of Prime Minister Jawarharlal Nehru, the Village of New Gourna was well under way in Cairo. Plans to develop it had begun as early as the mid-1940s reflecting the Egyptian government's desire to relocate the impoverished village of Gourna al-Jadida, an impoverished squatter constructed atop the ancient burial sites of the Theban Necropolis. For generations, the poor residents of Gourna al-Jadida had made their living by looting and selling burial artifacts, which the Egyptian government sought to curtail. In 1945, the Egyptian Department of Antiquities purchased 45 acres of sugarcane fields some two miles west of the archaeological site and commissioned Hassan Fathy to design and supervise the construction of the new settlement.

New Gourna was a radical departure from the high Modernist dogma of the '40s. Instead of using contemporary materials such as steel or reinforced concrete, the village was constructed of handmade, sun-dried mud bricks, an ancient Nubian construction material, used as a means of tempering the sunlight and reducing interior temperatures. As such it embodied an alternative modernity for a different socio-economic, climatic, and cultural context. Fathy consulted with local workmen and a team of Nubian master builders to create buildings sensitive to local rural lifestyles. Buildings were designed of handmade mud bricks and capped by Islamic-style domes. Homes were organized around central courtyards and the entire village was anchored by a main public square with a mosque, educational facilities, and theater. Fathy also expressed great interest in the social structure of the Gourna al-Jadida community, frequently visiting them to observe the social structure. Concluding that Gourni society was organized around two key units: the family and the *badana* (or group of families), he designed New Gourna's plan with individual family houses arranged in clusters around small squares. Fathy was not merely attempting to create a model settlement for the Gourni people, but seeking to create an international prototype to house the modern world's less privileged.

Le Corbusier on the other hand had a different agenda – almost a mandate from the Prime Minister of India himself to create a city that would break away from the traditions of India's past, and overwhelm newly-sovereign India's colonial complex. Within less than six weeks of his arrival, Le Corbusier re-planned the city of Chandigarh: He 'rationalized' the curved streets of his predecessor Albert Meyer's scheme into an orthogonal grid, re-apportioned its proposed 'Villages' into 'Sectors' thrice as large, reduced the quantity of roads, and increased the overall density. But much of Chandigarh's magnetism lay less in the city plan, and more in the Capitol Complex the master architect was so meticulously designing in brutal gray concrete. Set against the Himalayan backdrop, and carefully positioned on Modular proportions, was a dramatic concourse of four colossal and three smaller monuments: With the Secretariat slipped behind it, the Assembly and High Court stood across each other framing the (un-built) Governor's Palace, with the Tower of Shadows, the Geometrical Hill, the Monument to the Marytr, and the Open Hand Monument (built in the '80s) and as smaller players around them. Together they centered on the Esplanade - a 440-meter-long barren expanse of gray concrete stretching between them.

By the time Prime Minister Nehru formally opened the city in October 1953, Le Corbusier's reputation had propelled Chandigarh to international attention. Architects and historians from all over came to witness what would be the largest built project of the master architect, a phenomenon that remains true to this day. New Gourna on the other hand largely escaped the public eye until 1976, and not until Fathy published his memoir for the project, "Architecture for the Poor," would it attract the global eye. In any case, from today's standpoint, both places bear the parallel of being incomplete utopias that now stand at the epicenter of a serious intellectual discourse about their future, and by extension, the future of other such recently designed iconic places across the world.

Beyond Le Corbusier: Chandigarh Today

Since 2006, the city administration of Chandigarh has been pushing for a UNESCO World Heritage Designation, inspired by Brazilia, Le Havre, and Tel Aviv, to celebrate what is a healthy and thriving city, embodying the qualities of a progressive, prosperous polis. Chandigarh has nearly doubled in size over five decades along Corbusier's proposed pattern. It has survived the political upheavals and terrorist threats of the '80s. Its citizens wear an intrinsic civic pride towards India's first Modern city, known for its quality education, where everyone knows about the man named Le Corbusier. Its markets teem with activity, overwhelming the bland concrete and brick facades with a riot of signage, canvas, and color. It is India's first 'green' city to ban smoking in public. Chandigarh has its act together – not because of its planning or architecture, but because it has, like other Indian cities, been appropriated and absorbed by the plebian Indian ethos.

Meanwhile, Chandigarh's Capitol Complex tells a different story. Guard posts, gates, and barbed wires enclose the entire precinct today, interrupting the view of the famous Assembly and High Court from the central Esplanade. Trees grow randomly, blocking the same vista of the 240-meter long Secretariat that had not long ago been a carefully conceived visual composition. Secured entry to the Assembly and High Court occurs from the rear parking lots, which also becomes the setting for hawkers and commerce. Except as a space to admire the buildings, the 440-meter long Esplanade, the open space between the Assembly and High Court remains perpetually empty, with weeds and a few administrative cars sheepishly parked at its fringe. It stays that way even on India's Independence Day, with the parades happening instead in the field near Sector 17.

Image 1:

Assembly Building seen from the Esplanade, circa 2010 (copyright 2010 Artists Rights Society (ARS), New York / ADAGP, Paris / F.L.C. Photo by author).

Image 2:

High Court Building interrupted by security fences and guard post, circa 2010 (copyright 2010 Artists Rights Society (ARS), New York / ADAGP, Paris / F.L.C. Photo by author).

So whatever happened to Le Corbusier's Capitol? Circa 1985, some three decades after the Capitol's opening, Chandigarh had been gripped by the paranoia of Sikh terrorists killing people at will. A year later Prime Minister Indira Gandhi ordered a military attack on the Golden Temple in Amritsar, the holiest of Sikh shrines, killing hundreds of Sikh terrorists who had amassed weapons within, and eventually leading to her assassination. With everything from state to city wearing a somber garb, emergency security measures were implemented to safeguard the administrative center. Barbed wire fences with guard-posts, gates, and gunmen fortified the complex and entry to the Capitol became far more limited than ever before. Today the tortured, protected Capitol represents a helpless victim of unpredictable political circumstances on the one hand, and a mirror reflecting the darker colors of post-colonial India on the other.

Chandigarh's citizens hardly go to the Capitol. Its own link with the thriving city is Le Corbusier's Open Hand monument, not through its original democratic symbolism of being "Open to receive, Open to Give," but its ubiquitous scattering as a two-dimensional imprint throughout the city. From tourist hoardings and garbage bins to pamphlets and driver's licenses, it is the city's official symbol, though one may not exactly know its relevance then versus now. The only consistent inhabitants of the Capitol - besides the diurnal political menagerie, sanitation department workers and trash collectors, are the villagers of Kansal, the only retained village from the many demolished to build the city. They regularly visited the Complex without any invitation or permission, to wash, bathe, and carry home water for cooking. The lawns surrounding the deserted Open Hand have become their cricket fields and hangouts.

Not that all this has gone un-noticed. Since its founding in 2005, Hum Log (literally "We the People"), a local non-government organization (NGO) has sought to generate a wave of citizen activism through organized campaigns for the cause of the city. The "Free the Open Hand Campaign" organized street theater, debates, and conferences at the monument to make it accessible to the public. Thanks to such efforts, since January 2010, the Chandigarh government has lifted the ban on social gatherings at the Open Hand opening it to citizens daily between 10:30 and 3:30 (tourists and other outsiders must still apply to the city's administration for permission to visit). On August 15, 2010, scores of residents led by the same initiative, in an effort to highlight the Capitol's restricted access, sang the national anthem at the Open Hand to mark India's Independence Day. This was a watershed moment in the Capitol's recent history. As a performance of protest, it was not simply a mode of political expression, but also an indication of democratic success. It marked the beginnings of new meanings and identities for the city, taking it beyond its much-touted Modernist and Le Corbusian profile, and making it a site of populist contestation, redefinition, and reconstruction. Some two decades since its fortification, even as city elites were contemplating the city's UNESCO World Heritage designation, the question of who really 'owns' Chandigarh has come center-stage.

Beyond Hassan Fathy: New Gourna Today

Not many know that the even after the village of New Gourna was built, the Gourni people for years refused to transfer to their new homes and remained instead in their old village atop the Pharaonic tombs. It reinforced the naïve assumption in the first place that these people would willingly relocate to an unfamiliar settlement designed entirely by an unfamiliar agency. Many of the Gourni, antagonistic toward the relocation effort (and toward Fathy), began to vandalize the village by breaking its dikes, flooding and damaging the foundations. Construction of the new village ultimately failed mainly because of the Gournis' refusal to move to the new site, and the government's inability to force relocation coupled with political and financial issues. Fathy and the Egyptian government pulled out of New Gourna in 1948, and the project was abandoned following the Egyptian revolution of 1952.The Gourni largely continued to reside in their old village of Gourni al-Jadida. Gradually, squatters took over the neglected New Gourna buildings, and ignoring Fathy's original vision, unapologetically altered the village layout and mud brick structures to better serve their daily needs.

Today, New Gourna is in a state of deterioration. Continuing change and appropriation has compromised the material integrity of its structures. A rising water table, lack of an adequate sewer system, extreme heat and ad-hoc infill have destabilized many of the mud brick structures, with several on the verge of collapse. Most structures have been substantially altered - residents have covered the courtyards, filled in the wind catchers, and rebuilt collapsed domes in reinforced concrete – all in a manner antithetical to accepted Western historic preservation standards. These issues have aroused serious concern among preservation experts who see in such attitudes, a serious threat to Fathy's architectural master work.

Image 5:

New Gourna fabric circa 2009 (photo by Roland Unger. Source Wikimedia Commons).

Image 6:

New Gourna fabric circa 2009 (photo by Roland Unger. Source Wikimedia Commons).

In 2009, UNESCO, ICOMOS, and the World Monuments Fund (WMF) announced a rehabilitation initiative titled 'Safeguarding Project of Hassan Fathy's New Gourna Village.' The partnership between these three agencies was strategic: UNESCO and ICOMOS focused on technical concerns such as materials; the WMF brought in its diplomatic experience on issues of public relations and community development. In addition to placing New Gourna on its 2010 "watch list," that is, its annual list of endangered heritage sites, the WMF also reached out to the Gourni people and sought to educate them on the site's historical and architectural significance. The three agencies together released a report in 2011, but before any rehabilitation work officially began, the entire project came to an abrupt halt and to this day, it is unclear if it will ever resume. The agencies have hinted that the project was stalled because of Egypt's tenuous political climate.

Whether or not this is true is not the point. The point is that the UNESCO, ICOMOS, and WMF rehabilitation plan relies heavily on Euclidean methods of conservation. These include land use zoning, urban design guidelines, and building regulations - though such methods carry minimal efficacy in legally ambiguous nations such as Egypt, and particularly in appropriated places like New Gourna. The rehabilitation plan emphasizes architectural and material integrity and encourages the removal of insensitive modifications to Fathy's buildings. But as Susan Sachs has reported, the people who live in New Gourna claim that Fathy's houses no longer meet their needs. There is an increasing desire to replace the original mud bricks because fired bricks can better withstand the climate. Many of the modifications made to the Fathy structures reflect the residents' desire to have amenities like running water and adequate space to house extended families - issues certainly not adequately accounted for in the original plan. The question of what heritage means to the Gourni inhabitants, and even more significantly, who 'owns' New Gourna, remains at the heart of this discussion.

Who's Heritage?

In many ways, the 2011 UNESCO, ICOMOS, and the WMF's rehabilitation plan for New Gourna is similar to what is currently happening with Chandigarh's UNESCO World Heritage Designation discussions. From the inhabitants' standpoint, New Gourna's rehabilitation plan arrived unwanted and uninvited, seeking to impose and insinuate its own conception of heritage and methods of conservation without necessarily taking the residents' needs or interests into account. The agencies took a paternalistic approach to heritage using Western ideals and means to achieve their goals in a distinctively non-Western society. For them heritage could only be fully conveyed in an orderly, antiseptic environment, impeccably restored to its original state.

The same echoes in Chandigarh. The city's future today is the intellectual domain of a franchised elite, not the terrain of the city's inhabitants. In January 1999, to celebrate Chandigarh's 50th anniversary, a distinguished group of international architects gathered in the Capitol. They concluded among other things that Corbusier's original design for the un-built Governor's Palace was far more appealing that his succeeding alternative for the building as the un-built Museum of Knowledge. By December 2007, a year after Chandigarh officials submitted a bid to UNESCO's Paris-based headquarters to make the city a World Heritage site, it was made public that the Chandigarh Administration would build the Museum of Knowledge per the original design of the Governor's Palace, at the same location as initially planned. Who defines authenticity and heritage? Is construction of the Museum of Knowledge in the form of the Governor's Palace an acceptable 'authentication' of Corbusier's original vision? And who actually decides this and why?

Perhaps this has been Chandigarh's missing dimension all along. For all its democratic innuendos, it has evolved through anything but a democratic process. In fact its origins were 'non-democratic' to begin with. As Indian architect Romi Khosla has suggested, the making of Chandigarh was in a sense an 'Imperial Plan' not too dissimilar from colonial New Delhi. Despite their protest, 24 villages and 9,000 residents were displaced by a Euclidean vision. India's Prime Minister Nehru had the powers of the Viceroy and his dictum for an unabashed Modernity, however well intentioned, was never subjected to the litmus test of the native public - just as UNESCO, ICOMOS, and WMF sought to do at New Gourna.

Chandigarh and New Gourna then are telling instances of how visions, utopias, aspirations, and architectural prowess are rarely able to surpass the socio-political vagaries of time. They affirm that architecture and architectural conservation, however masterful, is but a pawn in a complex socio-political game. If the Capitol's guise from a national monument to a forlorn center, and New Gourna's natural take-over and appropriation tell us anything, it is that monumentality, social-justice, civic pride are eventually not architectural but socio-political phenomena. The intentions of places can become confused even at their inception, and certainly during their subsequent reception – at once an artistic, political, and anthropological problem. While visionary aspirations are important, the expectations and circumstances of those who inhabit, adopt, appropriate, and 'own' them are even more critical to their nurturing and long-term future.

The task at hand is to expand the lens through which we read, understand, engage with, and ultimately, envision the future of such places. Chandigarh and New Gourna should not be mistaken as the mere relics for mainstream preservation or heritage designations, but as the very seeds of larger evolving visions that are being tested and completed by generations to come. Whether or not Corbusier's city becomes a World Heritage Site, and whether of not Fathy's buildings ever get restored, what these places need desperately is a far more reflective examination of their complex cultural narrative. They need a deeper empathetic reassessment of the many other far more important forces and entities. This includes examining people, their needs, their preferences, their inclinations – all aspects that are shaping the identity of these places today. Chandigarh and New Gourna are not dead ruins to be embalmed, designated, restored, and glorified. They are living repositories of shifting histories that have gone far beyond their master architects or their original visions. It is these histories that should be brought to the forefront, to dominate the ongoing dialogues on their future.

References

Bharne, Vinayak. "Le Corbusier's Ruin: The Changing Face of Chandigarh's Capitol." Journal of Architectural Education 64/2. Association of Collegiate Schools of Architecture, March 2011.
Fathy, Hassan. *Architecture for the Poor: An Experiment in Rural Egypt*. Chicago: University of Chicago Press, 1976.
Hamid, Ahmad. *Hassan Fathy and Continuity in Islamic Arts and Architecture: The Birth of a New Modern*. Cairo: The American University in Cairo Press, 2010.
Iskander, Lara. "The Village of New Gourna." 9 June 2011. Available online at: <http://www.touregypt.net/featurestories/newgourna.htm>.
Pyla, Panayiota. "The Many Lives of New Gourna: Alternative Histories of a Model Community and their Current Significance." The Journal of Architecture 2009 (14:6), p. 715 - 30.
Sachs, Susan. "Honoring a Visionary if Not His Vision." *New York Times* (E:1). 4 April 2000.
Steele, James. *An Architecture for People: The Complete Works of Hassan Fathy*. New York: Whitney Library of Design, 1997.
Taragan, Hana. "Architecture in Fact and Fiction: The Case of New Gourna Village in Upper Egypt." Muquarnas 1999 (16), p. 169 - 78.
UNESCO Publications "New Gourna Village." Accessed online at: < http://whc.unesco.org/en/activities/637/>.
UNESCO Publications. Safeguarding Project of Hassan Fathy's New Gourna Village: A UNESCO Initiative. April 2011. Available online at: <http://unesdoc.unesco.org/images/0019/001925/192524e.pdf>.
World Monuments Fund. "Hassan Fathy's New Gourna: Past, Present, Future." October 2010. Accessed online at: http://www.wmf.org/video/hassan-fathys-new-gourna-past-present-future.

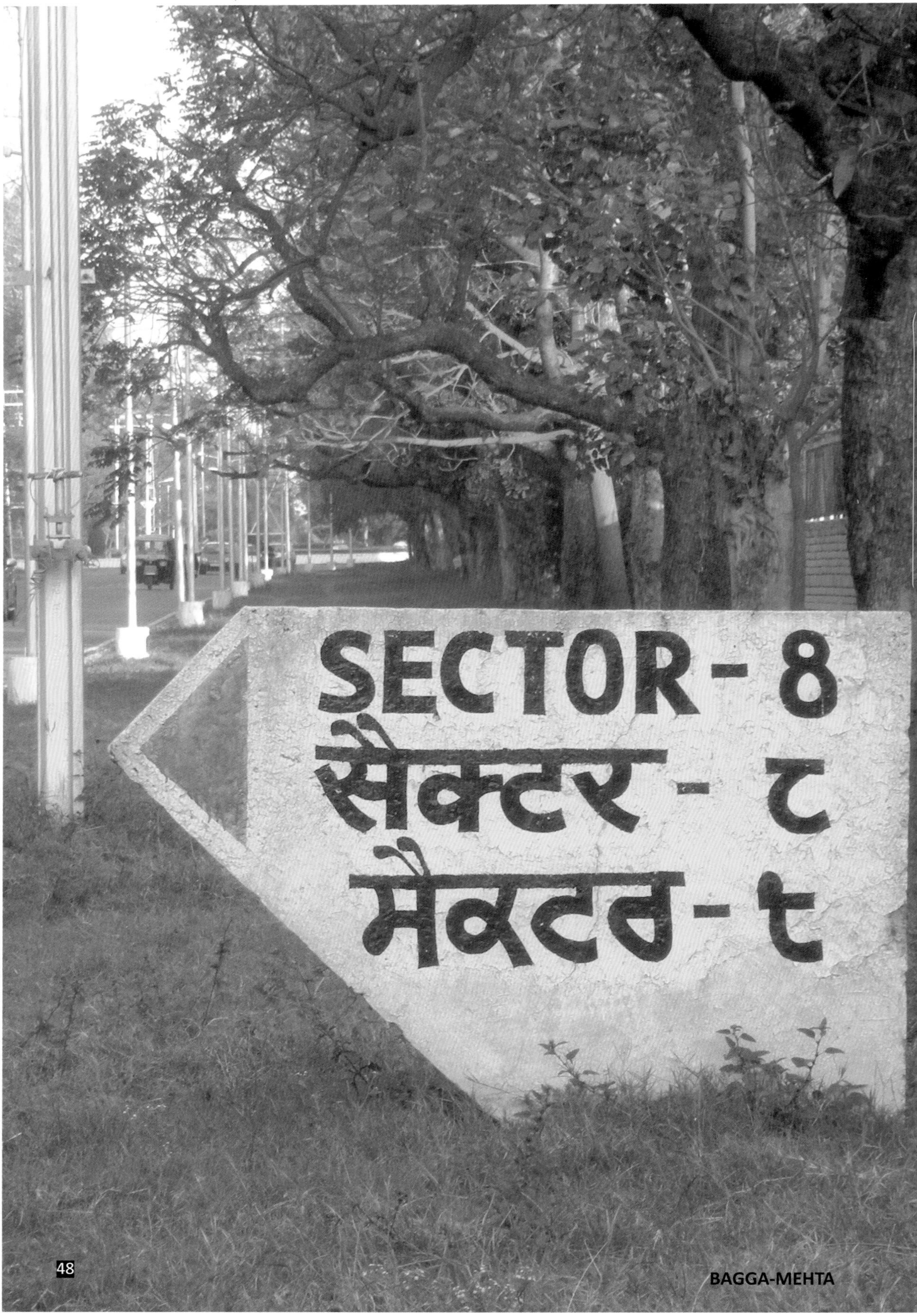

BAGGA-MEHTA

(Re) Defining The Typologies
Of Chandigarh's Urban Edges

SANGEETA BAGGA-MEHTA

ABSTRACT

Among the earliest examples of 'planned' cities in post-independent India, Chandigarh has attracted substantial attention within the urban scholarship. In a manner unprecedented (and yet uncontested), the conception of Chandigarh and its legislated urban limits where established vis-a-vis Le Corbusier's *Edict of Chandigarh and Statute of the land,* which reflects the city's unique relationship with its surrounding rural hinterland. It is the reflection of an urban environment defined by its edges - formalizing a sharply marked, urban-rural divide. In fact, this urban-rural divide is certainly not new. While urban settlements have always differentiated between these two realms, what makes Chandigarh's case especially unique is the specific geo-morphology of the city's urban landscape and the natural denominators that have marked these described edges. Few Indian cities have recognized or acknowledged specific natural constraints as sital elements in their urban plans. Chandigarh is defined by the Shivalik range to the north, while the Sukhna Choe and Patiali Ki Rao constitute its eastern and western riverine edges. The urban canvas is completed by the gently southwards slope, where the city grid is met by the zigzagging political boundary with the state of Punjab.

Culminating by the mid-1990s, the last few decades have witnessed a series of political, economic, and socio-cultural forces that have redefined these originally conceived urban boundaries. Simultaneously, these processes have lead to the creation of some 'new' internal edges and borders. Of these edge interventions in Chandigarh, the first manifestation is the enlargement of the boundary edges of the city to now include developments that effectively enlarge the Corbusian plan. A second development is the intensified link between the Corbusian city and its so-called 'peri-urban' areas. Third is the creation of an expanded zone of influence mediating between the city and its hinterland alongside the creation of new urbanities. The fourth is the retention of existing urban villages within the Corbusian city and their intrinsic interactions with the surrounding urbanity. In effect, while the Corbusian city continues to respect its 'original' sectoral grid, its system of 7Vs, its landscape plan of open spaces interspersed within sectors, a distinct patina of change is now visible, with newer developments coming up while older edges redefine themselves.

Within this background describing Chandigarh's move to towards her future, this research examines how original and new edges have modified and reinvented themselves since the city's inception and more recently in specific response to the pressures of urban expansion. Of particular focus is city's connection (and re-connection) with its hinterland, a dichotomy that the original Corbusian plan never completely reconciled. Beyond this thorny issue, the discussion also seeks to bring to forefront how some of the city's edges have been modulated to accommodate the new developments without compromising the ideological basis that underscores the core values inherent in this city of Sun, Space, and Verdure.

Image 1:

Map of British-India (1947) - The dawn of freedom from colonial rule in the subcontinent has forever been marked by the agony of Partition. The bloodshed, sweat of terror, and the tears of helplessness made India's partition and the creation of Pakistan simultaneously the most signifying and the most traumatic moment in South Asia's history. The map shows undivided Panjab in India just before the end of British rule.

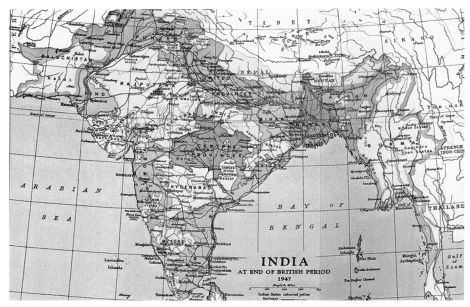

Edges that Matter

In contrast to their historic counterparts that lie embedded and 'organically' emerge from their site geographies; planned cities are pre-determined by the limits of their urban geographies and political boundaries. As layered configurations, within these urban environments reside overlapping boundaries called *edges*. While these edges occasionally remain as independent entities, more frequently, these also merge into one another. These edges operate at various levels and remain in a continual state of flux and change. While some represent physical limits of deeper, geopolitical and economic upheavals within the urban fabric, others are but barriers containing discrete parts both within and outside the legal confines of the city, some even serving as perimeters of no-man's land. The holistic understanding of these edges within planned cities remains a complex one, especially within the Indian subcontinent. This research seeks to better understand the emergence of such edge conditions - termed interchangeably as borders, boundaries, and seams under different lenses.

Among India's first few planned modern cities, Chandigarh was created following India's partition in 1947. Punjab was divided into east and west, separated by a national border, which formed the nations of India and Pakistan. The genesis of this divisive, political edge was marked by the mass migrations for Hindus and Muslims, emotional turmoil, and, indeed, the loss of the cultural capital at Lahore that had served both religious communities before partition. This edge condition also created emotional disconnects and permanent barriers for the countless refugees who would never be able to return to their native homelands. This bitter truth, etched in the minds of the displaced, was apparent soon following the process of partition. Chandigarh must therefore be viewed within this context. As the brainchild of India's first Prime Minister Jawaharlal Nehru, it came to fill the void created by this geopolitical edge and one especially exaggerated by the loss of Lahore with its institutions of culture. With the foundation of Chandigarh was seeded a microcosm – the Punjab University. This institution 'travelled' from Lahore, reorganized with its refugee faculty and administrators, and was compelled to operate with teaching departments temporarily scattered in the Amritsar, Jullundur, Ludhiana, Hoshiarpur, and Delhi, while administrative offices remained at the hill resort of Solan. Following a Senate decision in 1956, it was finally consolidated in Chandigarh on 550 acres in the northwestern urban fringe bordering the *Patiali ki Rao* rivulet.[1]

Image 2:

The Chandigarh master plan (1953) - as it emerged from the geomorphic determinants of water courses and topography. Image courtesy: Foundation Le Corbusier, France

In 1966, a second political upheaval created yet another geopolitical edge around Chandigarh. Conceived originally as the capital of the Indian state of Punjab, Chandigarh, now not only became the seat of Union Territory Administration, but also the capital of the two adjoining states of Punjab and Haryana, the latter carved out of Punjab in the year 1966. In effect, Chandigarh, as the seat of three governments, realized a central location in the region.[2] Various government and corporate magnets favored the city as the location of their regional head offices. However, this primacy of status also came with a reduction in size for the city. Today, of the original 114 square kilometers of urban area defined for Chandigarh, only 64 square kilometers remain; the rest forms uneasy peripheries with the neighboring townships of Panchkula and Mohali. In fact, this may not even be the settled *status quo*, since ongoing constructions within these townships are constantly transgressing these boundaries.

Image 3:

The trauma of partition witnessed in 1947 with the loss of Lahore (the capital of East Panjab (left millions homeless and the division of British India between the two new dominions was accomplished according to what has come to be known as the "3rd June Plan" or the "Mountbatten Plan" UNHCR estimates that 14 million Hindus, Sikhs, and Muslims were displaced during the partition and it was the largest mass migration in human history.

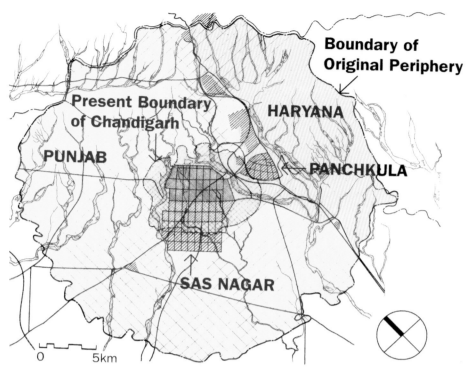

Image 4:

The division of the Chandigarh's periphery to carve out the states of Haryana and Panjab shrunk the city's hinterland and marked the beginning of pressure on the new capital. This pressure intensified with the development of Mohali and Panchkula, which were dormitory towns feeding on Chandigarh's educational, health, and urban infrastructure. (Kiran Joshi, Documenting Chandigarh- The Works of Pierre Jeanneret, Maxwell Fry and Jane Drew- Volume-1, Mapin, India, 1999)

Why did Chandigarh's periphery change and morph in this fashion? To start, Chandigarh's perimeter was no mere boundary line or an arbitrarily defined area. It was envisaged as a protective hinterland buffer that would protect the urbanity of the city and therefore remain sacrosanct in accordance with the *Edict of Chandigarh and the Statute of the land* as conceived by Le Corbusier.[3] This mechanism was intended to limit urban sprawl in the decades following the foundation of Chandigarh, providing adequate 'agricultural backup', strategically preserving the catchment basins of the watercourses that would help sustain life within the city. As per the legislation promulgated in 1952, the Periphery Control Act of Chandigarh was aimed at safeguarding these vulnerable peripheral wetlands and agricultural belts around the planned city. However, in decades following, and especially more recently, this has been violated by emergence of several townships, including Panchkula and Mohali, which have come up in Chandigarh's periphery, due to the reorganization of Punjab.[4] As a result, now, not only is the peripheral green belt being relentlessly depleted, but the city's infrastructure is also under grave threat.

Chandigarh and its Four Scales of Urban Edges

For the purposes of this chapter, Chandigarh has been examined at four hierarchical levels where borders, edges, or boundaries are recognizable both within and outside the urban plan of the city. These are the **XL** (extra large or monumental), **L** (large or city), **M** (medium or intra-city/sector), and **S** (small or the intra-sector, sub-sector, street and property) scales. While the borders within each of these scales may at times interchange to the next higher or lower scale depending upon the function, these scales remain largely constant.

a. The 'XL' (Extra-Large) Scale

Within Chandigarh, natural water systems, which are seasonal and natural in their manifestation, determine the geomorphology of the site and in turn influence the orthogonal plan of the city. Since its foundation, the relationship between Chandigarh and its ecological landscape elements (sun, space, verdure, and the water systems) has generated an urban structure of edges, which are location specific and thereby indigenous in their unique way. Corbusier's' chequer-board plan may be perceived as a density equation of sorts, wherein from north to south, there is progressive densification, with the north thinning out as its thin spaces merge into the folds of a mountainous landscape. The site selected for Chandigarh was a gently rolling plain located at the south of the foothills of the Shivalik Hills, ideal for its drainage and spatially contained within the natural confines of two seasonal rivulets that irrigated the land – the *Sukhna Choe* in the east and the *Patiali ki Rao* in the west. This southwards 'bias' of urban plan was also inherent in the expected (and intended) growth of the city in future decades. Meanwhile, perhaps best construed as intent to maintain a constant contact with nature, a shallow gorge traversing the urban site in the north-south direction was retained in its pristine state. Today, this central linear parkland or the Valley of Leisure, serves as a major recreational and lung space for this city.

Situated at latitude 300 50' N and longitude 760 48', Chandigarh has an altitude varying from 304.80 to 365.76 meters above sea level. The availability of elements such as an abundant natural groundwater supply, fertile soil, local building materials - clay, sand, and stone, have paved the way for development. Even climate has contributed as an important element in the making of the city. The city building process was on a shoestring budget, and with its climate responsive and site sensitive approach, Chandigarh became a city with regulatory measures to monitor its development in order to make it sustainable in the future as well as lend an environmental imageability to the city's urban form. The 3.7 kilometers radius of farmland for dairy and vegetables was extended to 6.2 kilometers and thus the periphery shared a natural border with its hinterland.

Tempered by geomorphic forms, seasonal rivulets and a backdrop of the Shivalik Hills, an urban form has been realized, which creates an identifiable city structure. Chandigarh has its unique, exclusive urban image-picturesque settings, large open spaces, and a well-ordered orthogonal matrix with a distinctive vocabulary of lowrise cubic forms. Planned as a finite entity, which would harness its resources for the present and preserve its assets for future generations, Chandigarh has served as a role model for the development of several new towns in India and abroad. Its master plan, based on the principles of CIAM (Congress, Internationale Architecture de' Moderne') afforded Living, Working, Circulation, and Care of Body and Spirit as the main city functions. Akin to the human body, the Capitol is the commanding head, the commercial center as the heart, its hand as the industrial area, its brain and intellect as the parkland. Within the city, the location of primary functions

Image 5:

The XL Scale – Le Corbusier's' checkerboard plan may be perceived as a density equation of sorts, wherein north to south, there is progressive densification, with the north thinning out as its spaces merge into a mountainous landscape. (Photograph by the author)

creates districts, defined by distinct streets that serve as edges for each - the Government Center, the City Center, the Industrial Area, and the University Campus. At Chandigarh, the XL or extra-large scale, binds the city to its hinterland, linking the gridiron to the natural environment created by the Shivaliks and the meandering watercourses of the *Patiali ki Rao* and the *Sukhna Choe*. One offshoot of the *Sukhna Choe* (stream) is the Sukhna Lake – a dam created to collect the runoff from the hills as a lake with flood-gates that could be raised should the monsoon discharge cross safety levels.

At Chandigarh, the matrix comprising the water channels, basins, and streams create their own borders and seams. In effect, undifferentiated edges are perceived. At the city level, the *Sukhna* Lake catchment - artificially created by an earthen dam across the seasonal *Sukhna* River, serves as a popular recreational place, besides supporting wildlife and serving as a migratory fauna sanctuary. However, Chandigarh has grown beyond its hydro edge; its urban matrix extending beyond the Sukhna rivulet to the Information Technology Park and NAC Manimajra township to the east. Another hydro edge feature are the Natural Ponds existing within the villages,[5] which serve the water needs and much beyond, and link the various elements together.

The eastern and western rivulets, with their watercourses, set limits to the city's growth, are the ecological wetlands that preserve the pristine character of the site, serving as borders to the hinterland beyond. Then, the *Leisure Valley* comprises the park system of the city. It also serves to collect rainwater runoff from the city and aids to replenish the water table level. The seasonal rivulet N Choe meandering through the middle of the site of Chandigarh was developed into a continuous green belt (the Leisure Valley) and the north to south slope provided natural drainage. Parallel to this are sector level open space systems that also run n-s and serve as rainwater catchments, and generate the spine network of catchments. Finally, at the sector level, the north-south green is the seam - a loose zipper that links and connects neighborhood level socio-cultural and health facilities. Yet somewhere in this division, a segregation of uses for the functional city has marginalized the inter-connectivity and the sector dividing V3 streets have created edge conditions between the limbs. Likewise, the horizontal V2s the Madhya Marg, Dakshin, and Vikas Marg have created economic divisions between the city due to the large plots with villa houses north of the town and increasing density with row housing and apartment blocks towards the south. This represents the classic case of the city edge remodeling itself at the XL scale.

b. The 'L' (Large) Scale

At the L or large scale, the edges of Chandigarh function as seams, or zippers – linking and laterally connecting different districts. Three areas within the city deserve particular mention in terms of the edges that are hence created. These are the Leisure Valley Parkland that runs through the length of the city, the so-called 'Urban Village' phenomenon occurring at the fringes of Chandigarh, and the developments within the Information Technology Park Boom and Industrial Area.

The Leisure Valley Parkland, which serves as the link between sectors and the intra-sector districts, is the first large seam within Chandigarh. As a component of the original realized plan of Chandigarh, it runs as a linear parkland – quite literally, 'the forest within the city', traversing north to south along the city's length. At another level, the development phases one, two, and three alongside the density equation of the city, creates borders with the horizontal V2 streets, namely, the Madhya Marg, the Dakshin Marg, and the southernmost Vikas Marg. The first phase is low rise and low density, gradually flowing into the second phase of medium-density with narrower units and 'marla' housing, culminating in the densest, phase three, where walkup apartments and group housing schemes have been realized to accommodate the growing population. The three horizontal V2 streets serve as the boundaries of this density equation.

Corbusier's plan, despite its urban rigor, also called for a green belt around the city - the second large urban seam. In response, the Development Plan for the 16 km belt around Chandigarh, brought under the Punjab New Capital (Periphery) Control Act (1952), summarily prohibited all building activities for non-agricultural purposes towards the preservation of this green belt. However, even in this plan, the so-called 'abadi-deh' areas of village hamlets falling in the Periphery Control Area were exempt from the provisions of this Act, while subject to certain restrictions. In the first phase of the plan, therefore, the 'Urban Village Edge' phenomenon can be seen, wherein not only agricultural land but also the area falling under the abadi-deh was acquired for development as part of the sector planning process. However, in the second phase, the abadi-deh of four villages, namely Burail, Attawa, Buterla, and Badheri, whose agricultural land was acquired, excluded from the acquisition process yet integrated within the sectoral plan. Thereafter, these mentioned villages are governed by their own development regulations and do not fall under the purview

of the Urban Planning legislative framework.[6] Activities such as dairy farming (which had been typical to these villages), are no longer allowed within the sector periphery. This has led to a mixed land-use at the village peripheries, along principal streets and important linkages. In extension, the introduction of the service industry is the most recent landuse to appear on these once-rural fringes abutting the city. Likewise, lower rentals and cheaper living has witnessed numerous migrants into the urban villages and they constitute the primary workforce of the surrounding city areas. In effect, the razor edge of the traditional urban village and the mother city has been negotiated and redefined to share a decent living and working environment.

Starting in 2006, the Government of India's directive[7] began to catalyze the urban diversification of the city's periphery into a plethora of educational and infrastructural additions. The Information Technology Park was set up on the eastern end, beyond Sukhna Lake and the township of Manimajra, creating what may be defined as a new economic edge. As Chandigarh's third large seam, this has consciously supplemented the economic instruments of Corb's plan. Other developments in the city's immediate vacant pockets have included the Education City and the Medicity. The Information Technology (IT) Park also propagated a demand for housing infrastructure to accommodate the new office goers in these round the clock global enterprises. In anticipation of these 'peripheral' populations (an antithesis to the original plan), entrepreneurs, and gourmet delights have occupied the mega-malls, some even included in their building programs. Likewise, the border of the Sukhna hydro-edge was redefined by busy traffic arteries now linking the city and the Information Technology Park along with the railway station, airport, and highway to Delhi and other neighboring states. Even beyond this urban growth, the syntax of architectural character employed at the Information Technology Park is in sharp contrast to the low rise cubic architectural forms of the Chandigarh city fabric raising provocative questions on the proximity of the two diverging architectural styles.

Yet another fourth edge transformation has occurred at the Industrial Area, which once constituted the eastern armature of the Corbusian grid. What was once separated from the city-proper by a 'substantial' border of mango groves and the industrial zone, keeping its noxious fumes from blowing towards the city, is today a heavy traffic zone, responding to the proliferation of additional, non-industrial activities. A revised 2006 legislation[8] has allowed industrial units to transform and amalgamate smaller plots into mega malls, multiplexes, and hotels. While land values of ailing

Image 8:

The L Scale is an edge condition in the abadi deh urban villages within the sectoral grid and even outside of it, whereby a rural urban exchange of goods and services is set up between Chandigarh and its urban villages. In effect, the razor edge of the traditional urban village and the mother city has been negotiated and redefined to share a decent living and working environment. (Department of Urban Planning, Chandigarh Administration UT)

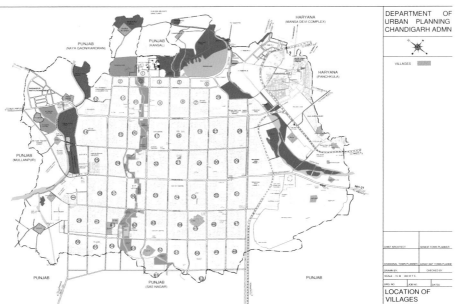

BAGGA-MEHTA

industries have skyrocketed, so have traffic congestion, parking woes, and overall character of the industrial area. This is a radical transformation from the earlier manufacturing industrial units, which had catered to the larger automobile industry in the region to the growth of an Information Technology Sector with white-collar workers replacing the indigenous definitions of industry.

With this industrial conversion policy, larger land parcels (larger than one acre) continue to conform to the building regulations, but the smaller industrial units are facing closure, with their owners moving out at low prices. Thus, while on one hand, the industrial area of Chandigarh is witnessing a building boom, on the other, large in-between tracts of single-story sheds present a discord in the absence of a holistic industrial policy backed by sound legislation. The original plot subdivision and building regulations displayed sensitivity to the concept of urban space and form, where an aesthetic regulation formed the necessary background of order against which individual architects could experiment and display their creativity interchangeably. The industrial conversion policy has failed to address the street picture, environmental psychology, scale, and urban density of the area. The high-rise emerging urbanity of the industrial area as compared to the two and a half-storied lowrise character of the city presents a new edge condition where diverse building materials, finishes, and contemporary architectural styles *border* the Chandigarh Style conceived by Pierre Jeanneret, Maxwell Fry, and Jane Drew.

c. The 'M' Scale

The V3 streets bordering and defining residential sectors are edges for the self-contained and introverted neighbourhood units 800 m x 1200 m, with the V4 and V5 streets defining the four predetermined entry points into the sector. Within the sector the vertically running north-south green 'fingers' support community buildings, sacred places, sports & medical institutions – while the more urban market street on V4 doubles as the edge within the sector demarcating north and south. At this scale, the single- and double-story section of the V4 street is important as it defines the pedestrian and vehicular segregation, the shop front and parking pockets of the

Image 9:

The Information Technology Park was set up on the eastern end, beyond the Sukhna Lake and the township of Manimajra, creating what urbanists have defined as a new economic edge. (Photograph by the author)

market, the row of flowering trees that borders the slightly curved market street representing the pack donkey's path as Le Corbusier himself called it. The V3 also defines the boundary of Le Corbusier's involvement in the sector, since the 'Spiritual Directeur' of the Chandigarh enterprise was preoccupied with the pieces of the monumental Capitol Complex and City Center, while the Chandigarh family of Fry, Drew, and Jeanneret were left to design the sector housing and its plethora of public amenities. At the block level and the architectural scale, boundaries are perceived which define sub-sectors.

Image 10:

The V4 market street, meandering as the 'pack donkey way' was the edge for the sub-sectors within the 800 m x 1200 m neighbourhood unit of the sector. (Photograph by the author)

d. The 'S' Scale

Seen as the intimate scale or the detail at the block level, the small/micro scale reveals the section of the V6 and V7 streets that convey traffic to the individual dwelling. At this level, the Drew Villages and the block typologies created within the sub-sectors, in addition to their identifiable architectural character constitute the defining markers of territoriality. Sector 22 was among the earliest of the sectors to be developed; it was characterized by the 'arched' borders that define the Drew Village. Within this community unit, larger Type 8 duplex homes cluster around central, sunny green spaces bordered by flowering trees much like an English neighborhood by Maxwell Fry, and the single-story stonewall units with box-like, sun breaker walls by Pierre Jeanneret. Chandigarh's mammoth housing plan comprising of 13 distinct categories of housing for all classes of people in the city represents the S scale. From within the variants of these 13 housing categories was born the characteristic Chandigarh Style of Architecture. And, in keeping 'good taste' in mind, the 'Chandigarh Style' was extended as a form of 'aesthetic legislation' to be fittingly extended to private housing design as well. With the development of Government Housing, privately owned plots also began to be constructed. Initially there were no laws to guide the private residential constructions, but the good taste set forth by the government architects soon set the tone for aesthetic legislation in private housing too.[9]

Chandigarh's Future on the Peripheries

In the 60 years since Chandigarh's inception, the city has grown inwards and exploded outwards. Not only have its borders, boundaries, and edge conditions faced the pressures of local and regional growth poles, but its ecological and geomorphic landscape edges have yielded to larger trends of global and economic liberalization. Many of these proposed liberalization policies have adopted entirely unprecedented ways of harnessing landscapes, ecologies, and cities within India's narrative towards development. How this restates the meaning of Chandigarh's urbanity in the next decades therefore remains to be seen.

Image 11:

Sector 22 - the earliest sector to be developed is characterized by the arched borders defining the Drew Village defining the S scale and creating the edge condition of territoriality within the subsector. (Photograph by the author)

Image 12:

Initially there were no laws to guide the private residential constructions, but the good taste set forth by the government architects soon set the tone for aesthetic legislation in Privately built housing too. (Photograph by the author)

Among the myriad of compelling issues that have emerged, the growth in urban population, both within and outside the urban limits of Chandigarh, is perhaps most important. Even if the population and density increase within the sectors could be accounted for, Chandigarh's growth as a regional magnet has brought about a proliferation of squatter settlements within the city's described hinterland. This has created its associated environmental problems, including, but not limited to, the edges of the city where squatters have come to reside. This especially includes lands alongside railway corridors, under high-tension power lines, along the flood and catchment areas of seasonal rivulets that form within the Sukhna Lake area, and within urban sectors that accommodate these incoming migrants.

Among these sites of migrant settlement, the development of new (and often in-formal) settlements within the original periphery creates a pressure for the mother city. It strains the urban infrastructure, and is reflected in the new economic edges that are discernible now. These new edges underscore a decided shift in the city's status from a purely capital/government city (as in the past) to a high-class, region-al locus encouraging commerce and production, while specializing as a center for medical and educational expertise in the north Indian region. Within this scenario, Chandigarh has often defaulted towards the urbanistic (and unrealistic) approach to relocate these informal (and slum) settlements currently positioned on the city's peripheries. The city has consciously devoted more than 2,000 acres of its urban land solely for parks, while strategically allocating precious little space for the poor populations within its future master plan. In opposition, urban thinkers have in fact suggested the in-situ upgrading of long established and unauthorized settlements instead of their arbitrary resettlement in other sites. Given that entirely stopping migrations to Chandigarh, or for that matter to any other Indian city, is neither an option nor a viable choice, this pre-emptive approach would at least alleviate pressures on the urban core and surmount the growing problem of land scarcity in Chandigarh.

The second issue, closely connected to the peripheral slums, is that of the sheer numbers of incoming migrants. The result has been the remodeling of earlier more or less predominant natural edge conditions by relatively aggressive, human-made ones. When conceived, Chandigarh was designed for a population of 150,000 persons to be accommodated in Phase I of the urban plan, followed by 350,000 inhabitants in Phase II, with an average density of 17 persons per acre in the former and 60 persons per acre in the latter. The current population of the city (as per the projections in the Chandigarh *Master Plan 2031*) is about 1,200,000. The city and its fringe areas contain pockets of habitation, which comprise slums and squatters crossing the 200,000 mark. In addition, development pressure from the satellite townships of Mohali and Panchkula are creating demands on the physical and social infrastructure of the city. Efforts to rehabilitate the squatter settlements under the minimum needs program can barely match the demand and is by no means putting an end to the inwards migrations.

Thirdly, with new townships, the growth along the urban corridors has led to land speculation and unplanned growth. These developer oriented dormitory suburbs further pressurize the city's basic urban services. Within Chandigarh's sectoral grid, four existing villages have been retained, which are facing land speculation owing to

Image 13:

There is a discernible shift in the city's status from a purely capital/ government city to a high-class regional locus of commerce, medicine, and education. The Master Plan 2031 suggests the remodelling of earlier, more or less predominant, natural edge conditions by more aggressive, manmade ones. (Chandigarh Master Plan 2031)

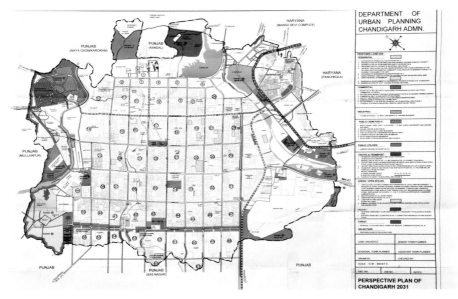

the absence of development controls or regulations. Within the villages themselves, rampant and unlegislated encroachments and vertical developments flout building byelaws. This is creating increasing pressure on the city and adversely affecting the surrounding residential sectors.

In addition to urban migrations, the ambitious Periphery Control Act of Chandigarh also appears to have riled, in past decades, urban legislators themselves. As a case in point, townships such as Panchkula and Mohali sprung up in Chandigarh's vicinity despite strict guidelines. In extension, by 1990, the State Government declared an area of 10,000 acres to be a Free Enterprise Zone (FEZ), wherein the setting up of industries was actually permitted around Corbusier's capital. While this appears to have substantially undermined the power of the Periphery Act, even the enforcement of this act has largely remained patchy. In 1998, the Punjab Government decided to permit an over-arching regularization of all existing unauthorized constructions, as well as permitting the future construction of educational and health institutions.

Image 14:

Chandigarh continues to be strongly embedded in its urban geography. There is a heightened and growing awareness of the citizens towards the heritage value of the city viewed now at the national and global forums. Its urban edges, above all, continue to re-define themselves to serve the particular focus - the city's connection (and re-connection) with its hinterland. (Photograph by the author)

Nevertheless, as a harbinger of change, Chandigarh has ushered India into a new era of urbanism. The city was conceived as an exemplar in the annals of town planning and its place in India's history of post-independence urbanism remains secure. It continues to be seen as a bold experiment for city planners with a moral and social commitment embodying improved living conditions; while recognizing the compelling needs of Indian society, its cultural milieu, as well as the inseparable contact between humankind and nature. Chandigarh is a living city, where the original ideas of foundation have been translated into a spatial plan, allowing flexibility to accommodate growth and manage change. All cities are embedded in their urban geographies. In a similar fashion, the intrinsic character of Chandigarh arises and relies upon its ecological determinants. The north is defined by the Shivalik foothills, whereas in the confines of its eastern and western wetlands is arrayed the sectoral grid defined via a 800 x 1200 meter neighborhood sector. Given this embedded-ness and hierarchy of edges, Chandigarh continues to maintain the spirit of the city of Sun, Space, and Verdure. At the XL scale, it must contain its limits of growth defined by its geographical constraints and be equally protected by a political will to conserve its character. At the L scale, the Master Plan 2031 is a legal instrument ensuring regulated development, urban fabric and character. The scales at the M and S levels are safeguarded as a trickle effect of the XL and L scales. Further, these are also affected by the heightened awareness of the citizens towards the heritage value of their city viewed now at national and global forums. Chandigarh's urban edges, above all, continue to remodel and reinvent themselves to be ecologically viable and serve the particular focus - the city's connection (and re-connection) with its hinterland. Nevertheless, Chandigarh continues to take up these challenges to show the way forward as a city of Sun, Space, and Verdure through its interchanging borders, edges, and seams.

Endnotes

1. Many, who had walked miles barefoot seeking refuge in transit camps, were awarded graduation degrees within the transit campuses - such were the ramifications of the geo-political fissure caused by the partition of Panjab.
2. Aptly hailed a city of convenience and comfort, Chandigarh was to occupy an area of 70 square kilometres, whose places of residence, work, and recreation (based upon the principles of CIAM) would be easily accessible from all parts of the city. Beginning in 1951, Le Corbusier played a significant role in orchestrating the present urban form of the city. Chandigarh has been developed in two phases: Sectors 1-30 in Phase One, and Sectors 31-47 in Phase Two, designed for a population of 150,000 in the first phase and 350,000 in the second phase. Presently Phase Three comprising of sectors 48-56, 61 & 63 is being developed to provide an additional area of 8.47 sq. km. The population in 1961 was 119,881 and by 2011 it was 1,054,686.
3. Capital of Punjab, Periphery Control Act, 1952. This act initially allowed for an urban a periphery extending 8 kms beyond the limits of Chandigarh, which was further extended to 16 km in 1962 under the Periphery Control Area Plan.
4. Following the re-organization of the State of Punjab in 1966, the Periphery Control Area got divided between the Indian states of Punjab, Haryana, and the Union Territory of Chandigarh with the majority of share going to state of Punjab. (Source: Chandigarh Master Plan 2031 document). In 1966, the re-organization of Punjab created Chandigarh as a Union Territory with 114 square kilometers area wherein Chandigarh city comprised of 70 square kilometers and 44 square kilometers were designated as periphery (Punjab occupied1,021 square kilometers and Haryana occupied 295 square kilometers out of the periphery which had a total area of 1,360 square kilometers).
5. Dhanas, Sarangpur, Khuda Jassu, Dhanas, Sarangpur, Khuda Jassu, Khuda Alisher, Behlana, and Khuda lahora have one pond each, Kaimbwala has 2 as per the Chandigarh Masterplan 2031.
6. At present, the Union Territory of Chandigarh has 23 villages in all. Manimajra village, which is located on the eastern edge of the city, was a small village at the time of preparing the original plan. This has today developed as a census town and is an integral part of the Chandigarh master plan.
7. In recent decades, the Chandigarh Administration has focused on the promotion of the Information Technology (IT) industry, which requires less space and is considered largely non-polluting. Accordingly, high-speed data communication facilities for software development and technology export have been arranged by providing a NODE at Punjab Engineering College (PEC), Chandigarh through the Software Technology Parks of India (STPI). STPI has set up an earth station at Mohali for the proposed Software Technology Park (Complex) set up by the Punjab Government. These economic propellers have rendered an economic edge condition to germinate within Chandigarh.
8. The industrial area of Chandigarh was sited, keeping in perspective the proximity to the railway station, inter-city highways, and the airport to cater so as to facillitate easy receipt of raw materials and distribution of manufactured goods to other towns. Sixty years later, with policy level changes in the industrial development of the country from a predominantly government and state owned entity to an industrial house and public sector enterprise along with liberalization in terms of foreign investment and global exchanges in both technology and resources, the industrial scenario of Chandigarh (like most Indian cites) has dramatically transformed.
9. The desire by Maxwell Fry, Jane Drew, and Pierre Jeanneret to develop an apparatus that would prevent 'visual anarchy' in the public domain and thereby ensure that the good urban form conceived by them would take root, caused private housing at Chandigarh to come under the purview of progressive architectural control. Local building materials such as brick, stone, and lime plaster played a key role in contributing to the homogenous character of the sector while responding to the mandates of climate, economy, and local construction techniques.

References

Capital of Panjab (Development and Regulation) Act 1952. The Controller - Printing & Stationery, Government of Panjab, 1953.

Casciato, Maristella, Gulinello, Francesco and Alessandrini, Elisa (eds.). *Abitaire à Chandigarh - Pierre Jeanneret, Maxwell Fry and Jane B. Drew.* Bologna: CLUEB, 2014.

Chandigarh Aesthetic Legislation: Documentation of Urban Controls in Chandigarh (1951-2001). Chandigarh College of Architecture, UT Chandigarh, 1999.

Chandigarh Master Plan 2031. Chandigarh: Department of Urban Planning, UT Chandigarh, 2015.

Evenson, Norma. *Chandigarh.* Los Angeles: University of California Press, 1966.

Joshi, Kiran. *Chandigarh - The Indian Architecture of Pierre Jeanneret, Maxwell Fry and Jane Beverley Drew* (Vol.1). Ahmedabad: Mapin Publishing,1999.

Le Corbusier. *Edict of Chandigarh & The Statute of the Land- Chandigarh*, 17 December, 1959.

Moss, Stanislaus von (ed.). *Chandigarh 1956. Le Corbusier, Pierre Jeanneret, Jane B. Drew, E. Maxwell Fry.* Zurich: Scheidegger & Spiess, 2010.

Sarin, Madhu. *Urban Planning in the Third World: The Chandigarh Experience.* London: Mansell Publishing Limited,1982.

Walden, Russell (ed.). *The Open Hand - Essays on Le Corbusier.* Cambridge, Mass.: MIT Press, 1977.

Discarding Corb's Shoes: Marginal Voices and Local Histories from the Urban Edge

ARIJIT SEN

ABSTRACT

This chapter offers a critical alternative to the Urban Edge Symposium's goal of "stepping vicariously into Corb's shoes" and argues that transforming notions of city and urbanity in the 21st century necessitates that we actually "forget Corb's shoes"—at least initially—as a way to build the 21st century city. By rethinking authorship (who builds and who designs the urban tabula rasa) and aesthetics (what constitutes spatial and formal ordering) we may challenge the professional hierarchy of architects and planners in the way cities are conceived. The research therefore engages the concept of the urban edge by pointing towards a novel way of thinking about order and aesthetics as an emerging frontier of urban thinking and architectural design, beyond the narrowly conceived visual and aesthetic culture developed by modernist architects and planners that continue to frame much of contemporary professional work. Using example of events and projects in the city of Milwaukee the research argues how current practices may force professionals to reevaluate and redefine entrenched concepts of beauty, aesthetics, and authorship in the making of urban spaces and cultures. The new city no longer emerges from the plan and sketch in an designer's office to be deified and preserved for perpetuity; rather it begins with, what the SARUP Urban Edge calls, "visceral urbanity," a concept that requires us to rethink the design process as we know it.

For architects and planners, urban design has always been a holistic process, a process where the big picture is the goal as well as a point of origin. Corbusier's design of Chandigarh and subsequent scholarship on the city's urbanism continue to take this universal point of view beginning with a view from the top - distant, objective, and cartographic. Chandigarh's plan, a proto-anthropomorphic grid shifted in order to accommodate existing settlement and topographical conditions, is ensconced within a mountainous terrain with a green corridor running through it. This grid-form urban layout tends to be fetishized and is often used as a rhetorical point of entry to any discussion of the city's overall relationship to the region.[1] The map of Chandigarh and its cartographic logic lead any explanation of the organization of the residential, administrative, commercial, and recreational territories, as well as the lived experience of the city itself.

This paper suggests a critical alternative to the Urban Edge Symposium's goal of "stepping vicariously into Corb's shoes" and asks, that given transforming understandings of city and urbanity in the 21st century, what happens if we "forget Corb's shoes" as the initial point of entry into a discussion of Chandigarh? Will that allow us to dramatically rethink Chandigarh as a twenty-first century city or will such a move be futile? What would our analysis look like if we rethink authorship - is the city also produced by those who live in it or is it the sole product of a designer or planner's vision? I argue that the city no longer emerges from a plan and sketch in an designer's office to be deified and preserved for perpetuity; rather it begins with "visceral urbanity," a concept that requires us to rethink the design process as we know it.[2] When we juxtapose these two forms of urban productions we begin to get a better understanding of urbanity.

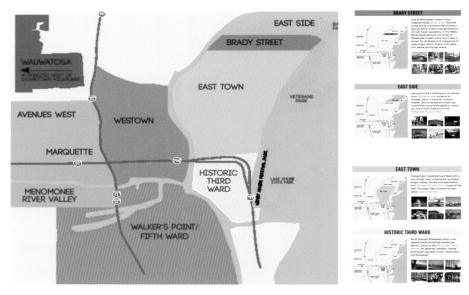

Much has changed in urban historiography in the last 50 years. Globalization, re-surgent local resistance, an emerging DIY culture, new technologies, social media, movement of people, and new infrastructures have transformed urban living in the new century. These changes frame the way in which scholars such as Aboumaliq Simone, Susan Ossman , Brian Larkin, Jeffrey Hou, or Ash Amin—emerging from vastly different disciplines and contexts—describe cities as visceral, contingent, unexpected, transient, and insurgent systems.[3] This chapter works within these emerging genealogies of urban analysis in order to offer a critical alternative to the cartographic epistemologies that frame the way we form knowledge of cities. I focus on grass-roots storytelling and examine how such methods produce an alternative urban cartography.

The following narrative is not about Chandigarh. It's content is centered around Mil-waukee, a city distant from the latter, geographically, culturally, and politically. But even though Chandigarh and Milwaukee may not be comparable case studies, this discussion of methods, or *ways of seeing* that frame our knowledge of Milwaukee may contribute to the way we study other cities, including Chandigarh.

Methods: Maps versus Stories

Central to our discussion is the question of epistemology: how we know, we know, what we know. For an architect interested in urban landscapes it means that we need to enrich our ways of seeing, deciphering, and judging these landscapes. When we view contemporary urban space in the form of plans, maps, and aggregate data we miss an aspect of urbanity that this point of view renders invisible, perhaps intentionally. The point of view that remains masked is the human experience of the city, a view from the ground, that suggests that everyday world-making produc-es a transient, fragmentary, and perspectival worlds that, at first glance, seems to lack coherence. Different individuals *know* and *construe* their city in personal ways. While many agree on certain urban descriptions, there are myriad disagreements and diverse mental maps of the city and its neighborhoods. An architect or plan-ner's analysis at the urban scale misses everyday dissonant practices of the human bodies, what Michel de Certeau terms tactics of daily life.[4]

The history of Corbusier's Chandigarh with the attendant cartographic analysis points towards a geographical logic that is distinctly different from the daily paths and worlds of urban residents. Yet in fact, these two urban imaginings—one, formal and top down and another, informal and bottom up—coexist. Saskia Sassen, points towards "analytic moments when two systems of representation intersect. Such analytic moments are easily experienced as spaces of silence, of absence.

They are analytic borderlands whereby discontinuities are given a terrain rather than being reduced to a dividing line."[5] Juxtaposing these two geographies renders an urban edge where two forms of urbanism meet—traditional and tactical, two forms of representation—specialized versus the quotidian, two kinds of aesthetics, visual and formal versus social and everyday, and two kinds of experiences, visual and visceral. A powerful story of disjuncture between the two modes of reading a city emerges when we examine a visitors map produced by the city of Milwaukee in order to promote tourism (Image 1). The Visit Milwaukee tourist map tells us the official story of Milwaukee's neighborhoods. It identifies historic and cultural attractions located along three rivers and a lake, rendering the historic growth of this riverine city - at least the history that the city's grand storyteller John Gurda likes to tell.[6] This map invests certain urban neighborhoods such as the Historic Third Ward, Walker's Point, and Brady Street with positive values, meanings, and histories, and delineates them as historically significant. However the urban description is not quite complete, because a dark gray section in the Visit Milwaukee map remains unmarked. This gray zone raises critical questions. Why does life seem to stop, tourism seem to end and land seem to disappear into a void in this unmarked region. Is this a territory that should be speedily passed over via a freeway marked in red or is this a merely land we need to cross in order to reach Wauwatosa, also marked as a destination on this map?

Coincidentally this cartographic erasure points us towards a more pernicious reality. If we compare the extents of this gray zone to a racial dot map of the city—an aggregate map produced using census data—we discover that the Visit Milwaukee's map correlates with race, income distribution and wealth.[7] The neighborhoods that hold some of the most affluent parts of the city and have majority white residents correspond to those spaces marked prominently as destination points in the Visit Milwaukee map. The tourist map leaves out large parts of the city that happens to be neighborhoods with urban poor and racial minorities such as African Americans, Hmongs, and Burmese. The stories, views, life, heritage, hard work, and struggles of those who are some of the most valiant citizens are not showcased in the official guide map of the city and neither are the architectural and cultural heritage of these neighborhoods celebrated in this rendition of Milwaukee's history. Aggregate maps crafted from census data, crime data, housing data, or environmental and geographic data tell us little more about the gray zone than what we already know: that the gray zones are minority-heavy, low income, high tenancy, low housing stock, and crime ridden neighborhoods. Sans any other narrative the gray zone remains known as a lumpen territory of disinvestment, decay, and blight, a "single story" of Milwaukee's segregated neighborhoods.[8]

Image 2:

The Buildings-Landscapes-Cultures summer field school participants, 2014.
Photo Credits: BLC Field School

This is where storytelling enters as a bottom-up strategy of historiography. Community storytellers render grassroots urban histories that are written from the margins. Analysis of stories narrated by local residents is a common strategy used by public historians to capture the diverse experience of living in urban neighborhoods.[9] Urban histories emerging from place-stories are also noted by preservation scholar Ned Kaufman who calls them storyscapes.[10] He calls upon urbanists, historians, and folklorists to help craft standards and methodologies "that capture the power of stories" in "heritage conservation." Scholars have demonstrated that people and buildings are repositories of stories of stewardship and heritage, and stories of places narrated by local residents render visible dreams and aspirations of people whose voices are often ignored in planning discussions.[11] Although, stories cannot *solely* generate a more equitable and sustainable discourse in the face of apathy, disinvestment, and neoliberal policies, nevertheless, they have the power to bring communities together. As Henry Louis Taylor Jr. puts it, when disparate strands of stories are collected and organized, there is "a synergy between people, physical and social environments. People are connected to their neighborhoods and each other, so these connections must be acknowledged and taken into account." Storytelling also produces accounts of the human body in everyday life, that elsewhere I call embodied placemaking.[12] Such stories produce an alternate kind of urban knowledge that may inform planners and urban designers engaged in collaborative and engaged practices such as tactical urbanism, performative urbanism, or integral urbanism.[13]

Picturing Milwaukee: An alternative epistemology

Since 2012, Project Picturing Milwaukee (thefieldschool.weebly.com) has explored urban historiography from the margins (Image 2).[14] This project uses storytelling as way to write urban histories of Milwaukee and examine how these alternative histories, in turn, can help us transform local landscapes.[15] Between 2014-16 the project concentrated on collecting place-based stories from Washington Park, a 20th Century streetcar suburb, now part of Milwaukee's segregated inner city, located on the northwestern edge of the metropolis. We collected oral histories from residents describing their physical environments, urban heritage, and personal accounts of Milwaukee's history and urban culture (Image 3). We also examined the built environment as a cultural artifact and social catalyst (Image 4, 6). We approached the material world not as mere containers of human activities, but instead, as an active agent influencing urbanity, human behavior, settlement patterns, and cultural activities. In other words our urban storytelling strategies involved collecting stories from local residents and local places, both voices otherwise marginal in the city. In this way our methods of urban historiography claimed to borrow from narratives from the urban edge.

Grassroots storytelling also involved crowdsourcing where digital media and smartphone technologies provided new innovative and multidisciplinary methods of data collection, curating, and dissemination (Image 5). We used technologies of digital indexing and organizing of information in order to very quickly extract story-clips from the interviews. We used Pixstori, an iphone-based digital application that captured soundscapes and human narrations of place and superimposed these audios over images of places (http://blcfieldschool2014.weebly.com/forum. html). Displayed on a public website we were successful in rendering audio-visual architectural histories and place stories directly to a wide cross section of non-expert audience. Stories generated a grassroots dialog and people responded by sending us their stories of their neighborhood and their unique urban experiences. This multi-year iterative spatial and ethnographic process generated new knowledge about ways local residents construct and construe the urban built environment.[16] Because this was an interdisciplinary and collaborative process that engaged local artists, architects, students, scholars, neighborhood residents, institutions, and activists, we found it necessary to rethink authorship (who builds and designs the city or who recounts and writes its history) and aesthetics (what constitutes spatial and formal ordering) in ways that challenged the professional hierarchy and creative agency of architects and planners. Our knowledge of the city no longer emerged from the plan and sketch, rather we saw the design process as narratives from the margins or edges.

  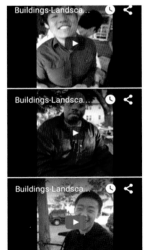

Image 5:

Website capture showing how we used digital oral history applications such as Pixstori, Summer 2015 Photo Credits: BLC Field School

Lessons from the urban edge: Plotting urban relations

Hayden White proposes "that to write a history meant to place an event within a context, by relating it as a part to some conceivable whole."[17] He called this act of historiography, *"emplotment,"* or assembling a series of historical events into narrative genres with a plot. We quickly discovered that grassroots urban histories from the margins too tended to revolve around central plots and followed particular narrative genres as discussed by White. Individual stories describing the city could be extracted from interviews and related to a host of other similar stories with narrative strategies and plots. In other words these stories were in conversation with each other and they could be plotted within a larger thematic matrix. These plots became our points of entry into a neighborhood and they helped us theorize an alternate to urban mapping and master planning *(http://blcfieldschool2014. weebly.com/relationships-and-ties.html).*

Stories of human lived experience of Washington Park, suggested that urban space is relational and overlapping, lacking the clear order observed in zoning maps or territorial demarcations produced by governmental and policy bodies. The latter includes historic districts, census tracts, functionally-zoned precincts, regulatory wards, and neighborhood boundaries. These 'official maps' help organize the city into manageable units for financial management, policing or governance. Spatial imaginaries culled from narratives and stories of lived experiences challenged, transgressed, and breached the official chorographies.

Image 6:

Juliana Glassco measuring and documenting Rosalind Cox's home, Summer 2014 Photo Credits: BLC Field School

The stories we heard were not simply accounts of selves, that is, individuals' location in this world or a collection of personal memories. They were ways by which people participated and acted in this world, forms by which they mapped a city made up of social networks. We met a variety of residents; recent immigrants such as Sahara who is Somali and Proctor Yang who is Hmong, or long term African American residents such as Rosalind Cox and Ulysses and Barbara Brown who lived in the neighborhood for 30 years, white residents such as Lois Luglio, who was born here, and Dave Boucher who owns a popular neighborhood café *(See http:// blcfieldschool2014.weebly.com/people.html)*.

Each of these individuals mapped 'their' physical city in different ways. They charted the residences of their neighbors, co-workers, church groups, and co-ethnics.[18] They described settings and sites that were associated with their social networks and everyday life. Their mental maps of the city varied over time. For instance, their world on holidays differed substantially from their world on workdays. Much like the "psychogeography" maps of the twentieth century Situationists, the city space of Washington Park was mapped by the words, memories, emotions, and actions of its diverse residents.[19]

These disparate, value laden, spatial networks were not idiosyncratic, isolated geographies experienced by individuals. Rather they overlapped and coincided at points that people had in common - producing true public nodes. At Washington Park we met Dave Boucher who manages one such node common to multiple narratives about relationships and ties. His café is a place where diverse individuals meet each other and create strong or weak bonds (Image 7). We also identified other public nodes such as an interconnected network of urban gardens and agricultural lands farmed by individuals, groups, institutions, and small farms. These spaces brought together Hmong elders, African American entrepreneurs, young adults, and Anglo volunteers from outside the neighborhood. Sahara, Rosalind, Proctor, and Dave's stories coalesced around these garden plots. Recently, Washington Park residents officially connected these productive garden spaces to create their own urban agriculture tour - a new geography that connected these locations within a coherent map created by the residents (Image 8).

Image 7:

Amaranth Café, Washington Park. Photo Credits: BLC Field School

Biologists and animal ecologist call such territorial reticulations as home ranges, or turfs where an organism lives and visits on a regular basis.[20] The way our respondents described their home range demonstrated that they straddled multiple worlds, within which they operated on a daily basis. The cities reproduced by Sahara, Proctor, Barbara, or Lois were different from the neat and well defined google maps, the neatly delineated GIS (geographical information system) property records from the City of Milwaukee, or the gridded plans of Corbusier's Chandigarh. Rather the view from the urban edges was multiple, disjointed, blurred, and overlapping. While each point in an urban grid in official city maps are equivalent, individual sites or nodes within mental map are weighted, valued, and charged with memories and meanings.

Our continuing semantic analysis helped us identify some key values that underpinned the ways residents mentally mapped these spaces (http://blcfieldschool2014.weebly.com/forum.html). One such concept is 'relationships and ties.' As examples of Hayden White's historiographical "emplotments," stories of real places, people, and buildings in Washington Park were woven around this term, implicating spatial networks of places.[21] These places gave material structure and order to human relationships within this community. Despite a common plot-line each individual described their world from different points of view and perspectives. Hannah Arendt, speaking of the public realm refers to this commonality when she says that "to live together in the world means essentially that a world of things is between those who have it in common, as a table is located between who sit around it; the world, like every in-between, relates and separates men at the same time." Yet she hastens to remind us that "though the common world is the common meeting ground of all, those who are present have different locations in it, and the location of one can no more coincide with the location of another. Being seen and being heard by others derive their significance from the fact that everybody sees and hears from a different position." The city became a "world in common" yet produced by "a plurality of perspectives."[22]

Image 8:

Washington Park Urban Garden Tour, 2015
Photo Credits: Phoua Vang, Washington Park Partners, 2015.

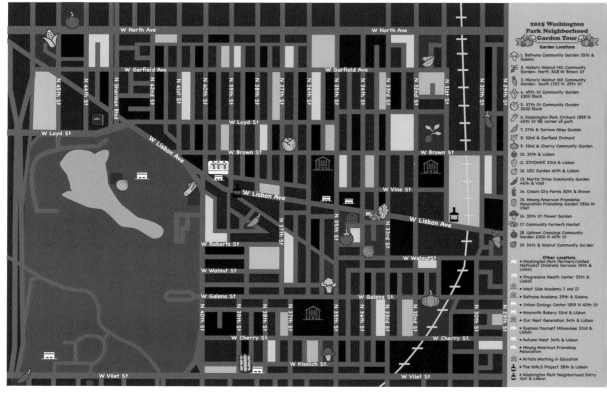

Conclusions: Why narratives from the margins matter?

The narratives from Washington Park demonstrate how transiently occupied spaces make their temporary presence felt more permanently within a collective memory and a collective geographical imagination of residents. These stories of geographical imaginations coalescing around residents' 'emplotments' of urbanity contests the singular histories proposed by hagiographies built around designers (such as Corbusier, Kahn, or Koolhaas) or around formative acts of government and planning bodies. But in order to capture the former narratives of this urban edge we need to move beyond opticentrism, i.e. our overdependence on the visual at the expense of the textual, historical, tactile, olfactory, sonic, or gustatory conditions. We have to rethink our ways of reading and interpreting cities and urban public places in ways that account for the workings of power and everyday resistance, guerilla appropriation of authorship and ownership of place, and local insurgencies against the silent hand of powerful ideologies and ontologies.

Saskia Sassen, talking about a growing popularity of tactical urbanism practices and new forms of urban action explains that "current conditions in global cities are creating not only new structurations of power but also operational and rhetorical openings for new types of actors and their projects." By that she means that cities offer opportunities for the powerless and the subaltern to make their presence felt, that "while many of today's urban struggles are highly localized, they actually represent a form of global engagement; their globality is constituted as a horizontal, multi-sited recurrence of similar struggles in hundreds of cities worldwide." The residents and other non-expert stakeholders often make their presence felt on urban space. The urban agriculture tour or the use of Amaranth Café described above suggest such alternative presences. These urban experiences may actually have something in common with similar practices and experiences of urban dwellers across the world. Therefore Washington Park stories open up ways to link myriad, horizontal, empowering possibilities of social action and new forms of urbanism.

I want to end with a related proposition that we rethink how we understand aesthetics in order to render visible these alternate urbanisms. It requires a shift in our interpretive vantage point to move towards an expanded discussion of aesthetics as a way to understand and experience our world. Ben Highmore's reading of Terry Eagleton suggests that "aesthetics, in its initial impetus, is primarily concerned with material experiences, with the way the sensual world greets the sensate body, and with the affective forces that are generated in such meetings. ... It is attuned to forms of perception, sensation, and attention; to the world of the senses; and to the body."[23] Aesthetics is also highly political and contested. Highmore refers to Jacque Ranciere's use of the term "the distribution of the sensible" as "a dynamic arena constantly managed by the policing activities of forces bent on maintaining what and who will be visible and invisible and constantly disrupted by aesthetic and political acts that will redistribute the field of social perception."[24] Therefore benchmarks of taste, practices of design, connoisseurship, and the sensory presence and visibility are contested terrains. The narratives from Washington Park point towards the emergence and presencing of a new aesthetic, it also points towards the failure of traditional forms of aesthetic evaluation that is predominantly visual and formal - and based on object-form and top-down expert knowledge of architects. If we were to reconsider aesthetics, we would have to rethink our dependency on the visual, formal, and the architectural object as a *tabula rasa*, turning instead towards the human body and the transient, experiential, and somatic acts of placemaking, we can't begin with Corb's shoes. Instead, we have to begin with the acts of everyday placemaking, tactical urbanism, and social aesthetics that reconfigures grid, place, and urbanity in contemporary Chandigarh.

1. Ravi Kalia. *Chandigarh: The Making of an Indian City*. New Delhi: Oxford University Press, 2000; Vikramaditya Prakash. Chandigarh's Le Corbusier: The Struggle for Modernity in Postcolonial India. Seattle: University of Washington Press, 2002.
2. During the 2014 Urban Edge symposium, Dr. Manu Sobti used the term "visceral urbanity" to refer to the quotidian, embodied and dramaturgical experience of the city.
3. Abdoumaliq Simone. *For the City Yet to Come: Changing African Life in Four Cities*. Durham: Duke University Press, 2004; Susan Ossman. *Picturing Casablanca: Portraits of Power in a Modern City*. Berkeley: University of California Press, 1994; Brian Larkin. *Signal and Noise: Media, Infrastructure, and Urban Culture in Nigeria*. Durham: Duke University Press, 2008; Ash Amin and Nigel J. Thrift. *Cities: Reimagining the Urban*. Malden: Blackwell Publishing Inc., 2002 & Jeffrey Hou. *Insurgent Public Space: Guerrilla Urbanism and the Remaking of Contemporary Cities*. New York: Routledge, 2010.
4. Michel de Certeau. *The Practice of Everyday Life*. Berkeley: University of California Press, 1984.
5. Sassen argues that the street and public space in the twenty-first century lends itself to performative activities and occupation that contradict the logic of top-down urban histories. "[T]o occupy is to remake, even if temporarily, a bit of territory, and therewith to remake its embedded and often deeply undemocratic logic of power" she argues. See p. 44 and p. 47 in Saskia Sassen. "Complex and Incomplete: Spaces for Tactical Urbanism" in Pedro Gadhano (ed.). *Uneven Growth: Tactical Urbanisms for Expanding Megacities*. New York: The Museum of Modern Art, 2014, p. 40 - 47.
6. John Gurda. *The Making of Milwaukee*. Milwaukee: Milwaukee County Historical Society 1999 & John Gurda. Milwaukee: *City of Neighborhoods*. Milwaukee: Historic Milwaukee Inc., 2015.
7. For a racial dot map of Milwaukee, see Dustin Cable. *The Racial Dot Map*. Demographics Research Group, Weldon Cooper Center for Public Service, University of Virginia, July 2013, http://www.coopercenter.org/demographics/Racial-Dot-Map, (Accessed May 12, 2016).
8. Chimamanda Ngozi Adichie. "The Danger of a Single Story" in TedGlobal 2009, https://www.ted.com/talks/chimamanda_adichie_the_danger_of_a_single_story?language=en, (Accessed May 12, 2016).
9. Dolores Hayden. *The Power of Place: Urban Landscapes as Public History*. Cambridge, Mass.: MIT Press, 1997 & Setha M. Low and Denise Lawrence-Zuñiga. *The Anthropology of Space and Place: Locating Culture*. Malden, MA: Blackwell Publishing, 2003.
10. Ned Kaufman. *Place, Race, and Story: Essays on the Past and Future of Historic Preservation*. New York: Routledge 2009.
11. Lived experiences and conversations create place. According to folklorist Gerald Pocius, place based conversation " … involves characters and events that fit into particular chronologies and time periods. … the discussions themselves deal with a community space, a specific landscape feature, a particular space … " in Gerald Pocius. *A Place To Belong: Community Order and Everyday Space in Calvert, Newfoundland*. Montreal: McGill-Queen's University Press, 2000; Leonie Sandercock. Making the Invisible Visible: A Multicultural Planning History. Berkeley: University of California Press, 1998; Nihal Perera. *People's Spaces: Coping, Familiarizing, Creating*. New York: Routledge, 2016.
12. Arijit Sen and Lisa Silverman. *Making Place: Space and Embodiment in the City*. Bloomington: Indiana University Press, 2014.
13. Mike Lydon and Antonio Garcia. Tactical Urbanism: Short-term Action for Long-term Change. Washington DC: The Streets Plans Collaborative Inc., 2015; Sophie Wolfrum and Nicolai Brandis. *Performative Urbanism: Generating and Designing Urban Space*. Berlin: Jovis, 2015 & Nan Ellin. *Integral Urbanism*. New York: Routledge, 2006.
14. Our curriculum drew upon the ethics of collaborative storytelling by encouraging scholars and community residents to identify common values and narratives that are important and central to both parties. Collaborative anthropologist Joanne Rappaport calls this co-theorization or a "collective production of conceptual vehicles that draw upon both a body of [academic] anthropological theory and upon concepts developed by our interlocutors … from local non-specialists." This form of collaborative ethnography suggests that we conduct research and teaching in ways that reduce the gap between the production of academic knowledge, everyday life, and community knowledge. It means that we no longer "look over the shoulder of our informants … " but rather "look with them … " Such an outlook has two further methodological bearings: mere interviews and participant observations are inadequate. Instead community members are collaborators and co-participants in the making of new knowledge and such knowledge should be developed in the context where such engagements occur, not in the classroom or a laboratory. That context is what we at BLC call "the field … " Joanne Rappaport. "Beyond Participant Observation Collaborative Ethnography as Theoretical Innovation" in *Collaborative Anthropologies* 1 (2008), p.1-31.

Endnotes (continued)

15. The project began as a summer immersive field school that was offered jointly by the Buildings-Landscapes-Cultures (BLC) program, a joint doctoral level initiative between the Department of Art History, University of Wisconsin Madison and the Department of Architecture, University of Wisconsin Milwaukee. Since 2009, students and scholars associated with the BLC field school have collected and interpreted stories of our built environment, with an assumption that such knowledge promotes values such as stewardship and civic pride. We speak to residents, but we also talk to buildings and landscapes—the material world that is often overlooked as mute— but they too tell us stories of heritage, values, struggles, and resilience. See www.TheFieldschool.weebly.com

16. For a description of spatial ethnography as a method see Arijit Sen and Lisa Silverman. *Making Place: Space and Embodiment in the City*. Bloomington: Indiana University Press, 2014, p. 8 - 10.

17. Hayden White. *Tropics of Discourse: Essays in Cultural Criticism*. Baltimore: John Hopkins Press, 1978, p. 94.

18. Anna Grosch did additional studies where she asked the research participants to draw cognitive maps of the neighborhood. She demonstrated that these scholars too developed their own maps of this neighborhood as a result of their engagement with the local residents. See Anna Grosch. Enacting Place: A Comparative Case Study, Theses and Dissertations. Milwaukee: University of Wisconsin Milwaukee, 2015.

19. For more on Situationist analysis of psychogeography see Simon Sadler. *The Situationist City*. Cambridge Mass.: MIT Press, 1999, p. 76.

20. Roger Powell and Michael Mitchell. "What is a home range?" in Journal of Mammalogy 93:4 (2012), p. 948 - 958 & Jeremy Anderson and Margaret Tindall. "The Concept of Home Range: New Data for the Study of Territorial Behavior" in W. J. Mitchell (ed.). Environmental Design Research and Practice, Proceedings of the EDRA 3/AR8 Conference. Los Angeles: EDRA, 1972.

21. White. *Tropics*. p. 66 - 67.

22. Hannah Arendt. *The Human Condition*. Chicago: University of Chicago Press, 1958, p. 50 - 58; Andrea Brighenti. "The Publicness of Public Space. On the Public Domain" in Quarderno 49 (Marzo 2010), http://web.unitn.it/files/quad49.pdf, (accessed May 16, 2016).

23. Ben Highmore. "Bitter After Taste: Affect, Food and Social Aesthetics" in The Affect Theory Reader, Durham: Duke University Press, 2010, p. 118 - 37.

24. Ben Highmore. *Ordinary Lives: Studies in the Everyday*. New York: Routledge, 2010, p. 45.

References

Amin, Ash and Thrift, Nijel J. *Cities: Reimagining the Urban*. Malden: Blackwell Publishing Inc., 2002.

de Certeau, Michel. *The Practice of Everyday Life*. Berkeley: University of California Press, 1984.

Ellin, Nan. *Integral Urbanism*. New York: Routledge, 2006.

Gadhano, Pedro (ed.). *Uneven Growth: Tactical Urbanisms for Expanding Megacities*. New York: The Museum of Modern Art, 2014.

Hayden, Delores. *The Power of Place: Urban Landscapes as Public History*. Cambridge, Mass.: MIT Press, 1997.

Highmore, Ben. *Ordinary Lives: Studies in the Everyday*. New York: Routledge, 2010.

Hou, Jeffrey. *Insurgent Public Space: Guerrilla Urbanism and the Remaking of Contemporary Cities*. New York: Routledge, 2010.

Kalia, Ravi. *Chandigarh: The Making of an Indian City*. New Delhi: Oxford University Press, 2000.

Kaufman, Ned. *Place, Race, and Story: Essays on the Past and Future of Historic Preservation*. New York: Routledge, 2009.

Larkin, Brian. *Signal and Noise: Media, Infrastructure, and Urban Culture in Nigeria*. Durham: Duke University Press, 2008.

Low, Setha M. and Lawrence-Zuñiga, Denise. *The Anthropology of Space and Place: Locating Culture*. Malden, MA: Blackwell Publishing, 2003.

Ossman, Susan. *Picturing Casablanca: Portraits of Power in a Modern City*. Berkeley: University of California Press, 1994.

Prakash, Vikramaditya. *Chandigarh's Le Corbusier: The Struggle for Modernity in Postcolonial India*. Seattle: University of Washington Press, 2002.

Sadler, Simon. *The Situationist City*. Cambridge Mass.: MIT Press, 1999.

Simone, Abdoumaliq. *For the City Yet to Come: Changing African Life in Four Cities*. Durham: Duke University Press, 2004.

Sen, Arijit and Silverman, Lisa. *Making Place: Space and Embodiment in the City*. Bloomington: Indiana University Press, 2014.

White, Hayden. *Tropics of Discourse: Essays in Cultural Criticism*. Baltimore: John Hopkins Press, 1978.

Wolfrum, Sophie and Brandis, Nicolai. *Performative Urbanism: Generating and Designing Urban Space*. Berlin: Jovis, 2015.

Living on the Edge: Shifting and Re-shifting Boundaries and Evolving Urban Edges at Ahmedabad and Mumbai

ARPAN JOHARI

ABSTRACT

This essay explores the changes that transform the boundaries and edges of rapidly growing urbanities in the Asian context. As a complex process of learning and un-learning, it aligns urban growth with the drivers of change and identifies the intermittent phases that a city undergoes during these developments. The two examples covered in this examination are identified as those that fall between the industrial and post-industrial development phases, and are viewed to have achieved a recognized autonomy of modern planning in recent decades. More significantly, culture and history continue to be viewed as integral not just to the social setup of their urban lives, but also to the formal character that constructs their urbanities. In both Ahmedabad and Mumbai, while the last few decades have been marked by tremendous growth, these urban centers have also struggled to relate this growth with strategic planning. In both cases, it has been a phase of learning and experimenting with the design and running of modern civic infrastructures. Both examples have aimed to introduce superlative public transit systems, yet have continued to deal with the problems of land acquisition, while addressing an ailing civic infrastructure and the pressures of migration. In the scenarios that unfold, this essay shows how these two cities are just learning to spread their wings in terms of long term planning and sustained urban growth strategies. Finally, this study explores the range of urban edges in these great cities in contemporary times, especially as they transition from a past of relatively unlegislated formal ordering to the adoption of an integrated urban planning approach.

Ahmedabad - Three Cities in One

On its grand 605th birthday, the city of Ahmedabad in western India, celebrates its most recent laurel of being on track towards becoming one among the first smart cities of India. This modern city, despite multiple changes to its physical form, continues to retain its cultural roots and artifacts dating over several centuries of history. In fact, so resilient is the urban fabric of Ahmedabad, that despite outside (and often heavy-handed) interventions, it has changed little over successive generations. In making this observation, Kenneth Gillion (1968) described the city in the following words:

> *Unlike Mumbai, Kolkata, Chennai and Kanpur; Ahmedabad was not a creation of the British but a city which while remaining true to itself successfully adapted to the new industrial age carrying over commercial and industrial skills and patterns of traditional social organization. In no great city of India can the continuity of past and present be seen as clearly as in Ahmedabad.*

> - Kenneth L. Gillion (1968), Ahmedabad:
> *A Study in Indian Urban History.* University of California Press, p. 2.

Ahmedabad - as an urbanity growing and responding to its multiple internal pressures, but never succumbing—may be conceptualized today as three cities morphed into one—the so-called medieval, the 'classic' industrial, and the 'pre-modern' industrial. Of these three city types inherent in Ahmedabad's plan, Sultan Ahmed Shah in 1411 CE founded the earliest medieval and walled town as an important administrative and trading center. Following the consolidation of this fortified center, smaller settlements began to emerge on the Sabarmati banks—the urban waterway that bordered the city—coercing urban expansion into a semi-circular form. This phase of genesis was also characterized by the construction of several examples of monumental architecture, including a series of medieval mosques in the Indo-Islamic architectural style, within and alongside tightly packed residential neighborhoods clustered on narrow, winding lanes. By the latter half of the 19th century, and following the emergence of the textile industry and mechanization, classic industrialization arrived on the peripheries of medieval Ahmedabad. Sustained employment opportunities and the influx of migrant workers from the urban hinterlands, rapidly turned these medieval settlements around the previously fortified center into 'high-density' industrial townships and crowded *chawls*. In the last phase of this classic industrialization process, multi-storied concrete slums mushroomed specifically in the vicinities of the textile mills, to accommodate the jump in urban population. However, perhaps the most radical geographical expansion of Ahmedabad only occurred after the 1970s. Ahmedabad, now given its roots as a major textile production center, became home to a multitude of newer and commercial establishments. Her relatively elite 'new' or 'dual center' became home to an emerging, middle, and increasingly affluent class. The ways of the old city continued, but a re-balancing was apparent. Within the three described scenarios of change over time, the river Sabarmati separated new Ahmedabad from the other two, creating a physical edge - an edge that was also characterized by the complex economics of city growth.

Small-Scale Edges - The Pols of Ahmedabad

Gated, residential communities, known as pols, characterized medieval Ahmedabad, and it's many interconnected settlements. Within these pols, homes with common walls straddled on either side of the inner lanes, offering shade against the harsh Ahmedabadi sun. Traditionally, these *pol* houses were excellent examples of timber usage with intricately carved screens, and upper level balcony projections supported on carved brackets. Connecting lanes between *pols* carefully culminated into little squares where the local residents gathered. These squares often had ornate bird feeders and as a collective defined the urban edges of the walled city at the micro scale.

Image 1:

The Five Satellite towns and Growth Centers of Ahmedabad

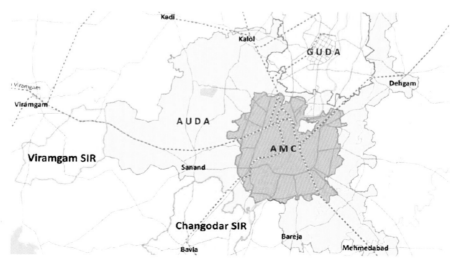

JOHARI

The present day *pols* of Ahmedabad paint a picture much removed from these descriptions. Exponentially increased housing demands in the old city have responded to population explosion in the last several decades, coupled with competitive rents, and an increase in the number of industries and job opportunities. An ever-increasing density in the walled city area also exerts a considerable (and detrimental) impact on its edges. The city responds to this surge by offering a quick fix to the problem. This involves more concrete and brick structures, relatively cheaper to build and maintain and not requiring highly skilled labor, versus the ornate homes of the past. The integrity of many *pol* neighborhoods has also been compromised; urban land use has drastically changed - for the once socially-specific *pols*, it creates an environment where private-public gradations no longer serve their intended purpose. Finally, lax legislation has caused the old city's fabric to to fray and create a new definition at its edges via sprawl over multiple kilometers beyond what had once constituted its periphery, creating a building morphology much at odds with its recent past. In the last decade (since 2005), a substantial part of the old city was identified as a heritage site making similar alterations to building fabric substantially difficult.

New Edges - Modern Ahmedabad

Beyond its *pols*, residential districts, and associated edges, modern Ahmedabad also displays a variety of boundaries and edges connected to its modern and larger infrastructure elements. These changes are critical, since, like most modern Indian metropolitan cities, large parts of Ahmedabad lack formal ordering that would identify areas and allocate usages based on any long-term development plan. Moreover, uneven density distributions lead to fragmented urban edges and consequently a strain on available resources. From this perspective, the Sabarmati Riverfront Development Project (2005 - present) and the Bus Rapid Transit Service (BRTS), inaugurated in 2009, are the two largest urban catalysts rapidly inflicting change at the edges. The Sabarmati Riverfront Project creates a new public space for cultural and civic institutions through the reclamation of a 10.5 kilometer stretch of the Sabarmati River banks. Via this space for recreation purposes and markets, the 'Ahmedabad stretch' of the river is effectively transformed from a geographical divider in the middle of the city towards becoming a focal point for public leisure and recreation. The Bus Rapid Transit Service (BRTS) corridor interconnects diverse parts of the city. In its architecture, it bisects any given road width and forms a screen of organized infrastructure edge on at least one side of the fabric and visible in a given direction of movement. This gives some relief from otherwise monotonous and unstructured edges.

Besides the government supported Sabarmati Riverfront and BRTS Projects, whose impact is visible throughout the city, large scale edges within the public realm are also created through active public engagement. Certain areas of Ahmedabad have 'wall lengths' stretching many kilometers. These mostly constitute the boundary walls of government owned properties, including convention grounds and civic utility complexes. Common citizens of the city get involved in the painting of colorful murals on these walls. In effect, the distance between every two columns on these walls serves as an individual canvas and themes are popular issues trending in society at different times of the year. These murals change about three to four times a year thereby creating an interesting dynamic edge through urban engagement, and distinctly in the public domain, much like the Sabarmati Riverfront and BRTS Projects.

Image 5:

Bus Rapid Transit Service BRTS (inaugurated 2009) corridor bisecting the existing road width creating a visual relief

Image 6:

BRTS Transit corridor aligning the non-uniform edges of the street thereby creating a visual relief

(Re) Making the Street Edge - Ahmedabad's CG Road & Public Domain

Beyond change at the urban edges occurring in response to population and
economic pressures, or via catalysts, Ahmedabad has also experimented with
focused urban legislation towards transmitting change. The first serious attempt to
introduce urban legislation within select pockets of Ahmedabad in the mid 1990s
involved the development of the upcoming Central Business District (CBD) around
the Chimanlal Girdharlal Road (also known as CG road). Ranked by Cushman &
Wakefield in 2010 as an exemplar of strong growth in the Asia Pacific region, this
new urban hub within Ahmedabad's new city was situated east of the Sabarmati,
combining business and residential functions. It was the brainchild of planners
understanding and executing how the built should relate with the un-built (in this
case the users). The new rendition of CG Road was meticulously designed and
aimed at creating a powerful public realm with retail spaces on the ground/street
levels and offices located in the floors above. Design decisions were visualized
as the much-needed injection into Ahmedabad's modern growth and real estate
aspirations. CG Road's urban guidelines visualized buildings with 'non-obstructive'
edges that accommodated well planned, public services and amenities for the
many pedestrians. The roads running through the development were planned to
accommodate a regulated traffic flow and parking lanes were clearly defined. Entire
road sections followed a hierarchy of transiting into a retail area from a public road.
The project even acknowledged the thousands of street vendors—an inseparable
element of the Indian city—who had traditionally converged on this area. In
showing the importance of their continued interaction with urban society, planners
envisaged a special area between the built and parking which was identified as a
permanent slot for licensed street vendors. This promoted healthy open spaces and
the entire scheme gave identity and structure to the idea of a modern Ahmedabad.
With the purview of the CG Road project, the 'architecture' of the commercial plots
on CG road and their 'urban character' was down to the plot owner, as long as it
fell within the broader framework of the urban byelaws. These byelaws determined
Floor Space Index (FSI) ratios and relationships between public and private spaces.

Image 8a:

CG Road
visualization of
the public realm
- the Urban
Edge identified
as key to built
engagement and
public contact
(Source HCPDPM
Report 2011)

The CG Road project was an important start, but a problematic experiment. Almost immediately, following the project's inauguration, the telling lack of facade regulatory norms allowed for violations to happen. In their zeal to extract maximum sellable real estate, developers attempted to maximize the number of floors and floor space on their properties, resulting in the callous under-sailing and over-sailing of retail floors. In time, these developments brazenly destroyed the desirable relationships of the sidewalk with the buildings fronting CG Road. Not only did this generation of edges not evoke any connection with built form, but that these facades looked dead and discouraged the originally intended character of the project and its spaces. CG road was also an important lesson on how the failure of having a defined edge, undermined the concept of its interaction with the un-built. Open spaces that were built out as part of the public realm became dreary and unusable. This was further exaggerated by not having a standardized system and size for signage elements. In their race to promote their products, brands came up with hoardings, one bigger than the other, often hiding the building fenestrations and other visible architectural elements, and destroying the synergy that should prevail at the edge of a vibrant CBD. In effect, at the CG Road approach, plazas to the many edge buildings slowly lost their spatial purpose, were increasingly encroached upon, and succumbed to the ever increasing pressures of vehicle parking space.

Image 8b:

CG Road
visualization of
the public realm
- the Urban
Edge identified
as key to built
engagement and
public contact
(Source HCPDPM
Report 2011)

*I*mage 9a:

CG Road, as built
(about 2013)
- Under-sailing
and over-sailing
sidewalks have
negative effects
on relationship of
customer to retail

Extra-Muros Edge Developments - Ahmedabad-Sanand & the Transforming Rural Context

As the plan of CG Road came into shape and progressed, so did the need for additional housing in this area. Towards this purpose, land was acquired in piecemeal fashion. In effect, housing developments with multiple phased densities emerged behind the facades of the CG Road, generating a range of building typologies, including individual bungalows, low and high-rise apartment blocks. All buildings were designed with individual plot lines as a reference, undermining the larger impact that these constructions could have had on the making of the new urban edge. This new development also lacked the hierarchy of space transition and building heights. Since plots were not aligned, it led to staggering building edges as developers built to plot lines. The result was a degraded public realm with poor quality open spaces and the absence of points for social interaction and exchange.

Image 9b:

CG Road, as built (about 2013) - Under-sailing and over-sailing sidewalks have negative effects on relationship of customer to retail

Ahmedabad's current growth phase can be placed somewhere between the industrial city and the post-industrial city. This is signified with a saturated inner city and its many industrial suburbs with satellite towns that develop around the core. Public utility, transport infrastructure, and entertainment buildings cover up the voids in-between. Once in this phase, the city grows outwards creating 'edge cities.' These edge cities are home to high tech, new industrial areas that bring about additional employment opportunities. It is interesting to note that edge cities are more than mere collations of factories with worker accommodations around them. Traditionally, set on agricultural lands (often by displacing rural townships), these fledgling cities have the capacity to drastically change the landscape and irreversibly transform social working, its inherent lifestyle and the way economic resources flow into a given area. In a rural setting 'so much, so soon' can therefore influence the way this changing environment is seen.

Following the financial crisis of 1991, 'agriculturally-driven' India liberalized her trade policies allowing for growth primed by private investments. This meant that apart from private funds, government instruments were more pro-business and willingly adopted market driven growth models. Around the same time, Indian industrialist Ratan Tata contemplated the idea of marketing a cheap, reliable, and all-weather vehicle for the growing Indian middle class (an extremely large cross section, comprising populations living in urban and rural areas, and lands in-between). By 1997, the so-called Tata Nano—touted as India's car for the common man—was born. Ironically, the 'common man's' Nano was also connected to land acquisition troubles that followed Tata's ambitious move to set up its first production center at Singnur, in the Indian state of West Bengal. By 2007, Tata Motors were forced to reconsider a suitable site at Sanand - Gujarat, located about 24 kilometers from Ahmedabad.

Following its humble beginnings as a rural township until the arrival of the Tata, Sanand in recent years has come to be known as 'The Detroit of India.' Now it is included under the Ahmedabad Urban Development Authority (AUDA) jurisdictional area, which is also responsible for its planning and development. As of the 2001 India census, Sanand had a population of only 32,348 inhabitants; by 2011 this figure was 41,530. Sanand, or 'Nano Town' today (owing to the Tata's plant of the same name), it has also gained importance given that it is located on the major trade corridors and Special Economic Zones in western India. Following recent developments, the city is connected to the Mundra Port, a fully operational—and growing—seaport in southeast Asia. The Sanand-Viramgam broad-gauge railway network connects the region to major industrial centers located across Gujarat and the rest of India. In anticipation that Sanand's growth is just a precursor to a bigger scenario, the state-owned Gujarat Industrial Development Corporation (GIDC) has acquired an additional 5,000 acres of land in and around Sanand for future industrial use.

The first phase of the Tata Motors project ushered in a new chapter in the consolidation and acquisition of land that belonged to the original six villages of Sanand. The initial resistance to relinquish ancestral farmland in 2009 gave way to a land-compensation process whereby the farmers grew rich by about US $30 million in just a matter of weeks. Over the next eight months, a total of about US $100 million was invested in this rapidly conceived, edge city. An area of 724 acres was speculatively acquired, of which 345 acres were specifically earmarked for setting up the vendor plants. Realizing the untapped potential and proximity of major transport hubs, soon other popular auto brands including Maruti, Ford-India, Honda, and Hero Motor Corp began investing in Sanand, boasting the combined production strength in millions of vehicle units. Tata's presence in Sanand spearheaded the rapid urbanization of this belt, re-defining its edge significance via proximity to Ahmedabad. It also created 100,000 direct and indirect job opportunities and kick started the local economy, including the hotel industry and housing, eventually propagating a demand for all basic amenities to be set up around the Nano plant itself. If Sanand had started as an anomaly, it ended as a

Image 10:

Ahmedabad and the 'balding' of farmlands - Ahmedabad (and Sanand's) urban expansion has happened on land that was once fertile, agricultural property. This aerial image shows how the city's farm lands are now bald, paving the way for prime real estate developments

*I*mage 11a:

Sanand and the
Tata Nano Plant

precedent for other regions within India - some attempting similar developments with products far removed from auto manufacturing.

The economic and urban changes unfolding at Sanand—still only at the beginning of their trajectories—have undoubtedly important repercussions for the societies residing within these environments. Post-acquisition of their lands, the locals claim that one among the biggest gains to result from the Nano project is that the environment of their villages have improved drastically. Official reports state that the Gujarat government has placed significant efforts into preventing pollution and improving environmental quality in Sanand. On these lines, it has given notice to factories and industrial plants, both small and large, to treat their pollutants. Meanwhile, some local newspapers have also observed that these 'agrarians' "were silent but happy spectators to their own transformations ...", perhaps indicative of their utter unpreparedness towards this edge city phenomenon unfolding around them. At Sanand, additional floors have been added to existing residences - an expected response attributed to the economic windfall created by the Nano plant. Moreover, buildings with multiple typologies have evolved to accommodate new (and often undesirable) functions, aggressively growing inwards and vertically. The increase in density has spiked the incidence of unregulated constructions, including drainage disposal in open channels and visible pits. Finally, the mushrooming of ancillary businesses and commercial establishments catering to the migrant populations has exacerbated the urban scenario. The resulting incongruous urban form strains the civic infrastructure, which was essentially a group of villages neither planned nor equipped with the logistics necessary to accommodate mega scale factories of the kinds that Nano introduced in the last decade. However, most importantly, the social fabric of the villages that once comprised Sanand has changed irreversibly; the residents have moved from being farmers to speculative investors, seeking to market their most critical possession - land. Within Sanand and in the villages in the environs, land deals and approvals for non-agricultural purposes have resulted in many kilometers of land remaining unutilized and untilled - an eye sore that extends well into the disappearing landscape and in stark contrast to the green belt that this used to be. What should have been a thriving community is now marked by large stretches of dead edges.

Image 11b:

Sanand and the
Tata Nano Plant

Image 12a:

Mixed building typology within vertical growth and unplanned placement of ancillary activities at Sanand

Image 12b:

Mixed building typology within vertical growth and unplanned placement of ancillary activities at Sanand

Urban Edges of Large Scale Transformation - Mumbai's Highways

> *[T]he principal function of the Third World urban edge remains as a human dump. In some cases, urban waste and unwanted immigrants end up together, as in such infamous 'garbage slums' as the aptly named Quarantina outside Beirut, Hillat Kusha outside Khartoum, Santa Cruz Meyehualco in Mexico City, the former Smokey Mountain in Manila, or the huge Dhapa dump and slum on the fringe of Kolkata. Equally common are the desolate government camps and crude site-and-service settlements that warehouse populations expelled in the course of municipal wars against slums. Outside of Penang and Kuala Lumpur, for example, slum evictees are marooned in minimalist transit camps.*

- Mike Davis. *Planet of Slums.* (Verso, USA: 2007), p. 47.

Image 13:

Derelict plotting schemes with many kilometers of land remaining unutilized and untilled around Sanand

As the second example in this essay, Mumbai's urbanity presents a distinct contrast both to the city of Ahmedabad and the satellite township of Sanand. Landlocked by its water edges, Mumbai's complex urban plan has extremely limited land space available for future expansion. Its politics of land control and urban legislation therefore enable an interesting response to the ever-increasing pressure of urban housing for new migrants moving into the city. Most choose to reside in Mumbai's inner-city slums as they seek alternative accommodations and employment. Others occupy shanty towns on the outskirts of the expanding city, while gaining access to the core via its efficient transportation network. Still others inhabit the upcoming townships of Navi Mumbai and most recently, Uran - the second and third cities existing alongside India's largest mega-city. In effect, the stereotypical rhythm associated with First World urbanism is seemingly reversed. No longer is it rich suburbia on the edges of a poor downtown; the emerging pattern in the Third World city is much removed.

Within Mumbai, the highways of the city often limit and demarcate informal, migrant settlements. Mumbai's Western Express (WE) Highway skirting around Mumbai's International Airport is a case in point. This WE Highway serves as a perimeter for two kinds of urban tissue—the first being the most upmarket areas of the Mumbai, the second being Asia's largest slum—Dharavi. Landing in Mumbai therefore does not present a pretty picture of India's commercial capital. Following the glimpse of the new terminal, the urban scenery transforms dramatically in traversing about a mile and crossing the highway. For one, it seems as if the Western Express Highway is trying to contain the bulk of slum that terminates at its edge. A similar action is intended towards the Mithi River, on the other side of Mumbai Airport where the slums are seemingly landlocked by yet another major artery - the Andheri Ghatkopar Highway. In both cases, these highways are strong physical edges containing the slums. Interestingly, the slums do not sprawl beyond the highways even though the space after crossing them is available and would seems an easy target for the ever increasing housing demand. Beyond the availability of easy, available land and lax laws, one wonders if the slum contained within the bounds of this highway is the result of building byelaws that prevent the construction of high buildings within the flight cone area. It could be well argued that slums, by definition do not adhere to any byelaws as are exhibited in this case as well. However, if byelaws had been a reason, then hotels exist within this zone and so do other high-rise buildings. One wonders what would have been the sprawl of this slum had it these highways been a mile apart from their current locations? Would they still have functioned as physical edges to separate two economically different building typologies?

What Happens Next?

Whether seen from within or without—urban edges—especially in case of growing Asian cities, are rapidly changing entities. While the physical scales of these edges would sometimes lead us to believe that they are permanent, these urban edges remain inherently mercurial. They influence the way urban (and more recently, rural) occupants relate to the built and un-built environments. A lot of pull-push factors like urban planning strategies, natural and geographical constraints, urban migration processes, social economics and structuring, cultural sensitivity, urban infrastructure, hydrology, and the politics of land go into deciding urban sprawl and its impact on the edges as we perceive them.

In the case of Ahmedabad, the edges are dynamic; boundaries constantly shift and edges are modified as the multiple urban systems across the city's history contend with each other. For Ahmedabad, the last 10 years have seen stringent, better-defined byelaws, and methodological planning attempts that are evident in the new edges displayed within the fabric of the city. On these lines, it would be worth identifying the transformations that would be brought about once future, and major infrastructure projects like the Metro rail and Bullet train are also executed. However, the edge-making process at Ahmedabad should be recognized as a compromised (if not dynamic) process - the city's mesh of earlier plans makes any 'full' implementation challenging. Sanand, on the other hand, while successful as a new industrial town model on Ahmedabad's periphery, remains a classic case of 'unhappy' urban edges. It is still in its early years of growth and what we see now of the Nano Capital is a snapshot in time and the resultant of sudden mega-industrial setup. Planning and adding ancillary infrastructures to Sanand would take time, it would be interesting to see how its new edges would react and interact with the old ones, which would have been dominant by the time, these facilities show up. Finally, Mumbai presents a case of fixed dimensions, yet has remained an unparalleled urban magnet, attracting migrants in the past, present, and future. How Mumbai's strongly legislated edges coerce its urban form alongside informal, social processes shall be questions for the future.

*I*mage 14:

Mumbai Airport & the WEH

References

Balleney, Shirley. *The Town Planning Mechanism in Gujarat, India.* World Bank Institute, 2008.

Ballaney, Shirley et al. *Inventory of Public Land in Ahmedabad, Gujarat, India.* Policy Research Working Paper 6664. The World Bank, Sustainable Development Network, Finance Economics and Urban Department, 2013.

Damyanti, R., Asri, A. and Teguh, W. "Urban Shape Of Ahmedabad City Triggered By Industrial Activity, Case Study Of Industrial Estates Of GIDC" in *Proceedings of the 4th International Conference of the International Forum on Urbanism (IFoU)*, Amsterdam/Delft, 2009.

Dutta, Shyama. *Partnerships in Urban Development: A Review of Ahmedabad's Experience. Environment & Urbanization*, Vol. 12 No 1, 2000.

Gillion, Kenneth. *Ahmedabad: A Study in Indian Urban History.* University of California Press, 1968.

Joshi, R. et al. "Urban Heat Island Characterization and Isotherm Mapping Using Geo-Informatics Technology in Ahmedabad City, Gujarat State (India)" in *International Journal of Geosciences*, 6, 2015, p. 274-285.

Kaul, B. A. "Industrialization, Peasant Mobilization and the Conflict over Land Acquisition in India: The Case of the Nano Car" in *APSA 2010 Annual Meeting Comparative Politics of Developing Countries Report*, 2010, p. 2-22.

Lynch, Kevin. *The Image of The City*. Cambridge Mass.: MIT Press, 1959.

Profile of City Ahmedabad. City Development Plan. Amdavad Municipal Corporation, 2015.

KIM

Towards Edge Spaces of Productive Inclusivity: A Subversive Act

DONGSEI KIM

ABSTRACT

Recognizing that spatial design does not offer solution to all social issues, this essay interrogates how spatial design could become a catalyst for a productive inclusivity, especially in edge spaces. This catalytic role is mainly interrogated through a series of design studios conducted by the author. These studios are part of an ongoing research that examines one of the world's most impermeable spatial divides— the Demilitarized Zone (DMZ)—between North and South Korea. The essay first presents a research animation on the DMZ. This illustrates how contested spaces under stalemates entangled by strong structural hegemonies can be emancipated from perpetuating prejudices. Following this, subversive examples within art and architecture are explored to examine the potency of spatial design in addressing contested edge spaces. Lastly, the essay explores sample studio projects that combine 'imagining the impossible' aphorism with subversive strategies within the DMZ. Sample projects illustrate attempts at producing novel proposals that amplify productive inclusivity latent in edge spaces. This directs us to a conclusion where we can state; an agency of spatial design for contested edge spaces can be found in; how well we can make latent 'realities' visible so they can become active ingredients for imagining novel futures.

'Archetypal fact' of twenty-first century architecture and urbanism will be the enclosure, the wall, the barrier, the gate, the fence, the fortress.

- Lieven De Cauter -[1]

Introduction: Edges, Borders, and Boundaries

The edge is where one entity meets the other. It is a place where identities start to be defined and constructed through spatial inclusion and exclusion. Moreover, whether an entity is inclined towards inclusion or exclusion can be corroborated by its spatial configuration at its edges. In this sense, an edge space may be comprehended as a *border* or a *boundary* depending on its character. For example, philosopher Edward Casey explains how edges construct identities and are used as exclusionary instruments. In his "Border verses boundary at La Frontera"[2] he employs the US-Mexico border as an example to argue that edges matter as they enable differentiations, where places and persons are expressed, and established.[3]

Here, Casey distinguishes *borders* from *boundaries* according to their porosity and character. He states that a *border* may be construed as a "clearly and crisply delineated entity and is established by conventional agreements such as treaties or laws; thus it is a product of human history and its vicissitudes." In contrast, for Casey, *borders* are specifically "designed to be impervious, seemingly resistant to the passage of good or people as possible."[4] This contrasting description highlights *borders* acting as exclusionary instruments, versus permeable boundaries. The resistance that multitudes of refugees faced in attempting to cross nation-state

borders in 2015 is one of these examples. This clearly illustrates how impervious *borders* can become a regressive exclusionary instrument that impacts many individuals and societies.

In contrast to *borders*, Casey's *boundaries* are porous, lack exact position, and admit various substances to pass through them. He proposes natural elements such as forests or rivers as examples of *boundaries*.[5] In short, we can loosely equate the characters of *boundaries* to *productive inclusivity*; and the characters of *borders* to *regressive exclusivity*. In saying so, perhaps edges and their spaces can become more inclusive when they take on the positive characters of *boundaries.*

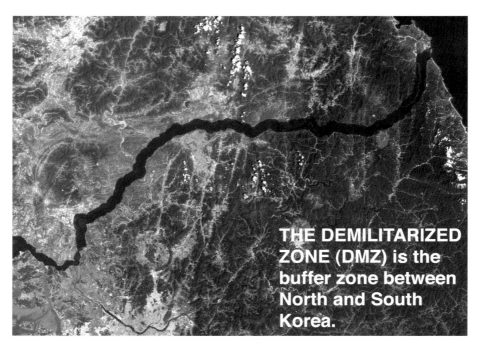

THE DEMILITARIZED ZONE (DMZ) is the buffer zone between North and South Korea.

Acknowledging that edges and its spaces can either act as instruments of exclusion or inclusion, this essay examines subversive approaches for the Demilitarized Zone (DMZ) between North and South Korea (Images 1 and 2). Employing examples, it suggests how constantly applying subversive approaches at the edges can engender robust platforms for inclusionary spaces to emerge for highly contested border regions.

The Agency of Spatial Design

I believe that spatial design[6] has a unique agency in constructing novel futures, possibly even better ones, through intentional provocations. In refelecting on this agency, this essay examines ways of imagining the seemingly impossible—yet more human, alternatives—through deliberately illustrating how borders and their spaces are represented, and re-imagined through subversive strategies.

If we assume that most contemporary borders and their spaces are symptoms of accumulated habitual thinking based on dominant hegemonic structures, the Demilitarized Zone (DMZ) between North and South Korea is a perfect example. Considered to be one of the most militarized and impenetrable borders in the world, it remains as not only the last ideological battling ground of the Cold War, but also among the only remaining frontiers for global capitalism. It is also an exemplification of the range of absurd conditions that can arise when nation-states attempt to sustain their highly contrived borders. These conditions become even more apparent when influenced by entrenched hegemonies. How then does one emancipate oneself from this hegemony? One among the ways to approach this is perhaps to imagine an alternative future that is beyond the accepted (or normative) status quo. I suggest that in order to go beyond this status quo, we need to proactively *construct* these alternatives through critical deconstructions.

Deconstructing the DMZ for the Imaginary

In order to imagine alternatives that break away from habitual ways of thinking, we need to first critically deconstruct the existing conditions. This conscientious deconstruction could engender novel foundations and ingredients for the DMZ. These new foundations and ingredients can bring about expanded imaginations for the contested DMZ. Moreover, these deconstructions uncover a range of absurd contradictions produced by nation-states that attempt to control their borders. This uncovering, furthermore, prompts a re-think on the nature of nation-state borders, inspiring us to imagine alternatives.

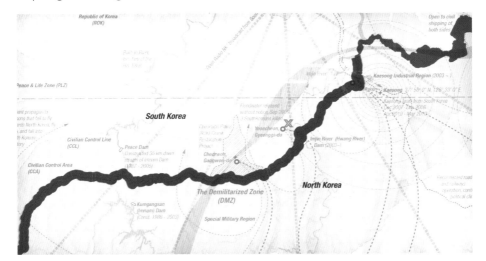

Image 3:

Conventional north–south orientation is questioned in the *A Construct the Koreas (Never) Made Together: Deconstructing the DMZ for the Imaginary* animation. © 2014 Dongsei Kim.

The research animation titled *A Construct the Koreas (Never) Made Together: Deconstructing the DMZ for the Imaginary*[7] is this critical attempt at deconstructing the DMZ (Image 3). This animation contributed to the border section of the Golden Lion Award winning Korean Pavilion exhibition *Crow's Eye View: The Korean Peninsula* at the 14th International Architecture Exhibition in Venice (2014). Using the instruments of spatial design and visualization, the animation offers an alternative understanding of the DMZ dominated by preconceptions, and destabilizes its habitual perceptions. Further, this animation—essentially a moving image—emphasizes the dynamic mutations over time that the DMZ has engaged over the last century. Among many things, it reveals the DMZ's fluidity and transgressions that uncover its dynamic spatial negotiations, contrary to prevalent static understanding. In the beginning, the caption of the animation states:

> By consciously deconstructing and reconstructing the DMZ, this dynamic mapping attempts to uncover its alternative future. Further, it attempts to emancipate one's preconceived perceptions dominated by the habitual.[8]

The animation starts with an intense pulsating red diagonal line that divides the screen into two. This red traced line of the DMZ represents the Korean division. The red diagonal line is then transformed into a straight line that becomes the 38th parallel north line. This locates the Korean peninsula within the context of the world and East Asia. This further alludes to the fact that the division of the Korean peninsula operates under the narrative of the unfinished Cold War and its local specificities.

This visual technique and narrative situate the DMZ within a larger historical timeframe. Here, 'history' is used as a lens to investigate the forces that cause the border between North and South Korea to fluctuate. This timeframe specifically investigates the period just prior to the Japanese colonial rule over Korea to when the Armistice Agreement was signed in 1953 after the three-year long Korean War. This historical lens traces the roots of the Korean division that shed light to late 19th century global imperial ambitions in northeast Asia. The animation then examines the DMZ through a 'barriers' lens. This lens describes how the DMZ performs and functions as a barrier hindering flows and crossings. These barriers range from the obvious physical border fences to the psychological barriers that emerge from land use restrictions and pervasive landmine accidents near the DMZ. An estimated 2 million landmines scattered within and near the DMZ intensify how this border region performs as a barrier for the entire Korean peninsula. These various forms of barriers are constructed on top of the literal 'line-on-the-map' over time since the armistice of 1953.

This lens further illustrates how Military Demarcation Line (MDL) and its 2-km offset line on both sides drawn on the military maps become a prelude and choreography

Image 4:

Migratory birds flying over the DMZ in the *A Construct the Koreas (Never) Made Together: Deconstructing the DMZ for the Imaginary* animation. © 2014 Dongsei Kim.

Anbyon Plains
Crane Restoration Project

Cheorwon Plains Crane
Restoration Project

Han River Estuary
Seasonal Bird Migration Site

for the current DMZ's spatial order. Moreover, the animation illustrates the expanded zone that operates under the logic of the securitized and militarized DMZ. Zones such as the Civilian Control Zone (CCZ) on the South Korean side that severely limit public access and use of lands near the DMZ are visualized.

The most important third lens, "transgressions, flows, and mutations" displays how the seemingly impenetrable DMZ is contaminated and circumvented. It illustrates the ecological, economic, political, and military forces that continuously push and pull the DMZ. The rivers that flow through the DMZ, migratory birds that cross the fences, the propaganda balloons deployed from the south toward the north via air, and underground infiltration tunnels are some of the transgressions that overcome the DMZ as a barrier (Image 4). They all vividly illustrate the absurd nature of these human-made divisions. At the same time, these transgressions demonstrate human ingenuity in imagining alternative use of this impenetrable border. This lens is important because it shows hope. The hope here is appropriating this inhumane regressive infrastructure of division—which performs to exclude—to become a catalyst for productive inclusion. This lens closely relates to the spatial subversions this essay further interrogates later. The last and fourth 'global' lens illustrates the unintended externalities that these impenetrable borders, such as the DMZ produce. In this case, the animation spatially visualizes the now well-known 5,000-km clandestine network that allows North Koreans to defect to South Korea. This example illustrates well one of the absurd aspects of nation-state border controls, and what impact this absurdities have on an individual basis.

The fundamental agency of spatial design in this particular investigation is visualizing existing information into meaningful knowledge. Here existing information of the border territory is visualized and spatialized, producing new knowledge that questions the status quo for new imaginations. This constant deconstruction and reconstruction starts to instigate alternative realities that open up new potentials for the contested DMZ.

Destabilizing the Status Quo

In addition to this act of deconstructing the DMZ, this animation acts as a rhetorical device. Based on facts and information, positioned statements are made. The agency of spatial design here lies in the way it attempts to destabilize the preconceived understanding of the DMZ through its deconstruction. It aspires to ignite conversations on what the North and South mean to whom, what the relationships between the two are, and how we can start to rethink these relationships from multiple perspectives. This dynamic spatial representation of the DMZ is not merely about how the DMZ operates and what it is. On the contrary, the important point here is making the subconscious perceptions of the DMZ visible. This addresses the prejudices prevalent on the DMZ. This uncovering perhaps has a greater impact on how the DMZ can be imagined for the future.

Now we return to the agency of spatial design and the animation acting as a rhetorical device. Rotating the conventional North and South Korea orientation prompts us to ask questions that challenge the status quo. This questioning ultimately prepares fertile grounds for critical engagement with the topic with reduced prejudice. This simple act of rotating the map challenges our conventional orientations that destabilize who might be 'us' and 'them.' This disorientation undercuts our current understandings of the DMZ but also grounds us in 'reality.' This grounding allows us to decipher media's surplus flow of stereotypical images that often demonize the 'other.' This subversive approach also contributed to the Crow's Eye View exhibition, where Minsuk Cho states:

> In contrast to a bird's eye view—a singular and universalizing perspective—it points to the impossibility of a cohesive grasp of not only the architecture of the divided Korea but the idea of architecture itself.[9]

To reiterate, one of the fundamental agencies of spatial design for contested border spaces lies in preparing fertile grounds and ingredients for imagining the seemingly impossible.

Subversive Approaches in Art

Understanding existing conditions in subversive ways is not new, and is found in many other disciplines. Nevertheless, many pertinent examples are found in conceptual and surrealist art that challenge the status quo. Subversive approaches are extensively interrogated though problematizing the object and visual/verbal relationships.

Following are some of the examples that illustrate this approach. They correspondingly become inspirations for the subversive approaches in the following studio interrogations. Marcel Duchamp's naming of an existing—ready-made object—urinal, the *Fountain*, from 1917, explores the disjunctive relationship between the meanings assigned to objects and their intended functions. The *Fountain* ultimately explores the relationship between 'signifier' and 'signified.' When René Magritte's painting of a pipe is juxtaposed with the text "Ceci n'est pas une pipe [*This is not a pipe*]" in *The Treachery of Images* (1928-9) a fragile relationship between images, words, and assigned meanings is exposed (Image 5).

Double reading afforded by the simultaneous depiction of a rabbit and a duck prompts us to question our preconceptions, what we can see and what we cannot see. Further, this opens up possibilities for identical objects to be perceived in different ways subject to who perceives them. Ludwig Wittgenstein discusses this complex relationship between signifier (object) and signified (concept) at length in

Image 5:

Fountain, Marcel Duchamp 1917; *The Treachery of Images,* René Magritte 1928-1929; *Rabbit and Duck,* Fliegende Blätter 1982; *One and Three Chairs,* Joseph Kosuth 1965. (In clockwise order from left top corner).

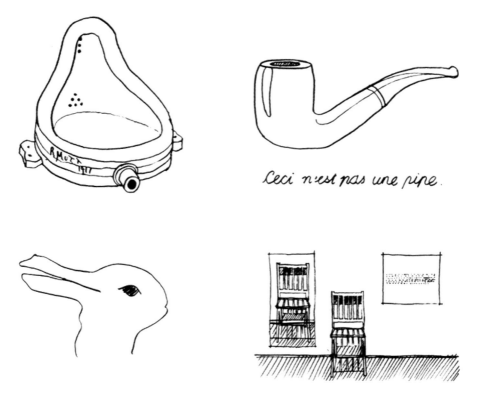

his *Philosophical Investigation.*[10] Lastly, Joseph Kosuth's *One and Three Chairs*, 1965 juxtaposes a *physical* chair with a *photograph* of the chair, and a dictionary definition of a chair. This work explores the disconnected and the connected relationship between the three different ways of representing and perceiving a chair. These novel ways of seeing and understanding existing conditions become an integral part of a studio and its design strategies. They ultimately become part of an attempt to subvert some of the regressive exclusionary spaces into a more progressive and inclusive space (Image 5).

Subversive Approaches in Architecture

As one might expect, many contemporary architects have also explored this issue of the signifier and the signified and how this might become subversive. For example, Robert Venturi explored this in his *Complexity and Contradiction in Architecture*. Venturi writes that Le Corbusier used juxtaposed *objet trouvés* to achieve such subversive effects. He further explains what the contradictions in meanings mean:

> Through unconventional organization of conventional parts he [the architect] is able to create new meanings within the whole. If he uses convention unconventionally, if he organizes familiar things in unfamiliar way, he is changing their contexts, and he can use even cliché to gain a fresh effect. Familiar things seen in an unfamiliar context become perceptually new as well as old. [11]

Bernard Tschumi is another architect and theorist who explored this subversive thinking. In his publications, such as *Architecture and Disjunction* (1996) and *The Manhattan Transcripts* (1981) he investigates the notions of subversions by attempting to answer the following question:

> How could architects avoid seeing architecture and planning as the faithful product of dominant society, viewing their craft, on the contrary, as a catalyst for change? [12]

Tschumi goes on to explain how concepts such as *objet trouvés* can overcome society's habitual ways of thinking and operating. Oswald Mathias Ungers also juxtaposes scores of city forms to other visually related objects yet unrelated artefacts in his *Morphologie: City Metaphors* (1982).[13] Ungers illustrates how seemingly unrelated forms and images offer provocations for imagining novel forms and narratives.

Aforementioned examples from these architects offer a way of deploying subversions for the design process. Whereas the next two examples offer specific illustrations on how these subversive design strategies can be applied to spatial borders. *Exodus, or the Voluntary Prisoners of Architecture* (1972) by Rem Koolhaas examines the "wall"—which was accused of being a "guilty instrument of despair." Following this, Koolhaas uses a subversive rhetoric to ask:

> Is it possible to imagine a mirror image of this terrifying architecture, a force as intense and devastating but used instead in the service of positive intentions?

Koolhaas then responds:

> Division, isolation, inequality, aggression, destruction, all the negative aspects of the Wall, could be the ingredients of a new phenomenon: architectural warfare against undesirable conditions.[14]

Koolhaas critically reflects on how architecture has been conventionally used as a tool in limiting freedom and establishing order. However, following the approaches seen in subversive strategies and *objet trouvés* Koolhaas attempts to subvert this instrumentality. He seeks the possibility of transforming this very same tool (architecture) for 'emancipation' rather than 'control.'

Lastly, architect Rael San Fratello's *Recuerdos: Snow Globes* examines the border between U.S. and Mexico (Image 6). Using subversive approaches Fratello playfully subverts existing walls and fences for positive intentions contrary to the original purpose of these walls to exclude. For example, he imagines inserting a playful Teeter-Trotter (Seesaw) into the existing wall structure, attaching a series of countertops for eating burritos together into the existing wall, and imagining the vertical components of the wall as an oversized xylophone to be played by people. Some of these selected examples from art and architecture offer inspiration for subversive way of framing contested border territories. They offer clues for uncovering latent potentials within the DMZ. These rhetorical subversions can act as catalysts for regressive and exclusionary DMZ to be reimagined as a space of productive inclusion.

Studio Interrogations: Imagining the Impossible in the DMZ

With a rhetorical statement, "imagining the impossible," the following interrogations explore how edge spaces that predominantly operate as instruments of regressive exclusions such as the DMZ, might be subverted into spaces of productive inclusions. The following design research studios (2014-16) investigate alternative futures for the DMZ through imagining seemingly impossible scenarios.

Following studios are a series of interrogations on the DMZ based on ongoing research. *Imagining the Impossible: Projecting the DMZ's Future,* RMIT, 2016; *What If the DMZ Became … ? Imagining the Impossible*, RMIT, 2015; *Projecting Future(s): Cosmopolitan DMZ*, Korea University, 2015; *Subverting Flows: A Folly for The DMZ Propaganda Balloons*, RMIT, 2014; and *The Epoch of Space Politics: DMZ Observation Platform for Peace*, RMIT, 2014 (Image 7). Above all, these series of studios offer a critique of the South Korean Government's DMZ 'World Peace Park' proposal. The overarching aim of these studios is to question the role of architecture for highly charged political spaces. Using the DMZ as a proving ground, the studio interrogates specific potency and limitations of spatial design in addressing such political tension. These studios build on top of extensive research materials accumulated over the past few years. As a first step students are first asked to engage the site through proactive mapping exercises.

While digesting the primary research materials, students produce proactive mappings. They are framed by seminal texts such as, "The Agency of Mapping: Speculation, Critique and Invention" (1999) by James Corner and "Defining Urban Sites" (2005) by Andrea Kahn. These mappings exercises deconstruct and recalibrate existing flows of the DMZ for further investigations. This step actively uncovers and 'constructs' fertile grounds for novel scenarios to emerge from the DMZ. Conventional views and habitual ways of framing the DMZ are fundamentally challenged through this process. All of these steps engage the aforementioned subversive design strategies. This active mapping of the territory enables a formulation of unconventional conceptual frameworks.

Image 6:

Teeter-Trotter (Seesaw) Wall, Burrito Wall, and Xylophone Wall; from Recuerdos: Snow Globes, Rael San Fratello 2013.

Image 7 (facing page):

Design Studios on the DMZ led by Dongsei Kim © 2014-2016 Dongsei Kim.

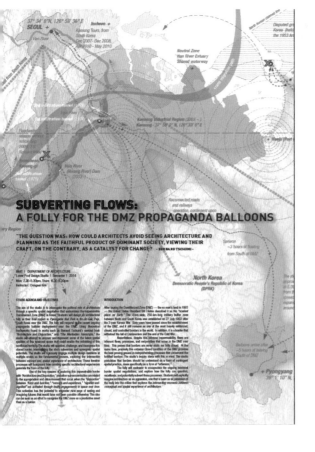

SUBVERTING FLOWS:
A FOLLY FOR THE DMZ PROPAGANDA BALLOONS

"THE QUESTION WAS: HOW COULD ARCHITECTS AVOID SEEING ARCHITECTURE AND PLANNING AS THE FAITHFUL PRODUCT OF DOMINANT SOCIETY, VIEWING THEIR CRAFT, ON THE CONTRARY, AS A CATALYST FOR CHANGE?" - BERNARD TSCHUMI -

THE EPOCH OF SPACE POLITICS
DMZ OBSERVATION PLATFORM FOR PEACE*

"THE QUESTION WAS: HOW COULD ARCHITECTS AVOID SEEING ARCHITECTURE AND PLANNING AS THE FAITHFUL PRODUCT OF DOMINANT SOCIETY, VIEWING THEIR CRAFT, ON THE CONTRARY, AS A CATALYST FOR CHANGE?" - BERNARD TSCHUMI -

What If The DMZ Became a...? Imagining the Impossible

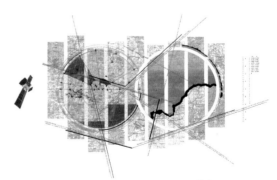

Imagining the Impossible:
Projecting the DMZ's Future(s)

Image 8:

A Carnival for the
Soybean. © 2014
Pei She Lee and
Darius Le. In an
architecture studio
lead by Dongsei Kim
at RMIT.

Student projects framed by these methods were diverse. Nevertheless, the more explicitly the projects engaged the subversive framework; the more fruitful were the resulting projects. Through this pedagogical framework, students' projects clearly begin to imagine seemingly impossible programs and spaces within the DMZ. Existing reciprocities and contradictory hybrid conditions of the DMZ are excavated, amplified, and combined into unlikely combinations. These critical uncovering and understanding of the DMZ driven by research, such as the abovementioned animation make the DMZ readily available as a catalyst for change. These sites framed as 'ready-made' or '*objet trouvés*' become ingredients to be appropriated into unlikely combinations that transcend our habitual understanding of the DMZ.

Subversive Propositions for the DMZ

Following this, a student project "A Carnival for the Soybean" by Pei She Lee and Darius Le critiqued the commodification of the DMZ (Image 8). Their proposal explored the DMZ's latent potentials as a culturally productive landscape. They first identified the voyeuristic tourists who flock to the Imjingak near the DMZ under the name of 'security tourism.' The students then identified extensive soybean fields near Jang-dan, Paju (near the given site) in their mapping exercise. Observing this paradoxical site condition, the students curated an unlikely journey that combined the movement of voyeuristic tourists and that of soybean manufacturing process at the site near the DMZ. This juxtaposition produced an unusual linear 'carnival' space. This unconventional space activates unorthodox interactions which in turn engender new forms of cultural production. The two main programs are experientially interwoven into one paradoxical existence while maintaining their programmatic separation as a tourist attraction and a soybean factory. A Carnival for the Soybean inspires its users to interact with the 'unusual others' through multiple senses that produce collective imaginations for the future.

"Unfolding Surveillance: The Arms of Cooperation" by Holly McNaught and Nirvana Hrustanovic proposed to transform the current DMZ into a Siberian tiger biosphere reserve. Also known as Amur tigers, they are endangered worldwide and are currently believed to be extinct in the Korean peninsula. This was inspired by late Nam June Paik's artwork, which light-heartedly suggested the DMZ become a tiger farm (Image 9). Unfolding Surveillance: The Arms of Cooperation assigns the Siberian tigers as a 'charismatic megafauna' to drive the proposal. In addition, existing heritage sites within and around the DMZ are amplified to engage the UNESCO World Heritage programs. This commitment reinforces the proposal's long-term viability and its implications on the global scene. Existing walls, fences, military buildings, surveillance platforms, observation decks, military guard posts, drones, and its related logistical systems reinforce and control the impenetrable border. However, these extensive military surveillance apparatuses within the DMZ are

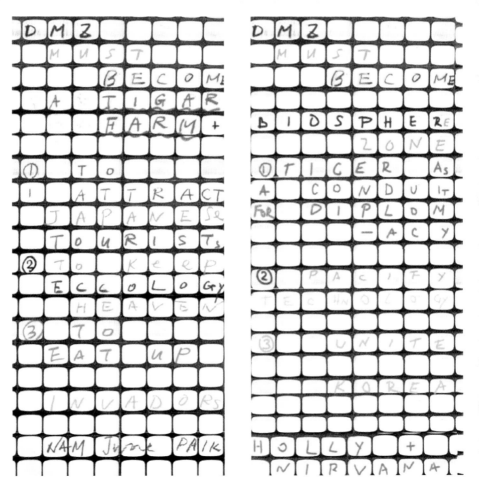

Image 9:

Unfolding
Surveillance:
*The Arms of
Cooperation* by
Holly McNaught
and Nirvana
Hrustanovic,
in a landscape
architecture
studio lead by
Dongsei Kim at
RMIT. This image
is a parody of an
untitled work of
Nam June Paik in
the Project DMZ
exhibition at the
Storefront for Art
and Architecture,
New York,
c.1988.

subverted into infrastructure that observe, maintain, and promote the tiger biosphere through subversive design strategies (Image 10). This proposal is also an illustration of how ecology and heritage combined can become a catalyst for change to produce a new culture of cooperation.

Towards Edge Spaces of Productive Inclusivity

These strategies are rooted in the kinds of subversive approaches seen in the examples of aforementioned artists and architects. Needless to say, these proposals are nascent and can be seen as naïve. Nevertheless, these constant explorations driven by 'imagining the impossible' aphorism informed by subversive design strategies seems to be one of the better ways to address these contested spaces. It particularly seems to be effective in addressing contested spaces that are entangled under long stalemates, such as the DMZ, constantly prejudiced by strong structural hegemonies.

The essay attempted to elaborate the agency of spatial design in engaging edge spaces. It aimed to illustrate how subversive approaches in spatial design could enable us to break away from habitual thinking often ingrained in the way borders operate. The research animation *A Construct the Koreas (Never) Made Together: Deconstructing the DMZ for the Imaginary* offered a concrete example of how the

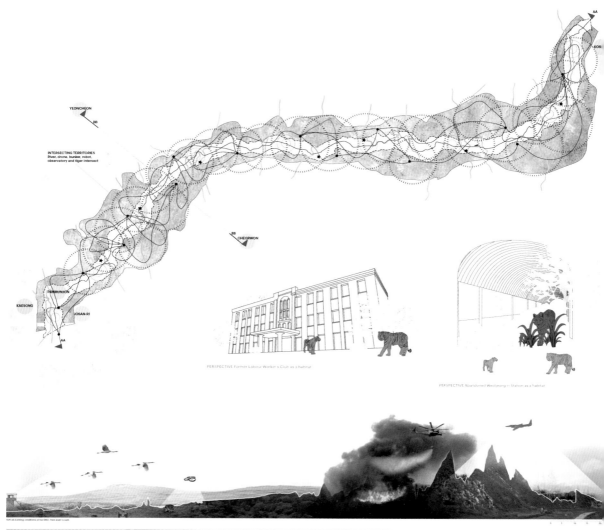

Image 10:

Unfolding Surveillance: The Arms of Cooperation © 2015 Holly McNaught and Nirvana Hrustanovic. In a landscape architecture studio lead by Dongsei Kim at RMIT.

existing conditions could be destabilized to question the status quo. This helps us start to question the functions, meanings, and potentials in contested edge spaces. This framework conceptually contrasts the regressive exclusive spaces and the productive inclusive spaces that are simultaneously inherent in edge spaces.

Subversive strategies within art and architecture were examined to underscore the potency of spatial design that could overcome habitual structures for contested edge spaces. This subversive framework was then combined with imagining the impossible aphorism to produce novel studio proposals. Studio proposals used the DMZ as a proving ground to amplify productive inclusivity latent in its edge spaces.

These amplifications came in the form of uncovering reciprocities and hybridity within the existing DMZ. These readings were then refined through subversive design strategies that endeavored to transform regressive exclusive spaces into productive inclusive spaces. This directs us to conclude that an agency of spatial design for contested edge spaces can be found in how well we can make latent 'realities' visible, so they become active ingredients for imagining novel futures.

Endnotes

1. De Cauter, Lieven. *The Capsular Civilization: On the City in the Age of Fear.* Rotterdam: NAi-publishers. 2004, p. 45.
2. Casey, Edward. S. "Border versus Boundary at La Frontera" in *Environment and Planning D: Society and Space.* Volume 29, 2011, p. 384.
3. Ibid. p. 384.
4. Ibid. p. 385.
5. Ibid. p. 385.
6. *Spatial design* here mainly refers to architecture, landscape architecture, urban design, and urban planning.
7. Kim, Dongsei. "A Construct the Koreas (Never) Made Together: Deconstructing the DMZ for the Imaginary" on Vimeo, 2014. (8 mins 24s). https://vimeo.com/93697167
8. Ibid. 0'24" - 0'33".
9. Cho, Minsuk, "Crow's Eye View: Prologue for the First Architecture Exhibition of the Korean Peninsula" in *Crow's Eye View: The Korean Peninsula.* Edited by Hyungmin Pai and Minsuk Cho. Seoul: Archilife. p. 8 - 9. Also Kim, Dongsei. "A Construct the Koreas (Never) Made Together: Deconstructing the DMZ for the Imaginary" in *Crow's Eye View: The Korean Peninsula.* Edited by Hyungmin Pai and Minsuk Cho. Seoul: Archilife, 2014, p.192 - 94.
10. Wittgenstein, Ludwig. *Philosophical Investigations.* New York: Macmillan, 1953.
11. Venturi, Robert. *Complexity and Contradiction in Architecture.* New York: Museum of Modern Art, 1953, p 43.
12. Tschumi, Bernard. *Architecture and Disjunction.* Cambridge, Mass.: MIT Press, 1996, p. 6.
13. Ungers, O. M. *Morphologie: City Metaphors.* Köln: Verlag der Buchhandlung Walther König, 1982.
14. Koolhaas, Rem. "Exodus, or the Voluntary Prisoners of Architecture" in Koolhaas, Rem. *S, M, L, XL.* New York: Monacelli Press, 1998, p. 5 - 6.

References

Casey, Edward. S. "Border versus Boundary at La Frontera" in *Environment and Planning D: Society and Space.* Volume 29, no.3, 2011, p. 384 - 98.

Cho, Minsuk, "Crow's Eye View: Prologue for the First Architecture Exhibition of the Korean Peninsula" in Pai, Hyungmin and Cho, Minsuk (eds.). *Crow's Eye View: The Korean Peninsula.* Seoul: Archilife, p. 8 - 9.

Corner, James. "The Agency of Mapping: Speculation, Critique and Invention" in Cosgrove, Denis (ed.). *Mapping.* London: Reaktion Books, 1999, p. 213 - 53.

De Cauter, Lieven. *The Capsular Civilization: On the City in the Age of Fear.* Rotterdam: NAi-publishers, 2004.

Kahn, Andrea. "Defining Urban Sites" in *Site Matters,* edited by Carol J. Burns and Andrea Kahn, 208-96. New York: Routledge, 2005.

Kim, Dongsei. "A Construct the Koreas (Never) Made Together: Deconstructing the DMZ for the Imaginary" in the *Crow's Eye View: The Korean Peninsula, at the 14th International Architecture Exhibition,* Venice. Vimeo. (8mins 24s). https://vimeo.com/93697167, 2014a.

Kim, Dongsei. "A Construct the Koreas (Never) Made Together: Deconstructing the DMZ for the Imaginary" in *Crow's Eye View: The Korean Peninsula,* edited by Hyungmin Pai and Minsuk Cho, 192-194. Seoul: Archilife, 2014b.

Kim, Dongsei. *The Epoch of Space Politics: DMZ Observation Platform for Peace.* Design Studio at RMIT University, Melbourne. March - June.

Kim, Dongsei. 2014d. *Subverting Flows: A Folly for The DMZ Propaganda Balloons.* Design Studio at RMIT University, Melbourne. July - October 2014c.

Kim, Dongsei. *What If the DMZ Became a... ? Imagining the Impossible.* Design Studio at RMIT University, Melbourne. July 2015a.

Kim, Dongsei. *Projecting Future(s): Cosmopolitan DMZ.* Design Studio at Korea University, Seoul. September - December 2015b.

Kim, Dongsei. *Imagining the Impossible: Projecting the DMZ's Future.* Design Studio at RMIT University, Melbourne. February 2016.

Koolhaas, Rem. 1972. "Exodus, or the Voluntary Prisoners of Architecture" in Sigler, Jennifer (ed). *S, M, L, XL.* New York: Monacelli Press. Storefront for Art and Architecture. 1998, p. 2 - 21.

Project DMZ. New York: Storefront for Art and Architecture. November 22 - December 18, 1988.

Tschumi, Bernard. *The Manhattan Transcripts.* London, New York: St. Martin's Press, 1981.
Tschumi, Bernard. *Architecture and Disjunction.* Cambridge, Mass.: MIT Press, 1996.
Ungers, O. M. *Morphologie: City Metaphors.* Köln: Verlag der Buchhandlung Walther König, 1982.

Venturi, Robert. *Complexity and Contradiction in Architecture.* New York: Museum of Modern Art, 1977.

Wittgenstein, Ludwig. *Philosophical Investigations.* New York: Macmillan, 1953

Intervention

Within the broad meanings ascribed to the term Urban Edge, the city of Chandigarh served as the focus of two Urban Design explorations at SARUP - the first completed in 2009, the second in 2015.

The Urban Design Studio from 2009 examined fabric interventions at the city center. In moving beyond the existing urban legslative code, it combined visions of Corbusier's unbuilt Post and Telegraph Building with relevant scenarios of commercial and institutional expansion in Chandigarh's Sector 17 (pages 108-21).

The Urban Edge Studio Award from 2015, built upon these 2009 studies and the multiple India Winterim visits (2008-15). Two action areas - Badheri (pages 122-93), and Kansal (pages 194-277) were selected in Chandigarh's fabric, and employed to provoke discussions on urban (and rural) edges.

Displaced migrants on the streets behind the Jama Masjid at Delhi. Delhi receives the equivalent of about 23% of its total population via incoming migrants each year. Of these, around 10% remain homeless and reside on the sidewalks of Delhi. Chandigarh's case is similar; Badheri, Kansal, and a host of rural places accommodate temporary visitors in the city.

PROVOCATIVE CHANGE - CRITICAL INTERVENTION
CHANDIGARH: LE CORBUSIER'S UNSURPASSED MONUMENTAL *TABULA RASA*

This project focuses on how conflict, contestation, adjustment, and reconciliation between the past and present are embodied in the making of achitecture and urban form in the Indian city.

Employing India and her fast-developing cities as a paradigm for rapid change following the process of modernization, this project concentrates on how pre-existing and relatively modern urban centers inevitably cope with these catalytic and unprecendented changes.

SECTOR 17: MORPHOLOGICAL ANALYSIS

Commercial Zone

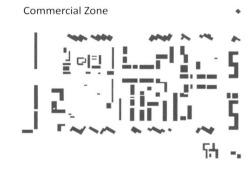

Residential Zone

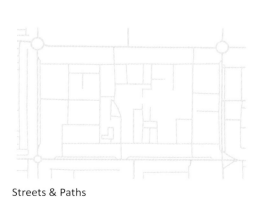

Streets & Paths

nd within the city is creasingly degrading without oper care and repair.

The scale of public spaces does not correspond to the demands of traditional social layout.

Wide city roads cut the city into isolated and disconnected chunks of land.

Endlessly stretching parking lots within a city change the scale and make it difficult to commute.

There is an abandoned waste land in the city, while there is a shortage for living space.

ormal use of space: vendors d sellers choose their vn spaces to conduct daily tivities.

Informal use of spaces: a barber sets his shop along the traffic road - spaces are used in unpredictable ways.

Facades that were originally meant to be clean are increasingly cluttered with posters and banners.

The original structural skeleton is getting filled with additional walls and other structures.

Residential code is particularly broken. New encroachments are built despite of the existing prescriptions.

Paths versus Commercial

Open versus Residential

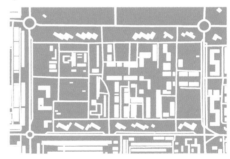

Open versus Green

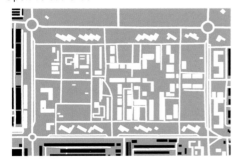

All Layers

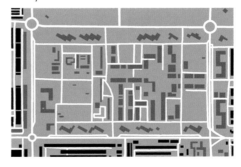

Image 1:

SARUP Chandigarh 'City Center Re-development' Studio 2009 (Hanna Rutkouskaya)

ORCHESTRATING CIRCULATION:

To propose a public, commercial center for Chandigarh's Sector 17 - this center would serve to invigorate the city center and create a nexus for diverse activities in the urban heart. The city center would embrace the scenarios of change, based on how commercial and public spaces may potentially transform in the decades to come - it therefore entertains design possibilities that recognize this continuous process of change.

PLAZAS: ORGANIZATION & RELATION

The site is organized around two plazas - public and private. Buildings around each plaza are organized and unified by common facades. Plaza 1 has a fenestrated 'punched' facade. The area in-between this facade and the buildings serves as a circulation zone. Plaza 2 has a 'thick' facade that can be inhabited.

FIRST FLOOR PLAN

Plaza 1: It is the most public and the biggest plaza. It serves as a gate introducing visitors to the complex.

Plaza 2: Is smaller, sunken into the ground and feels more private. Owing to its different function, its facades (inner faces) have thick walls that can be inhibited and are built on a shifted grid.

Plaza 3: This most private space is located on the second floor. It serves as a connecting point between the two lower plazas.

TIMELINE DIAGRAMS:

Public courtyard is the core of organization. It has a uniform facade, to which the rest of the buildings are attached.

The second courtyard serves as a gateway and a main point of arrival. It is fronted by a free-standing facade serving as a 'skeleton' for future developments.

All buildings are organized around the two courtyards. The new complex is connected to existing buildings by common circulation corridors, which terminate at the public plazas.

A second floor plaza is added as a unifying element. A uniform facade on the outside hides behind different juxtapositions of forms created through the combinations of two axis.

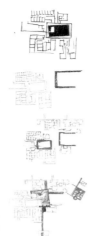

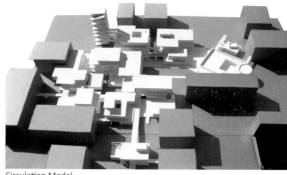

Circulation Model

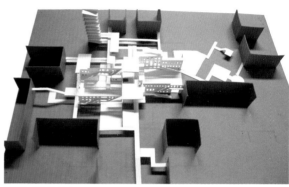

Volumetric Model

Image 2:

SARUP Chandigarh 'City Center' Studio 2009 (Hanna Rutkouskaya)

111

CORE OF THE INDIAN URBANISM:
CREATING THE IN-BETWEEN

Le Corbusier's Capital Complex at Chandigarh: The juxtaposition of the monumental Assembly Building against the 'informal' clothing line as a striking example of 'blurred borders' between the public and private in the Indian condition.

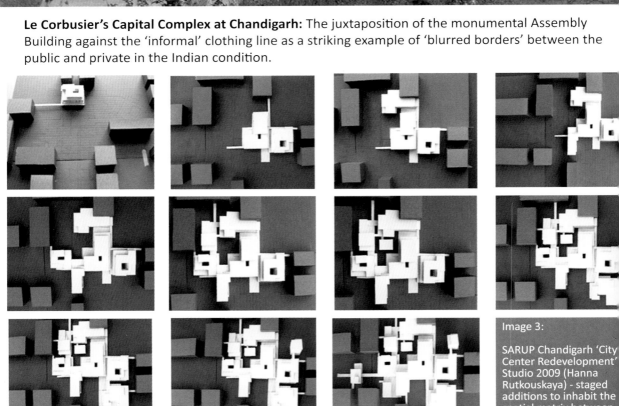

Image 3:

SARUP Chandigarh 'City Center Redevelopment' Studio 2009 (Hanna Rutkouskaya) - staged additions to inhabit the spatial matrix between buildings

FIGURE-GROUND DIAGRAMS

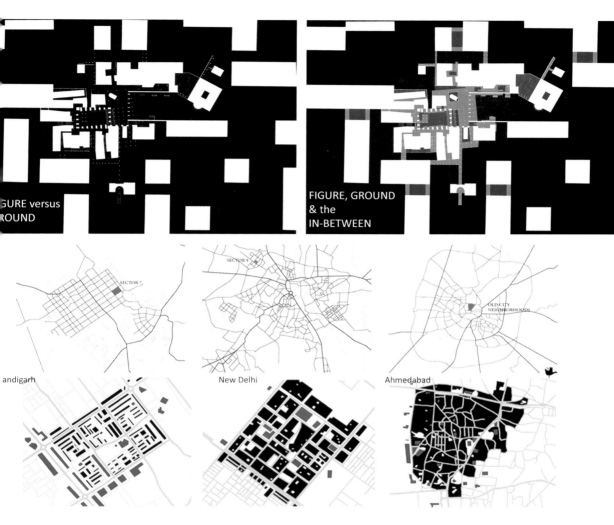

FIGURE versus GROUND

FIGURE, GROUND & the IN-BETWEEN

Chandigarh

New Delhi

Ahmedabad

...fferent scales and sharp contrast between the organic-accretive urban fabrics of traditional ...dian cities, such as Delhi and Ahmedabad, versus the rigid urban fabric of Chandigarh. Traditional ...dian urbanity and its buildings seem to gradually grow accretively over time in sharp contrast to ...anicured edges of formally-planned urban centers. The broader streets grow narrower, generous ...aces become smaller, and space cross-sections transform to canyons.

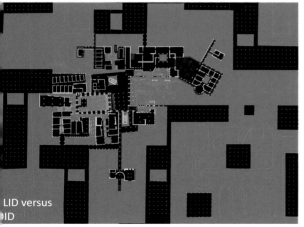

...LID versus ...ID

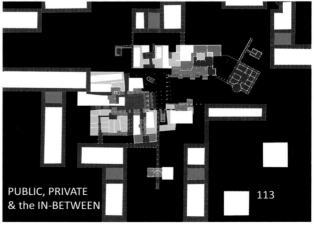

PUBLIC, PRIVATE & the IN-BETWEEN

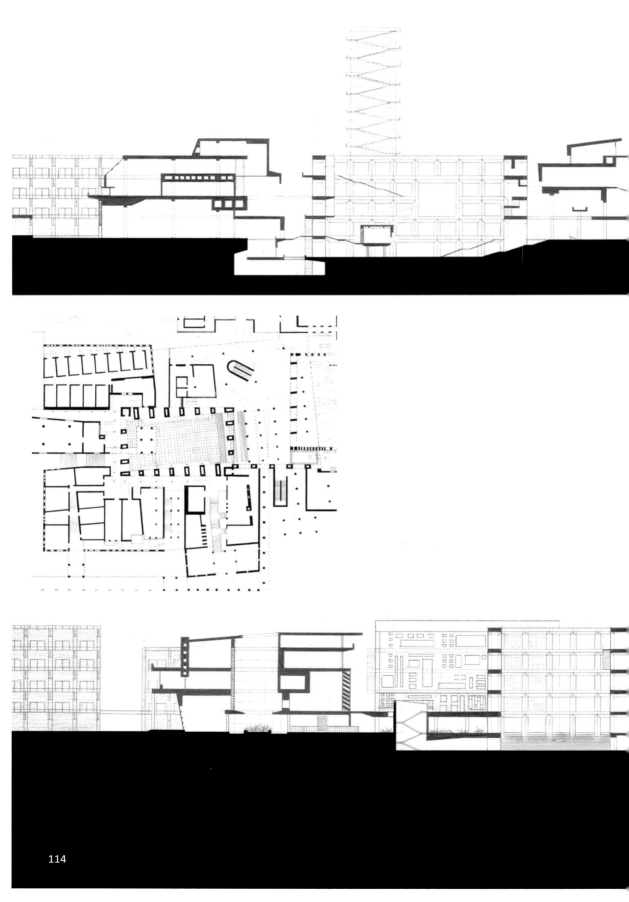

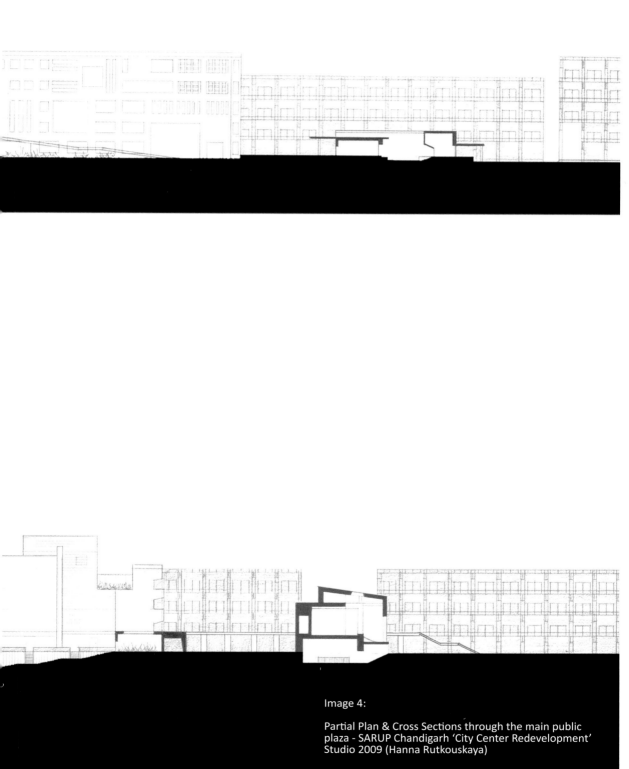

Image 4:

Partial Plan & Cross Sections through the main public plaza - SARUP Chandigarh 'City Center Redevelopment' Studio 2009 (Hanna Rutkouskaya)

Level gradients of infill

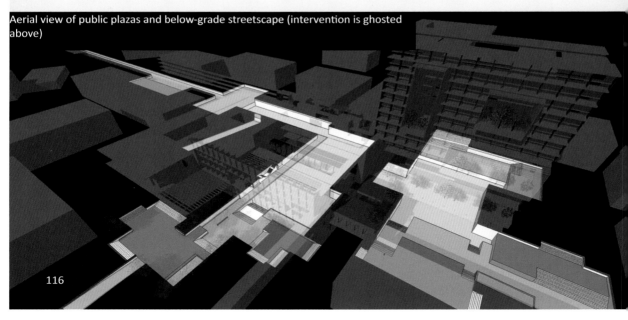

Aerial view of public plazas and below-grade streetscape (intervention is ghosted above)

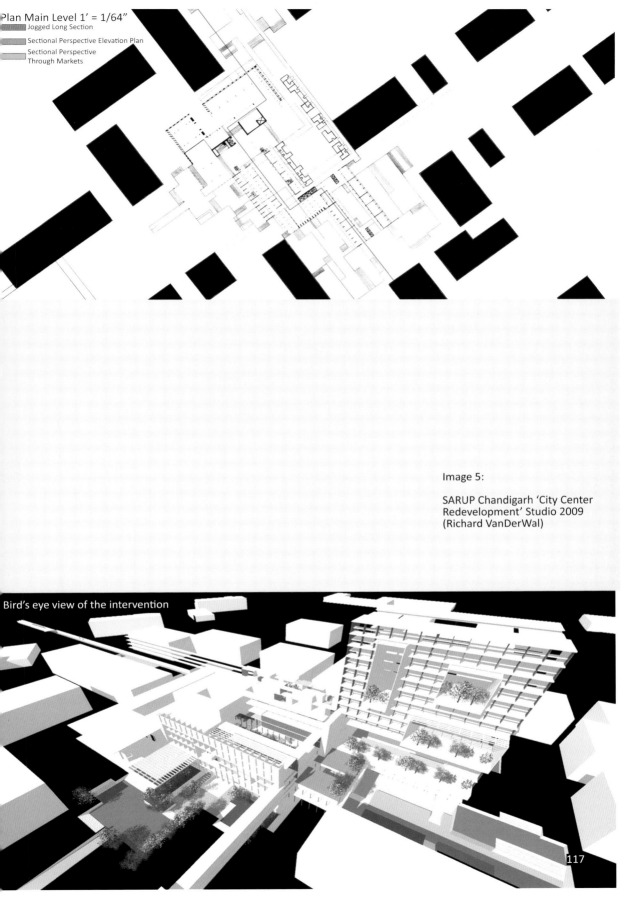

Plan Main Level 1' = 1/64"

Jogged Long Section

Sectional Perspective Elevation Plan

Sectional Perspective
Through Markets

Image 5:

SARUP Chandigarh 'City Center
Redevelopment' Studio 2009
(Richard VanDerWal)

Bird's eye view of the intervention

117

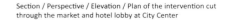

Early sections of markets and tower design with an emphasis on the lower plaza levels, interior streets, and voids or green spaces.

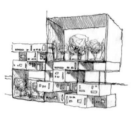

Encroachment study with modular system to accommodate hotels and green spaces.

Hotel rooms becoming a potential skin for the market. A courtyard developing from the tower footprint and the hotel emerging above the gathering space at the lower level pathway.

MARKET'S MORPHOLOGICAL SIMILARITIES TO THE INDIAN CONDITION

IIM-Ahmedabad complex interior street study.

Perspective of skin system and interior streets emerging from the ramp system.

Subtractive mass for public void space carve out the lower level streetscape.

Cut out mass admittting into building interior.

Markets Section Perspective 1' = 1/4"

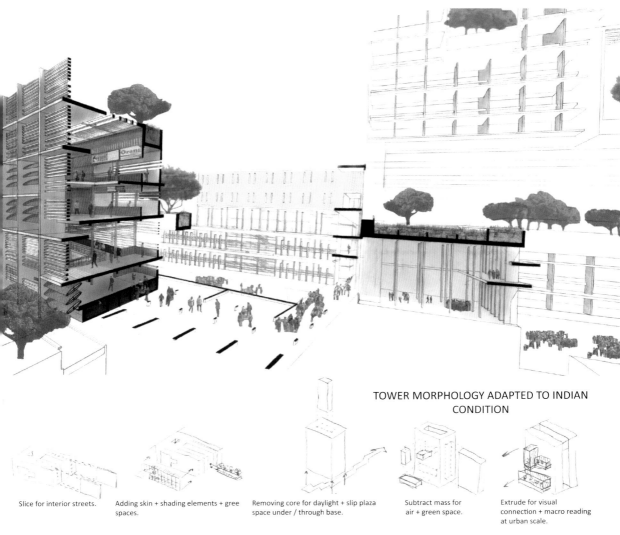

TOWER MORPHOLOGY ADAPTED TO INDIAN CONDITION

Slice for interior streets.

Adding skin + shading elements + gree spaces.

Removing core for daylight + slip plaza space under / through base.

Subtract mass for air + green space.

Extrude for visual connection + macro reading at urban scale.

The goal of this project is to transform the principles and rules put forth by Le Corbusier at Chandigarh and Modernism in general to more successfully inhabit and relate to the Indian condition and climate. To allow Chandigarh to remain the modern, forward-looking city that it was initially proposed to be, while creating an interpretation for how buildings outside the traditional could still remain true to the cultural conditions and urban fabrics that are inherently Indian.

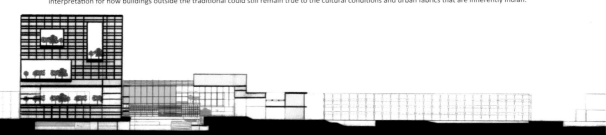

Site Section Looking South West 1' = 1/64"

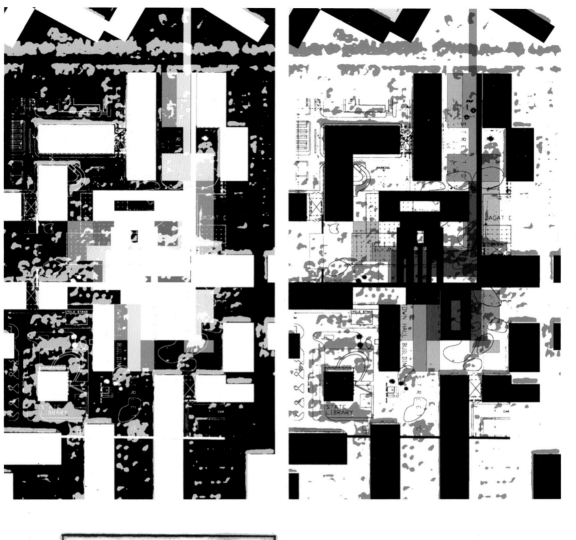

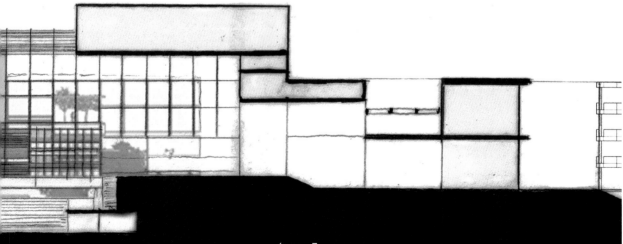

Image 7:

SARUP Chandigarh 'City Center Redevelopment' Studio 2009
(Richard VanDerWal)

1
Urban Edge Studio 2015
Baber Group

Chandigarh

PUNJAB

HARYANA

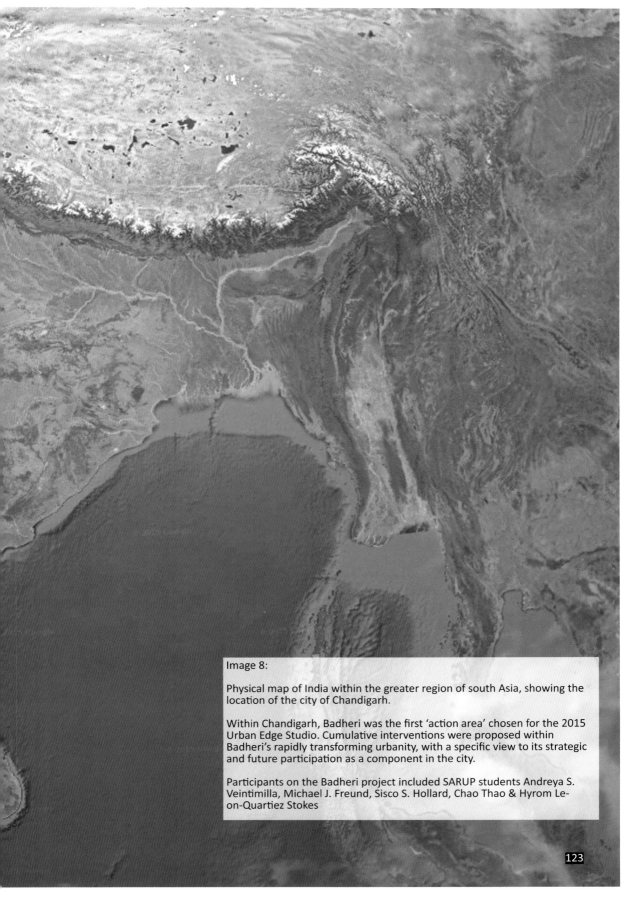

Image 8:

Physical map of India within the greater region of south Asia, showing the location of the city of Chandigarh.

Within Chandigarh, Badheri was the first 'action area' chosen for the 2015 Urban Edge Studio. Cumulative interventions were proposed within Badheri's rapidly transforming urbanity, with a specific view to its strategic and future participation as a component in the city.

Participants on the Badheri project included SARUP students Andreya S. Veintimilla, Michael J. Freund, Sisco S. Hollard, Chao Thao & Hyrom Le-on-Quartiez Stokes

Image 9: (Top left to top right, counter-clock wise)

a) Aerial view of Chandigarh's urban site, showing the Shivalik Hills serving as a backdrop to the city's location on the relatively flat, alluvial flood plain (1960s photograph).
b) Plan of Chandigarh showing its urban structure, sectors, and the two action areas for SARUP's Urban Edge Studio 2015 (Kansal & Badheri).
c) Plan of Badheri, showing dense, organic-accretive nature of the fabric organized around the village center.
d) Urban Fabric at Badheri.

1947
General Systems Theory
Ludwig von Bertalanffy

Game Theory
John von Neuman and
Oskar Morgenstern

Ecological
Anxiety

Relative World Events   World War I   Great Depression   Principles of modern computing
                                                                                        World War II

Modernism

**Architecture
Urban
Response**

1902
Garden City
Ebenezer Howard

1917
Constructivism
Iakov Chernikhov

1928
CIAM
Functionalism / Rationalism

1949
Neo Futurism
Buckminster Fuller

1914
Futurism
Antonio Sant'Elia

1932
Broadacre City
Frank Lloyd Wright

1893
City Beautiful
Daniel Burnham

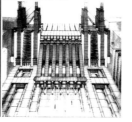

1924
Ville Radiuse
Le Corbusier

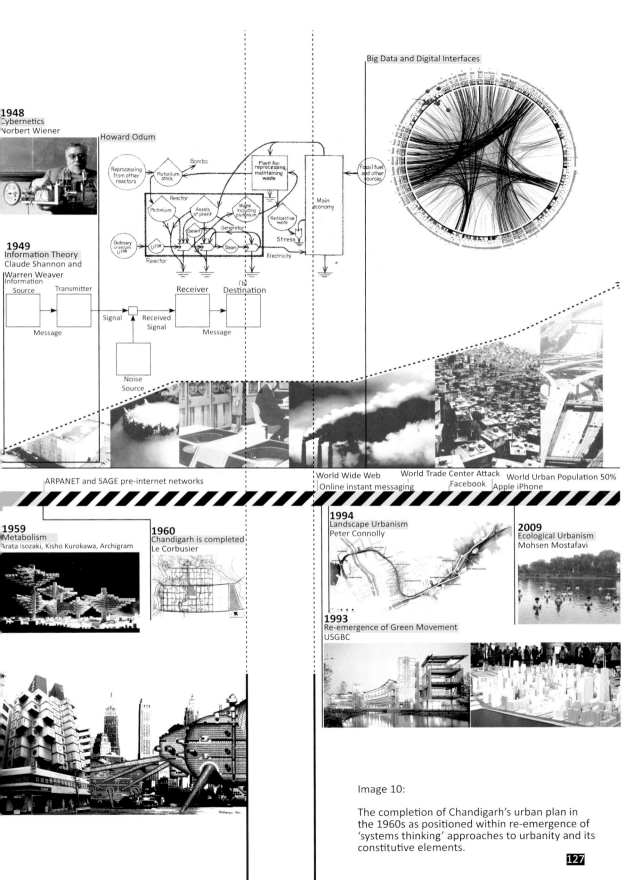

Big Data and Digital Interfaces

1948
Cybernetics
Norbert Wiener

Howard Odum

1949
Information Theory
Claude Shannon and
Warren Weaver

ARPANET and SAGE pre-internet networks

World Wide Web
Online instant messaging

World Trade Center Attack
Facebook

World Urban Population 50%
Apple iPhone

1959
Metabolism
Arata Isozaki, Kisho Kurokawa, Archigram

1960
Chandigarh is completed
Le Corbusier

1994
Landscape Urbanism
Peter Connolly

2009
Ecological Urbanism
Mohsen Mostafavi

1993
Re-emergence of Green Movement
USGBC

Image 10:

The completion of Chandigarh's urban plan in the 1960s as positioned within re-emergence of 'systems thinking' approaches to urbanity and its constitutive elements.

Population Concentration in Millions
per 2011 census

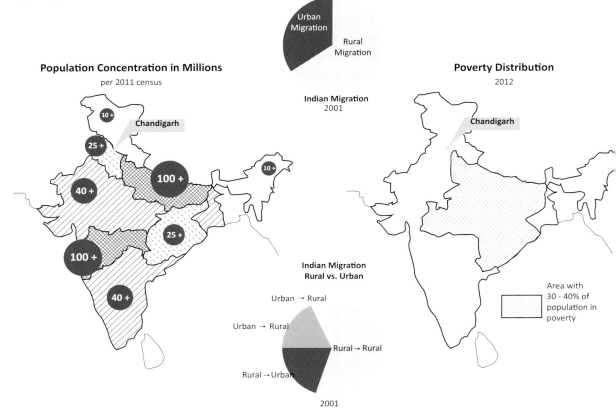

Chandigarh

10 +

25 +

40 +

100 +

10 +

100 +

25 +

40 +

Urban Migration

Rural Migration

Indian Migration
2001

Indian Migration
Rural vs. Urban

Urban → Rural

Urban → Rural

Rural → Rural

Rural → Urban

2001

Poverty Distribution
2012

Chandigarh

Area with
30 - 40% of
population in
poverty

Percentage Share of Urban Population
per 2011 census

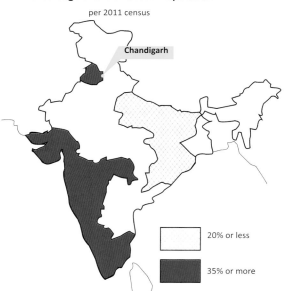

Chandigarh

20% or less

35% or more

Major Net Internal Migration Flows
2001

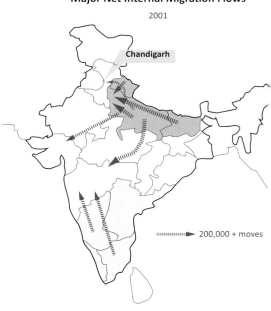

Chandigarh

200,000 + moves

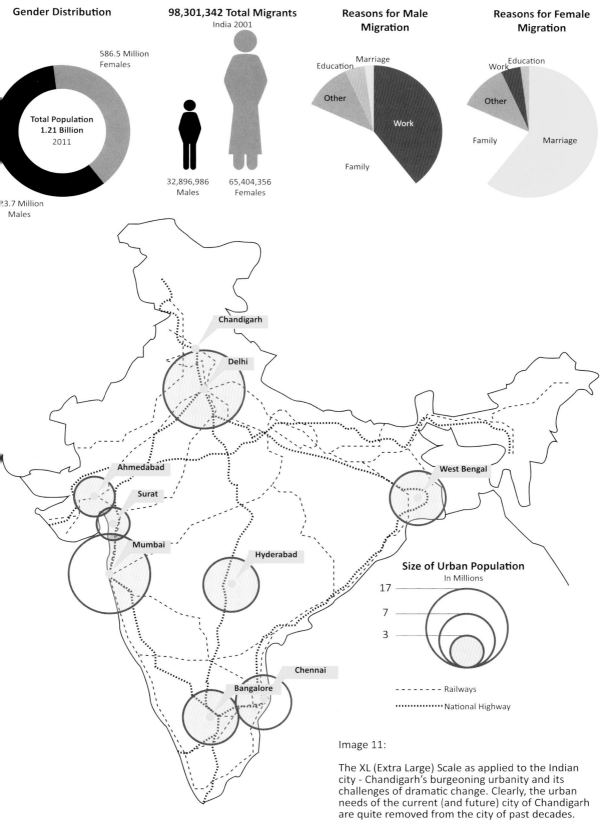

Gender Distribution

586.5 Million Females

Total Population 1.21 Billion 2011

23.7 Million Males

98,301,342 Total Migrants
India 2001

32,896,986 Males

65,404,356 Females

Reasons for Male Migration

Education
Marriage
Other
Work
Family

Reasons for Female Migration

Work
Education
Other
Family
Marriage

Chandigarh

Delhi

Ahmedabad

Surat

Mumbai

Hyderabad

West Bengal

Size of Urban Population
In Millions

17
7
3

Chennai

Bangalore

‑ ‑ ‑ ‑ ‑ Railways
•••••••••••• National Highway

Image 11:

The XL (Extra Large) Scale as applied to the Indian city - Chandigarh's burgeoning urbanity and its challenges of dramatic change. Clearly, the urban needs of the current (and future) city of Chandigarh are quite removed from the city of past decades.

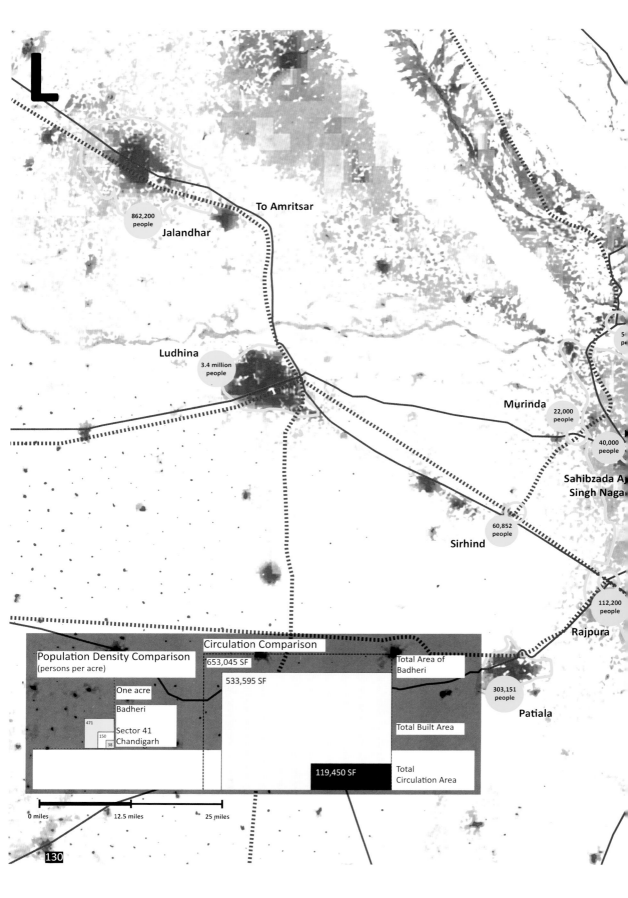

L

To Amritsar

862,200
people

Jalandhar

Ludhina

3.4 million
people

Murinda

22,000
people

40,000
people

Sahibzada A
Singh Naga

60,852
people

Sirhind

5
pe

112,200
people

Rajpura

Population Density Comparison
(persons per acre)

Circulation Comparison

653,045 SF

533,595 SF

Total Area of
Badheri

One acre

Badheri

471

Sector 41
Chandigarh

150

38

Total Built Area

119,450 SF

Total
Circulation Area

303,151
people

Patiala

0 miles   12.5 miles   25 miles

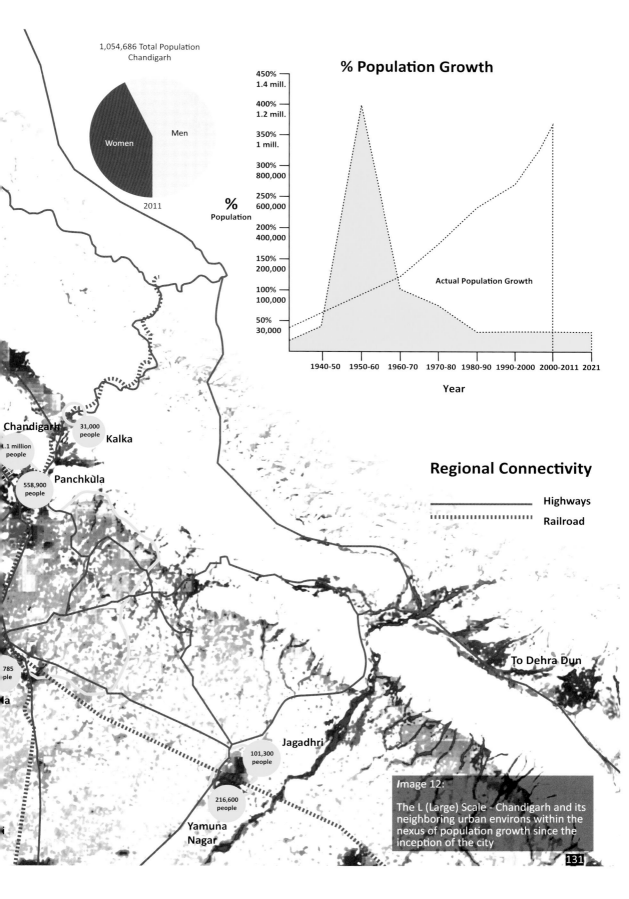

1,054,686 Total Population
Chandigarh

Women   Men

2011

% Population Growth

450%
1.4 mill.

400%
1.2 mill.

350%
1 mill.

300%
800,000

250%
600,000

%
Population

200%
400,000

150%
200,000

100%
100,000

50%
30,000

Actual Population Growth

1940-50   1950-60   1960-70   1970-80   1980-90   1990-2000   2000-2011   2021

Year

Chandigarh   31,000 people   Kalka

1.1 million people

558,900 people   Panchkula

Regional Connectivity

Highways
Railroad

785 ple

To Dehra Dun

Jagadhri

101,300 people

216,600 people

Yamuna Nagar

Image 12:

The L (Large) Scale - Chandigarh and its neighboring urban environs within the nexus of population growth since the inception of the city

131

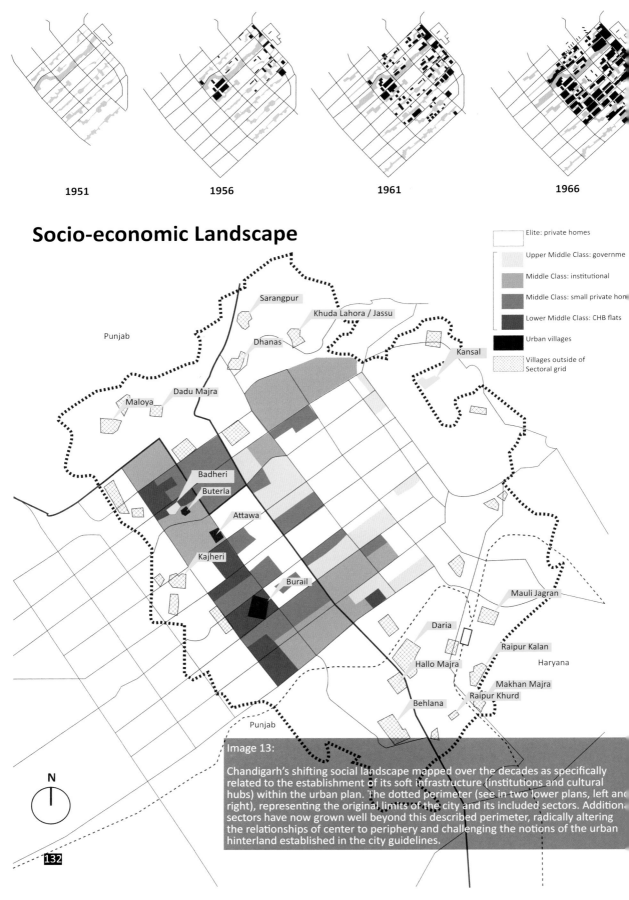

1951   **1956**   **1961**   **1966**

Socio-economic Landscape

Elite: private homes

Upper Middle Class: governme

Middle Class: institutional

Middle Class: small private hon

Lower Middle Class: CHB flats

Urban villages

Villages outside of
Sectoral grid

Punjab

Sarangpur

Khuda Lahora / Jassu

Dhanas

Kansal

Dadu Majra

Maloya

Badheri

Buterla

Attawa

Kajheri

Burail

Mauli Jagran

Daria

Raipur Kalan

Hallo Majra

Haryana

Makhan Majra

Raipur Khurd

Behlana

Punjab

N

Image 13:

Chandigarh's shifting social landscape mapped over the decades as specifically related to the establishment of its soft infrastructure (institutions and cultural hubs) within the urban plan. The dotted perimeter (see in two lower plans, left and right), representing the original limits of the city and its included sectors. Addition sectors have now grown well beyond this described perimeter, radically altering the relationships of center to periphery and challenging the notions of the urban hinterland established in the city guidelines.

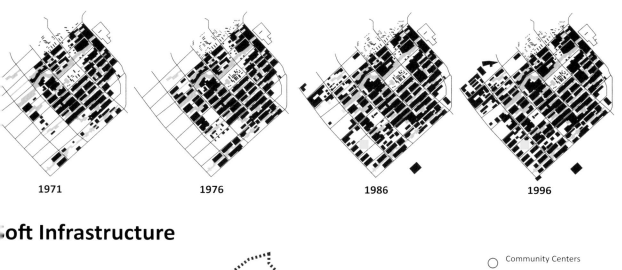

1971   1976   1986   1996

Soft Infrastructure

Community Centers

Cultural / Entertainment

Police / Fire

Governmental Services / Facilities

Educational

Healthcare

Punjab

Punjab

Haryana

0 miles   2 miles   4 miles

M

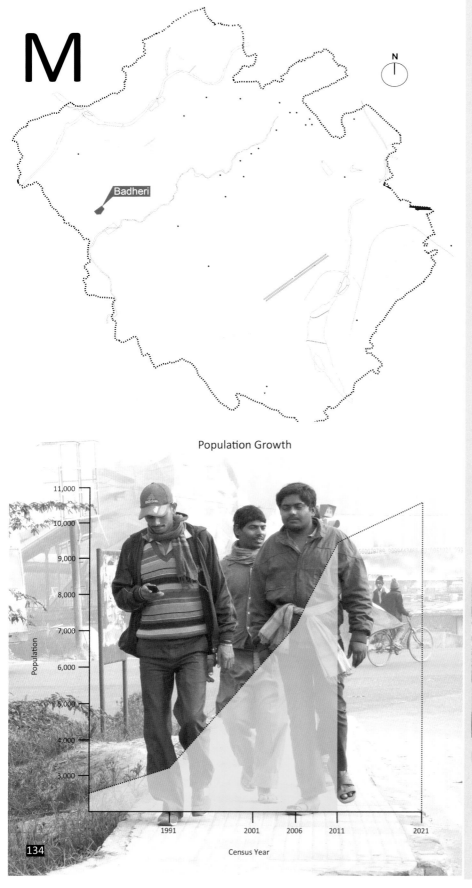

Badheri

Population Growth

Population

11,000

10,000

9,000

8,000

7,000

6,000

5,000

4,000

3,000

1991   2001   2006   2011   2021

Census Year

How did the village begin?
Originally resided in sector 20 but was overtaken by the growth of Chandigarh. Badheri began as agricultural fields with one of the gurudwaras's (Sikh temple) being t only remaining original building.

Any owned vs. rented divisions within the village? Mixed. It's up to the owners if they want to rent. Many migrants come from surrounding villages and states. Chandigarh is their "first stop." The left side of Badheri with the more organic organizational structure is the old part and the new part is th right and slightly more organized. The tree where the priest sits is the oldest place of worship. The kindergarten school is 12-14 years old. Things are available in Badher that aren't available in the sector housing.

He is a well-to-do migrant that worked for a life insurance compar Moved from Haryana to Chandigar with his wife but has knee trouble and couldn't climb the stairs in his sector home, so he moved to Badheri because a friend suggested that the rents for a ground floor apartment are cheaper. The facilities within Badheri are similar to the city but less expensive. Land surrounding Badheri was once all agricultural land with cows grazing between Badheri and Buterla, the other village located in sector 41.

People of Badheri

Badheri is a developed village, not yet a town or city. It is relatively safe. There are some petty crimes but not much. Sector 25, on the outskirts of Chandigarh, has higher crime. Badheri and Buterla were always separate villages.

He was originally from Punjab. His father worked in the Secretariat and now he does as well. He was a kid growing up in Badheri in the 1970s. He loved Badheri, he went to school in the old pond area, and says Baheri has really changed since then. In 1993 there was a flood, drainage was was blocked by dirt and trash. That year, he got married and moved into a house. His house was completely destroyed in the flood. Neighbors helped a lot but the government did nothing and there was no compensation. His only complaint about the village is that the roads are not wide enough and the encroachments are not safe because many areas are not accessible in case of emergency. He has a four person family and they are very happy. He did not want to comment on a success story but mentioned a man named Angrez Singh (which means a foreigner), whose land was taken by the government and he used the compensation money to purchase more land. He now owns most of Badheri and his family actually rents from this man who is now very old.

The village was originally settled based on caste divisions. The more organized area is now primarily rental while the older, more organic area is where the original villagers reside. Renting out apartments became very lucrative once the agricultural lands were all gone and the city developed around Badheri. In 1960, a single room rent was about $10 a month, then increased to $50; now it is about $100 a month and is the primary business. The villagers pay a commerce tax to Chandigarh.

There is no formal legislation within the village. As chief, he tries to make improvements on behalf of the village. He has tried to get the roads widened. The city also has a law that says buildings cannot be more than 35 ft high, and he tried to get limit raised to 45 ft. He believes that if they can build one more level higher the opportunities in Badheri will really open as people could build a hotel or open up the ground level to commerce. This would also help reduce overcrowding and allow more space to widen the roads. However, the city won't listen. He would like Chandigarh to accept Badheri but says they won't until the village becomes clean and more accessible.

He moved to the village in 1970 and was living in the surrounding area before that. Before 1970, most people lived in rental units. In 1996, a corporation formed in Badheri that began to look after the village affairs. Between 1970 and 1996, the village was mostly an agricultural trading village selling milk and raising cows. Then people started to rent out their properties for other more lucrative purposes. PG's, or paying guests, were a good way to make money. They were originally only short term paying guests that didn't make many demands. Over time the guests would rent for longer periods of time until eventually people were holding year-long leases. Taxes help pay for the streets in the village and other infrastructural work.

s the government assist or help village? Yes, the government ided plumbing, drainage, ricity, and assisted after a big d. There are two major Sikh oles in the village; one originally he lower caste and the other he higher caste that originally ed in the village.

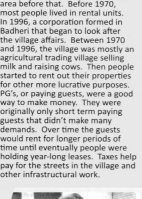

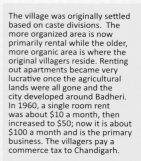

Image 14:

The M (Medium) Scale - Action Area Badheri as a nested, rural pocket positioned within the urbanity of Chandigarh, characterized by its densely built-up fabric and diverse populations who especially endorse their belonging to place. Their histories and the deliberate (strategic) continuation of these histories is as important as the tenets of a 'top-down' urban legislation. Should this effectively imply a 'repetition' of the past, or an opportunity for (re) invention?

Residential
Commercial
Mixed - Use
Institutional
Open Space
Road
Sector Housing

9% 5% 2%
20% 6%
13%
45%

LAND USE (CURRENT)

0' 25' 50' 100'   200'

0M 13M 25M 50M   100M

Residential
Commercial
Mixed - Use
Institutional
Manufacturing
Entertainment
Open Space
Road
Sector Housing

19% 5% 2%
12% 14%
11% 13%
8%
45%

LAND USE (FUTURE)

0' 25' 50' 100'   200'

0M 13M 25M 50M   100M

Commercial Activity

Road Use Intensity

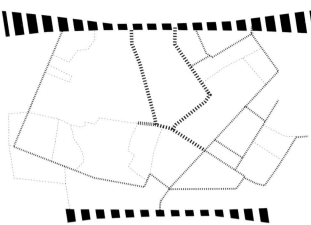

Major Roads
ıııı Internal Streets - 6 to 9m
.... Minor Streets - 3 to 6m
----- Gully - Less than 3m

Chandigarh Housing

Level Four: 35'-0"

Level Three: 25'-0"

Level Three: 25'-0"

Level Three: 25'-0"

Level Three: 25'-0"

Level Four: 35'-0"

Image 15:

Action Area Badheri's land use, demographic distribution, and traffic studies - the rapid commercialization of the accretive rural fabric exerts an alarming pressure not only on the current residents of Badheri, but is also detrimental to the lifestyles of populations residing in the formally conceived sectors around Badheri. If indeed Badheri's transformation towards a commercial (trucking and retail) hub and a migrant base for transient populations arriving in Chandigarh is accepted within the strategic development of Chandigarh, then a long-term scenario of change may be well imagined.

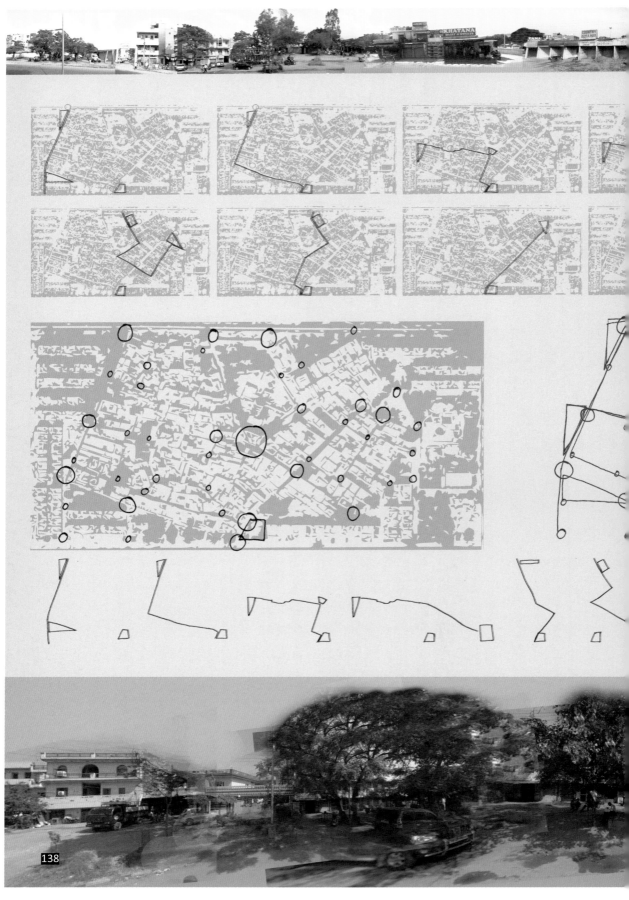

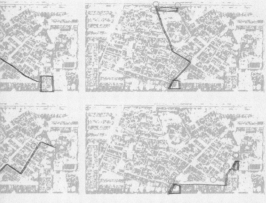

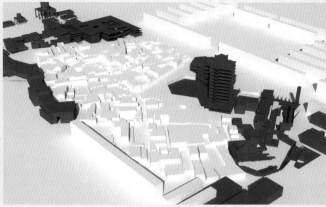

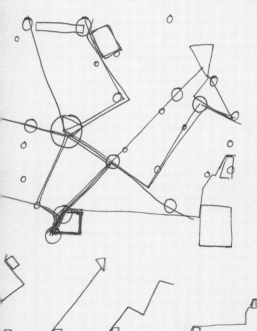

Image 16:

Elevations showing the sector edges of Badheri - these were undefined on the original plan and have been systematically encroached upon in recent decades. Removed of the agrarian properties that once surrounded the village of Badheri, urban legislative measures (and building typologies in adjoining sectors) have done little to 'contain' and consolidate the rural pocket.

The Urban Edge Studio 2015 interrogated if, at all, the conscious 'containment' of such a fabric was indeed a viable urban and social strategy, especially given that Badheri is among the multiple 'nested' ruralities within the urban fabric of Chandigarh. In anticipation that Badheri would grow in ways intrinsic to its fabric (and change from within), these design explorations identified viable 'points of intervention' within the sector edges - which were perceived as catalysts for systematic growth strategies in the future.

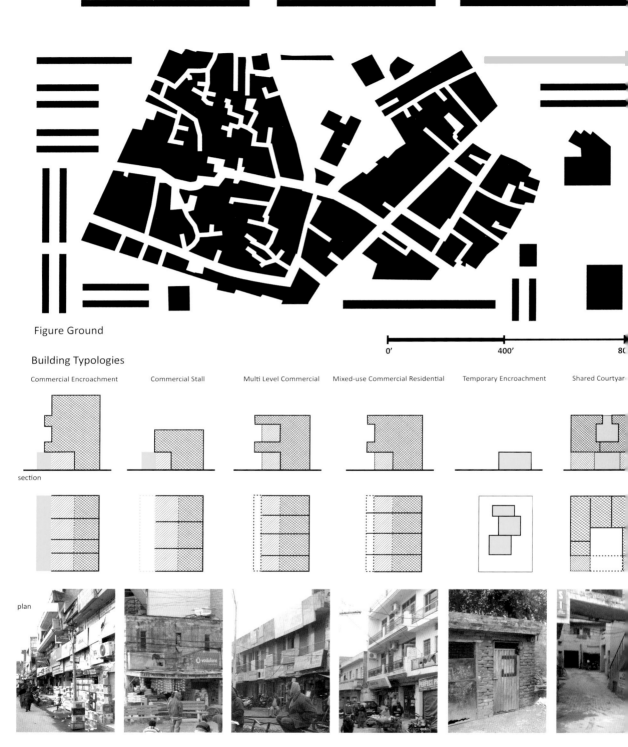

Figure Ground

0'   400'   8(

Building Typologies

Commercial Encroachment   Commercial Stall   Multi Level Commercial   Mixed-use Commercial Residential   Temporary Encroachment   Shared Courtyar

section

plan

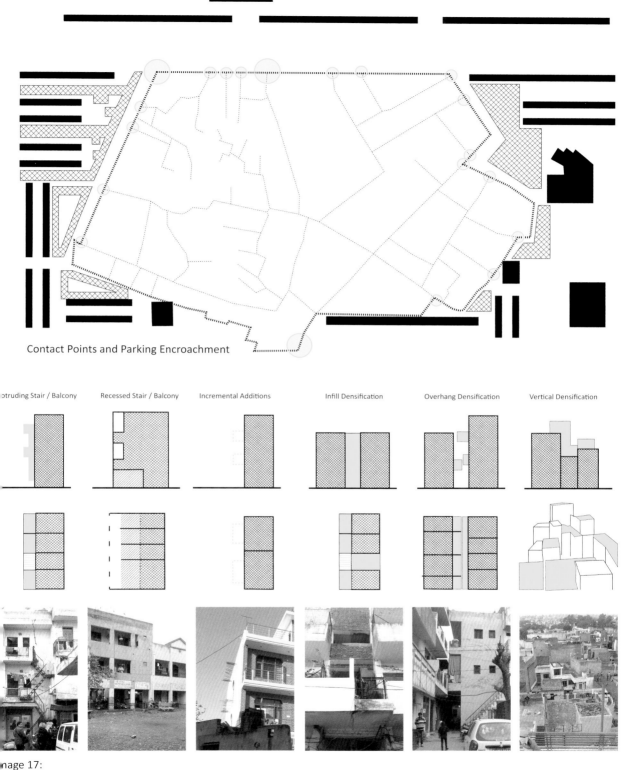

Contact Points and Parking Encroachment

| Protruding Stair / Balcony | Recessed Stair / Balcony | Incremental Additions | Infill Densification | Overhang Densification | Vertical Densification |

Image 17:

Studies on the urban fabric and its typological variations in Badheri - current building typologies in Badheri suggest multiple strategies whereby new interventions may modify and extend the existing strategies, allowing for the introduction of unprecedented building typologies, yet allowing for functional flexibility.

S

Gateway

Education

Housing

Cultural / Entertainment

Trucking / Warehouse Depot

Commercial Depot

Village Administration /
Migration Services

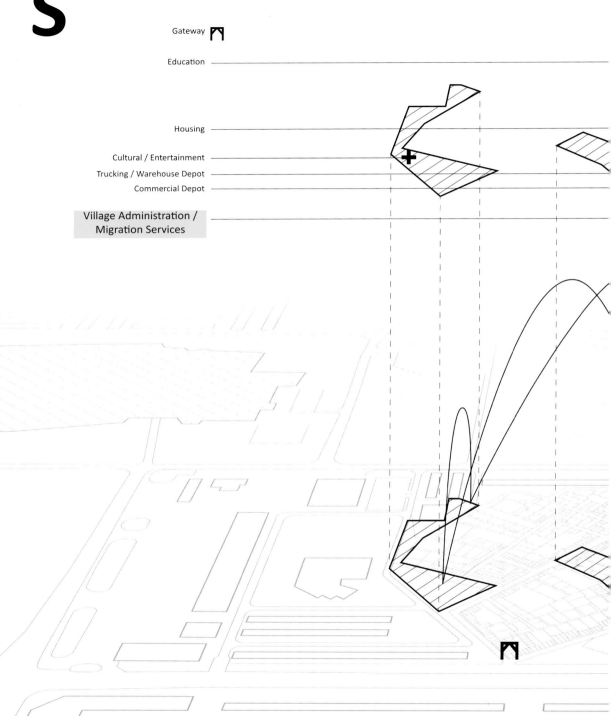

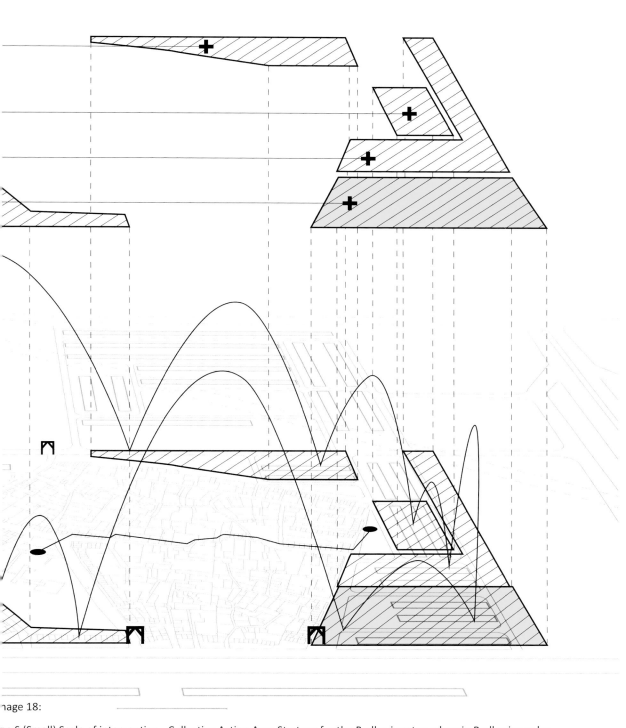

Image 18:

he S (Small) Scale of intervention - Collective Action Area Strategy for the Badheri sector, wherein Badheri may be
onceived as more than the sum of its parts, a veritable semi-lattice that allows for the development of a clearly discernable
rban character' emerging from the overview of the Chandigarh legislative mechanisms merging with currently identified
eeds.

Program Diagram

127,330 SF

Oasis / Resting Place (100,000 SF)

Other Projects in Badheri
Jobs: Trucking Depot
Housing: Rooms / Apartments
Education: Tutoring
Commercial
Cultural

Parking for up to 150 cars / bikes / scooters (90,000 SF)

Vertical park / recreation area
(10,000 SF)

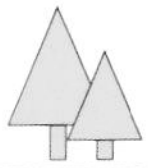

Village Administration
(3,690 SF)

(i)

Contracts and records
Legal aid
Migration control and monitoring
Community support organizations
Post office

Assembly space
(seating for 150 =
6,280 SF)

Design Strategy
Incremental Development

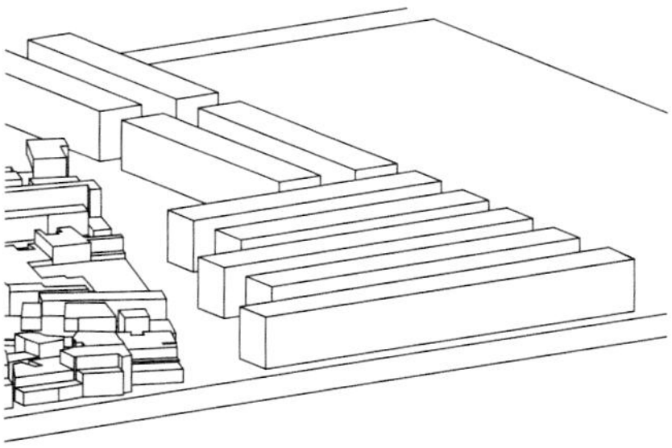

Existing Condition

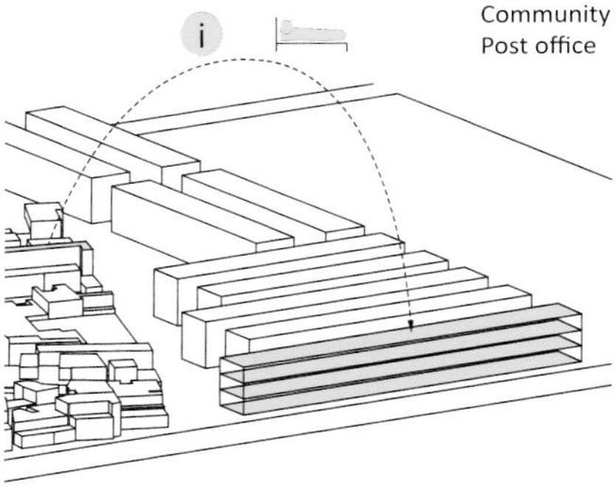

Phase One
Relocate Village administration
Adapt apartments for temporary housing

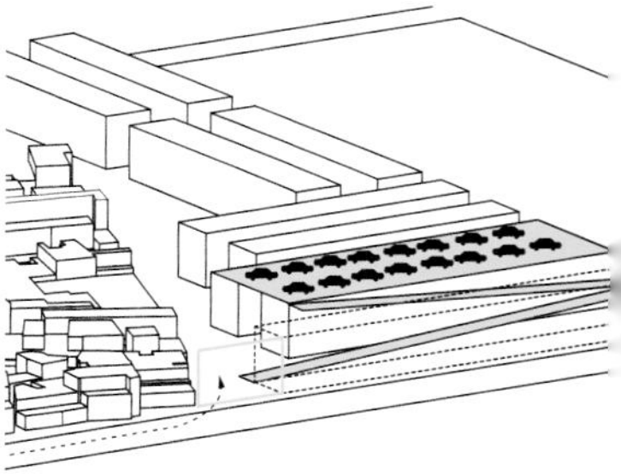

Phase Two
Add parking level
Establish gateway

Parking Structure Typologies

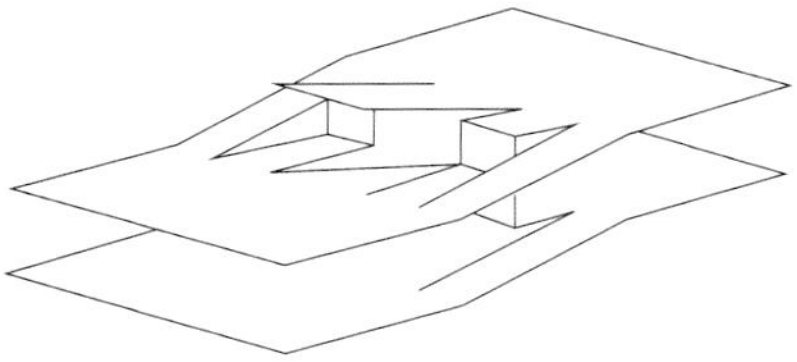

Staggered Floors
Two-way
circultation

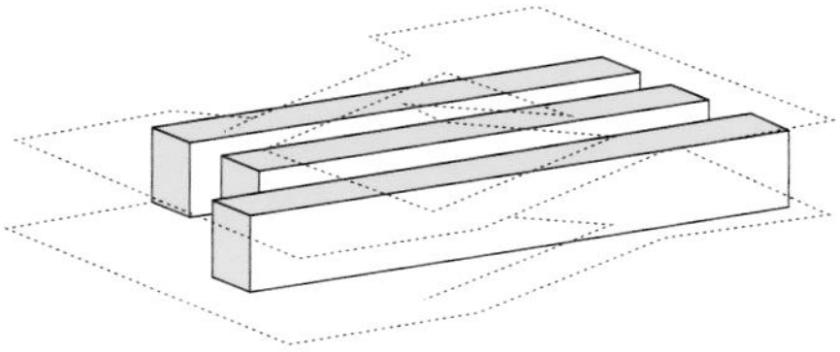

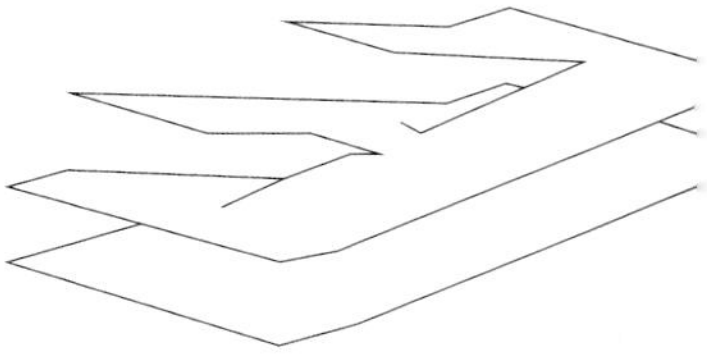

Sloping Floors
Cross connected two-way circulation

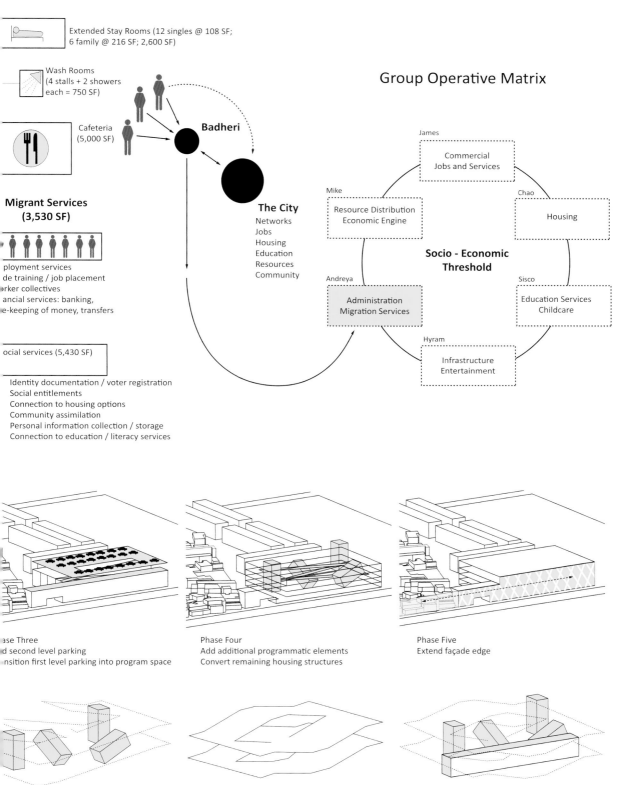

Extended Stay Rooms (12 singles @ 108 SF;
6 family @ 216 SF; 2,600 SF)

Wash Rooms
(4 stalls + 2 showers
each = 750 SF)

Cafeteria
(5,000 SF)

Badheri

Migrant Services
(3,530 SF)

ployment services
de training / job placement
rker collectives
ancial services: banking,
e-keeping of money, transfers

ocial services (5,430 SF)

Identity documentation / voter registration
Social entitlements
Connection to housing options
Community assimilation
Personal information collection / storage
Connection to education / literacy services

The City
Networks
Jobs
Housing
Education
Resources
Community

Group Operative Matrix

James
Commercial
Jobs and Services

Mike
Resource Distribution
Economic Engine

Chao
Housing

**Socio - Economic
Threshold**

Andreya
Administration
Migration Services

Sisco
Education Services
Childcare

Hyram
Infrastructure
Entertainment

ase Three
d second level parking
nsition first level parking into program space

Phase Four
Add additional programmatic elements
Convert remaining housing structures

Phase Five
Extend façade edge

Sloping Floors
One-way circulation

Image 19:

Badheri action area 'commercial hub'
proposal (Andreya S. Veintimilla)

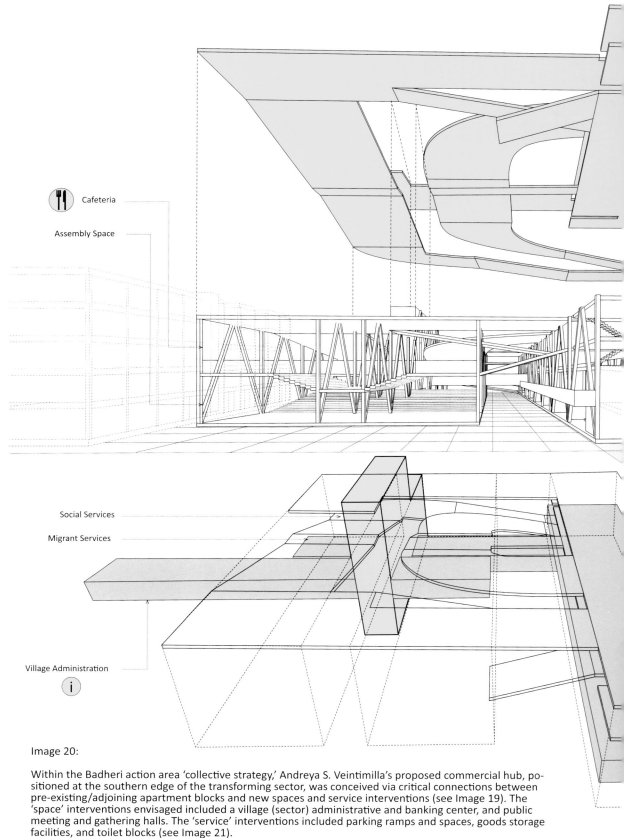

Cafeteria

Assembly Space

Social Services

Migrant Services

Village Administration

Image 20:

Within the Badheri action area 'collective strategy,' Andreya S. Veintimilla's proposed commercial hub, positioned at the southern edge of the transforming sector, was conceived via critical connections between pre-existing/adjoining apartment blocks and new spaces and service interventions (see Image 19). The 'space' interventions envisaged included a village (sector) administrative and banking center, and public meeting and gathering halls. The 'service' interventions included parking ramps and spaces, goods storage facilities, and toilet blocks (see Image 21).

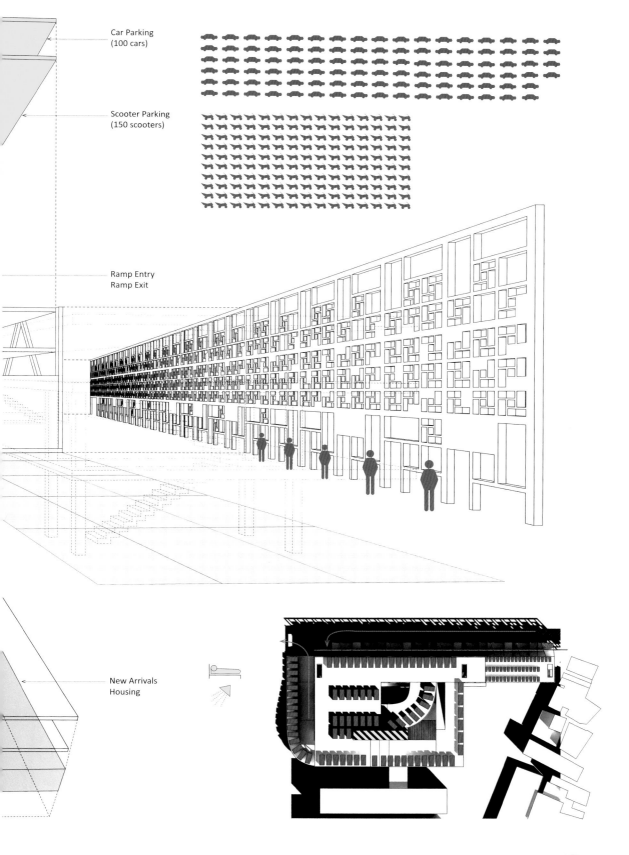

Car Parking
(100 cars)

Scooter Parking
(150 scooters)

Ramp Entry
Ramp Exit

New Arrivals
Housing

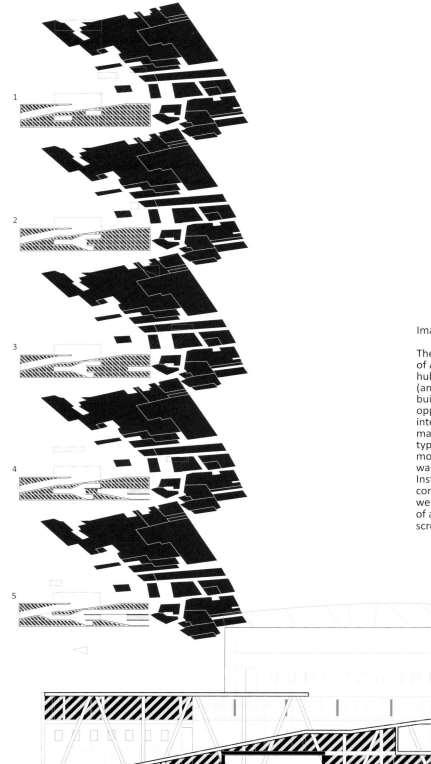

Image 21:

The deliberately disjointed architectur[e] of Andreya S. Veintimilla's commercia[l] hub consisted of disparate, yet closely (and programmatically) inter-related buildings that were perceived as opportunistic interventions over an intended timeline. Following a close mapping of existing and transforming typologies at Badheri, the convention[al] monumental, single building typology was therefore specifically avoided. Instead, the multiple disparate buildin[g] components (spaces and services) were kept together via the elements of a sweeping roof canopy and façade screens.

Fourth Floor

intersect with parking

Third Floor

intersect with village
administration core

Second Floor

intersect with migrant
services core

office spillover

First Floor

insert extra shop space

Ground Floor

mechanical space

temporary wall system

Image 22:

Image showing the activated roof-scape of Andreya S. Veintimilla's commercial hub, re-imagining these as public spaces accessible to the population of users, village inhabitants, and transient migrants.

Image 23:

Image showing Andreya S. Veintimilla's monumental façade screens transforming liminal spaces connecting the inside and outside. Building elements appear to move vicariously behind this perforated façade screen - touching it, transforming it, and occasionally even relishing their formal proximity. As a janus-faced urban device, the façade not only contains the built program within, but also defines the urban program without. In any case, given the social choreographies inherent to the Badheri sector and its everyday activities, it was this in-between (or liminal) space, that was of paramount importance.

Image 24:

Image showing the narrow, side alleyways of Andreya S. Veintimilla's commercial hub and connections to the residential district located beyond.

Image 25:

Image showing the active spaces contained by the public façades in Andreya S. Veintimilla's commercial hub. On weekdays, these spaces would bustle with truckers and transporters eager to arrange deliveries, local agents and buyers arranging payments, and day workers moving goods to storage sheds and rental pallets. On weekends and holidays, these spaces would be taken over by the resident population of the Badheri sector. Within the envisaged timeline, a certain 'adjustment' between these legislated and social functions would be expected, particularly one employing the buildings as background props. The buildings themselves would morph and change.

Image 26:

Image showing the public space just outside Badheri's committee hall, nested deep within Andreya S. Veintimilla's proposed commercial hub. Its resting places, vantage points, and dappled shadows - a perfect gathering place in the hot, summer afternoon.

159

Image 27:

Approaching the unabashed conundrum of movement elements positioned at staggered location within Andreya S. Veintimilla's commercial hub.

Image 28:

Parking spaces at lower levels of Andreya S. Veintimilla's commercial hub - potentially transformed spaces over the weekends (see Images 22 & 23).

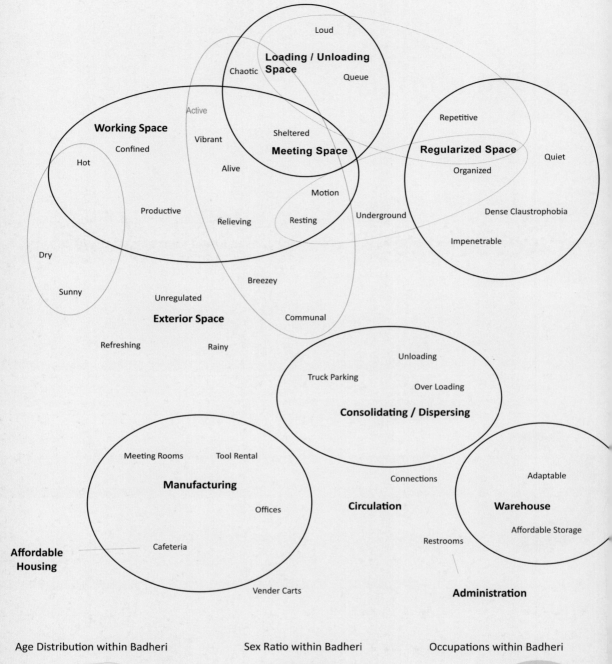

Loud

Loading / Unloading Space

Chaotic

Queue

Active

Repetitive

Working Space

Vibrant

Sheltered

Regularized Space

Quiet

Hot

Confined

Meeting Space

Alive

Organized

Productive

Motion

Dense Claustrophobia

Relieving

Resting

Underground

Dry

Impenetrable

Sunny

Breezey

Unregulated

Exterior Space

Communal

Refreshing

Rainy

Unloading

Truck Parking

Over Loading

Consolidating / Dispersing

Meeting Rooms

Tool Rental

Adaptable

Manufacturing

Offices

Connections

Circulation

Warehouse

Affordable Housing

Cafeteria

Affordable Storage

Restrooms

Vender Carts

Administration

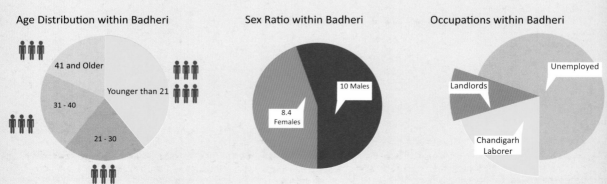

Age Distribution within Badheri

41 and Older

Younger than 21

31 - 40

21 - 30

Sex Ratio within Badheri

10 Males

8.4 Females

Occupations within Badheri

Landlords

Unemployed

Chandigarh Laborer

Image 29:

Michael J. Freund's Trucking and Warehousing Center adjoins Badheri's Commercial Hub (see Images 19 - 28 for Badheri's Commercial Hub). Conceived as two 'bar' (chromosome) buildings bridged together via multiple pedestrian bridges, the two parts effectively nest an urban and activity core between them. Organized at multiple levels, this core facilitates the arrival of market products via tempo and truck transportation, and its temporary and permanent storage (including retrieval) both within Badheri and beyond.

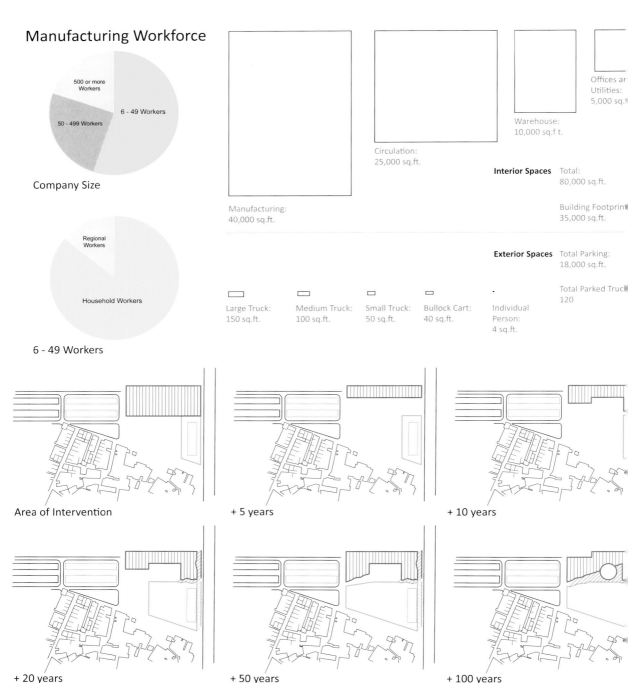

Manufacturing Workforce

Company Size

6 - 49 Workers

- 500 or more Workers
- 6 - 49 Workers
- 50 - 499 Workers

- Regional Workers
- Household Workers

Manufacturing: 40,000 sq.ft.

Circulation: 25,000 sq.ft.

Warehouse: 10,000 sq.f t.

Offices and Utilities: 5,000 sq.ft.

Interior Spaces Total: 80,000 sq.ft.

Building Footprint 35,000 sq.ft.

Exterior Spaces Total Parking: 18,000 sq.ft.

Total Parked Trucks 120

Large Truck: 150 sq.ft.

Medium Truck: 100 sq.ft.

Small Truck: 50 sq.ft.

Bullock Cart: 40 sq.ft.

Individual Person: 4 sq.ft.

Area of Intervention

+ 5 years

+ 10 years

+ 20 years

+ 50 years

+ 100 years

Image 30: (Top left to top right, counter-clock wise)

a) Population and Area Studies (top left);
b) Trucking and Warehousing Center within the action area timeline;
c) Building space and its connections to Badheri, via re-definitions of previously ambiguous spaces between the rural and urban fabric;
d) Within the Trucking and Warehousing Center, the buildings themselves accommodate commercial offices on multiple, upper floors, their curtain walls moving between transparent and reflective skins. Lower levels are lifted on pilotis, encouraging the extension of the street space, providing parking and enhanced by the addition of a service pavilion serving the community (top right).

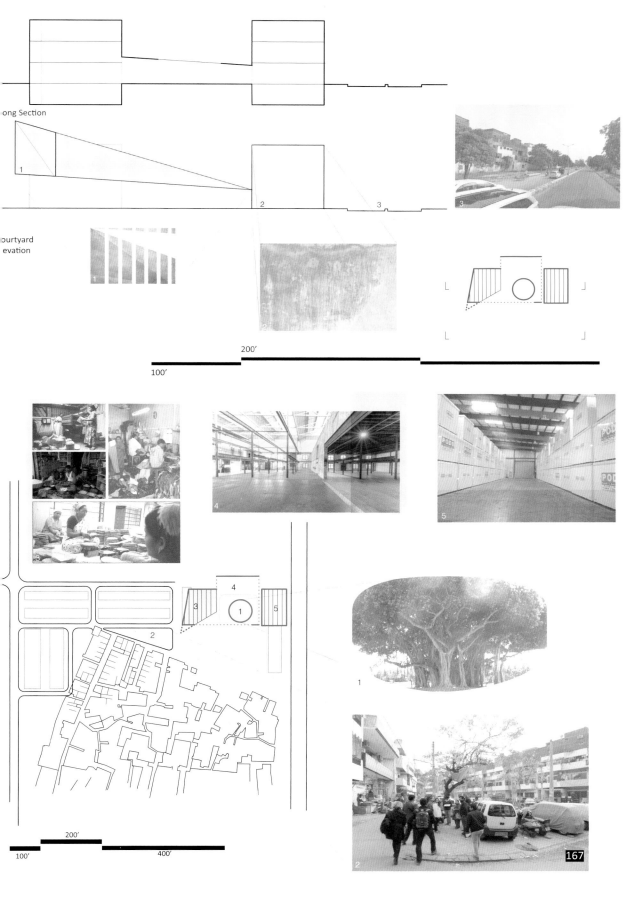

Long Section

Courtyard
Elevation

1

2

3

3

200'

100'

4

5

1

2

200'

100'

400'

167

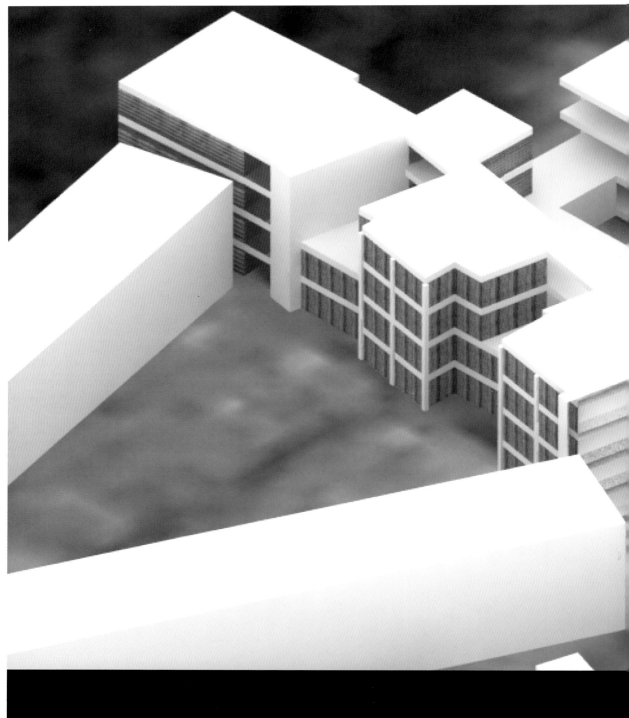

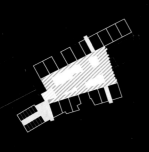
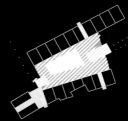
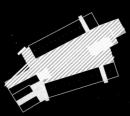

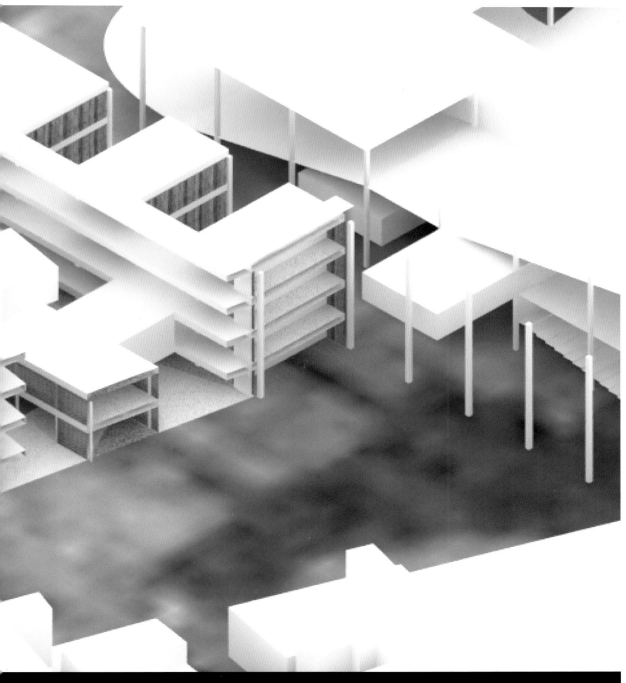

Image 31:

Axonometric view of the Trucking and Warehousing Center by Michael J. Freund, showing its interaction with the existing fabric (Lower), with the Commercial Hub (right), creating three vibrant urban spaces - two outside and one within the building cluster.

Bottom) Schematic Plans of the Trucking and Warehousing Center within Freund's proposed timeline.

Image 32:

Top) Sectional view of the primary circulation core of the Trucking and Warehousing Center by Michael J. Freund. Given the functional (and transient) nature of the intervention, this circulation core was viewed as an organizational locus to position the building on its site. It was also assumed that, as this 'matrix-building' would grow centrifugally and centripetally in time, similar 'cores' would be replicated elsewhere (especially in location where new interventions 'connected' to the existing fabric).

Bottom a) & b) Building spaces interacting with the shopping district of Badheri.

Storage

WC

Loading Zone
Loading Zone
Loading Zone

Trucking Entrance

Shower Facilities

Offices

Opent To Above

Meeting Space

WC

Storage

Storage

Manufacturing Rooms

WC

Light Well

WC

Storage

Offices

WC

Image 33:

Trucking and Warehousing Center
Michael J. Freund - Plans & Sections

Manufacturing Rooms

WC

Light
Well

Light
Well

WC

Meeting
Space

Open To Below

Offices

Meeting
Space

Storage

Patio

WC

Open To Below

Patio

Manufacturing Rooms

Storage

WC

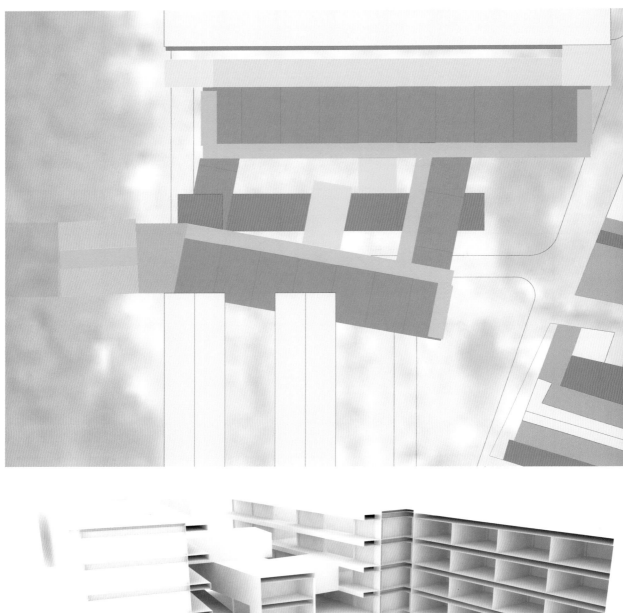

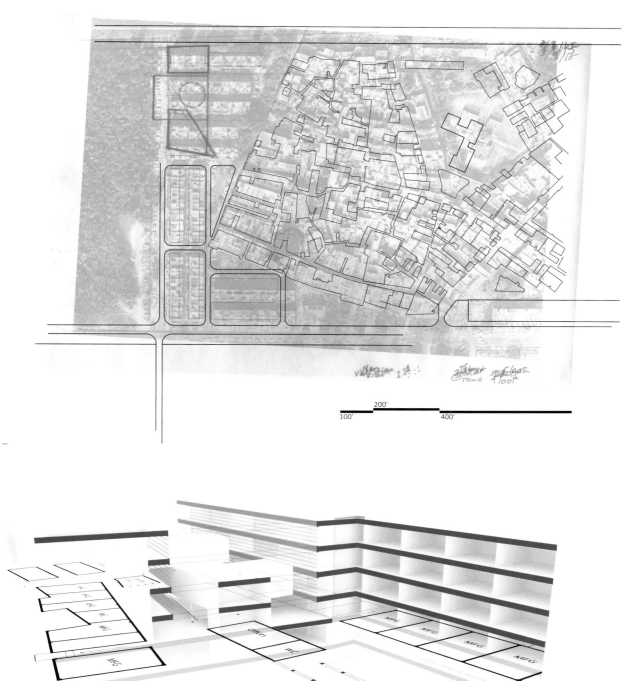

200'

100'   400'

Image 34:

Composite images (left and right), showing the genesis of the Trucking and Warehousing Center by Michael J. Freund. Pre-existing building blocks on the peripheries of Badheri are 'treated' at their envelope peripheries (marked in blue), gradually giving way to substantial physical change.

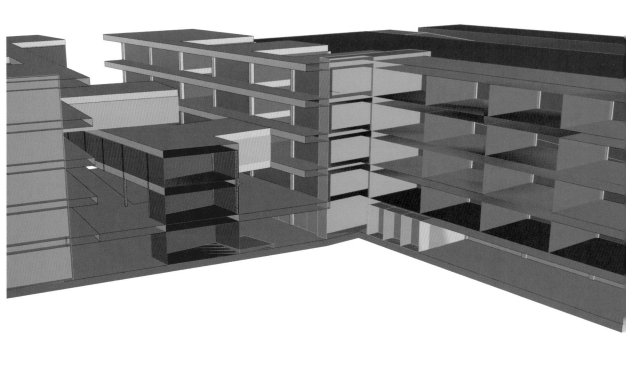

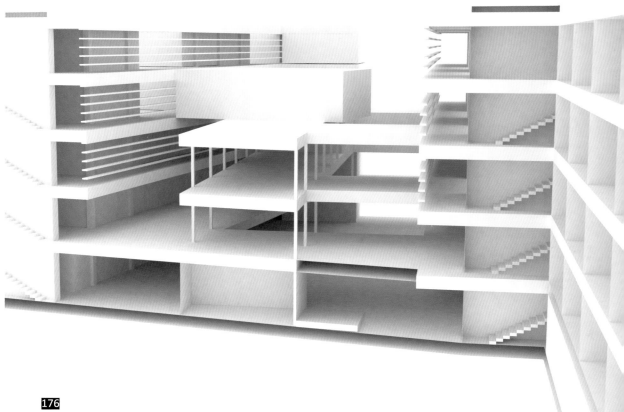

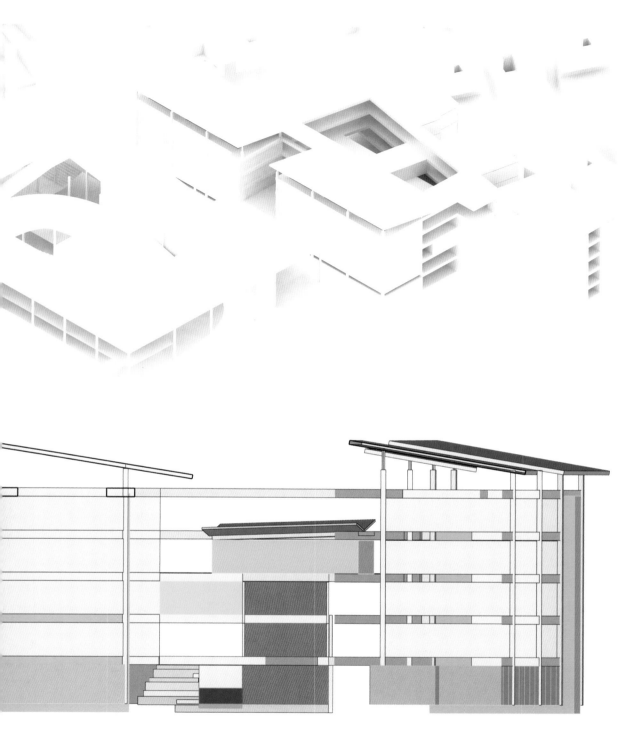

Image 35:

Following interventions suggested in Image 34, these piecemeal changes culminate in the development of building envelopes for Badheri's Trucking and Warehousing Center.

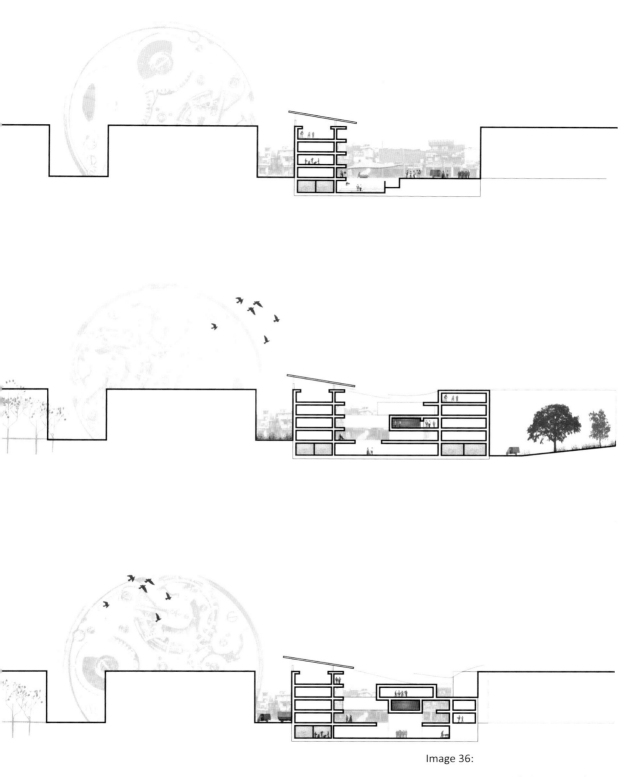

Image 36:

Composite images (left and right), showing views of the 'circulation core' (see Image 32) and its spatial presence in the Trucking and Warehousing Center.

Circulation

Typical Floor Plan

Residence

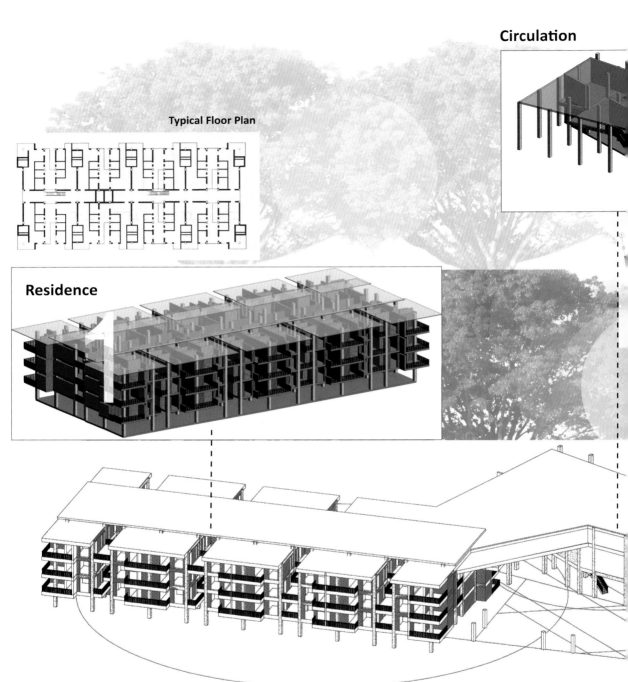

Image 37:

The 'Tree-Building' Badheri project by Sisco S. Hollard's incorporates and enlarges the footprints of pre-existing building blocks on the outer peripheries of the sector. The ficus like mega-block is the only one envisaged for the action area. It is composed of multiple trunks; each of these trunks representing a programmatic component of the building. The Tree-Building envisaged a mixed-use scenario comprising of educational facilities accommodated at the lower levels and residential facilities (units and apartments) at the upper levels. Urban spaces were consciously created by the built masses both within and without, and suitably exaggerated by the building's ability to connect spaces in front and behind via pedestrian pilotis in its under-belly.

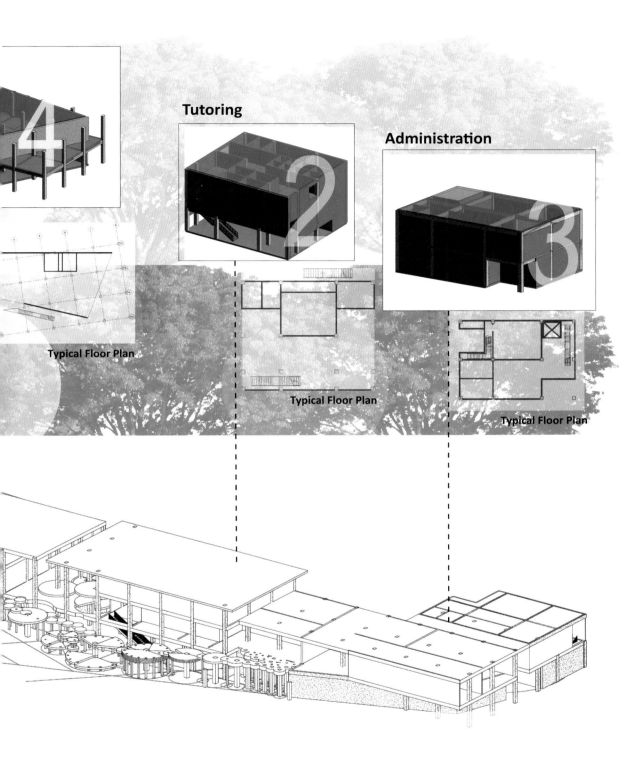

Tutoring

Administration

Typical Floor Plan

Typical Floor Plan

Typical Floor Plan

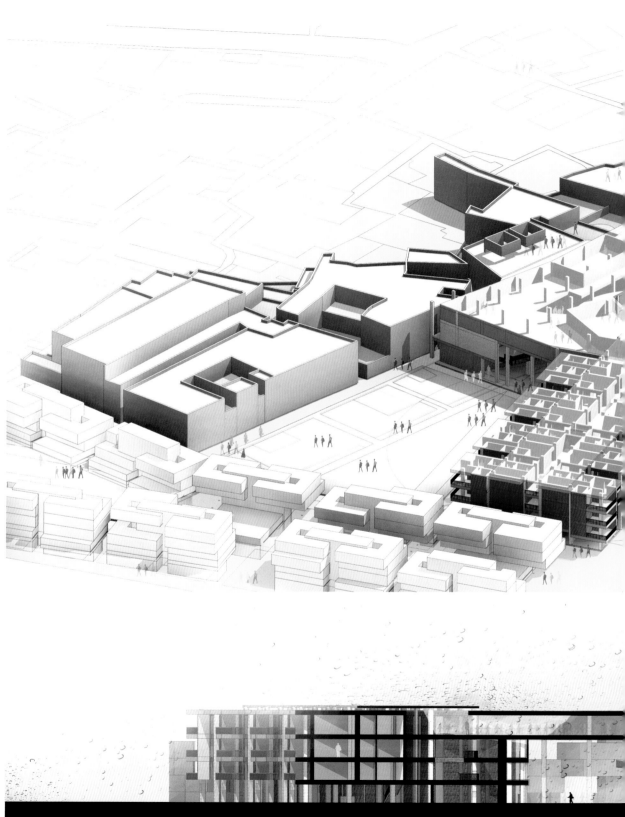

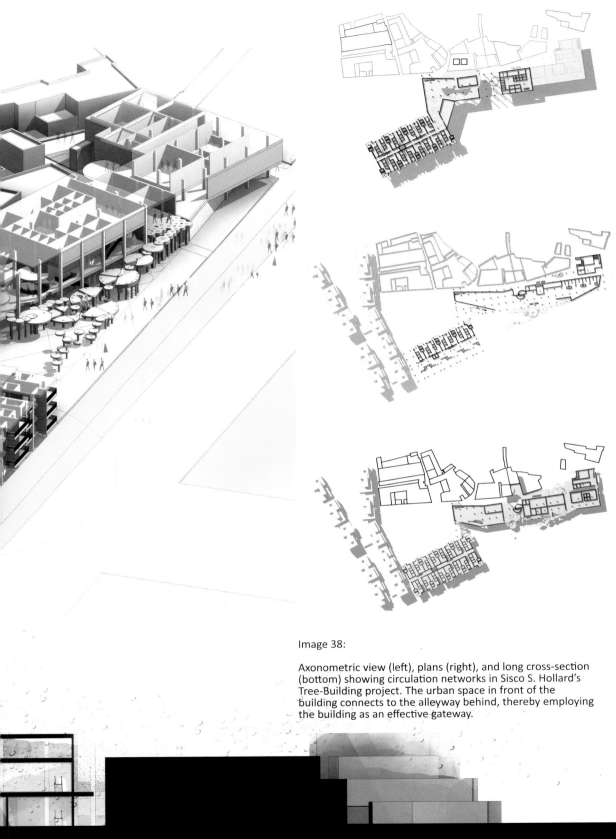

Image 38:

Axonometric view (left), plans (right), and long cross-section (bottom) showing circulation networks in Sisco S. Hollard's Tree-Building project. The urban space in front of the building connects to the alleyway behind, thereby employing the building as an effective gateway.

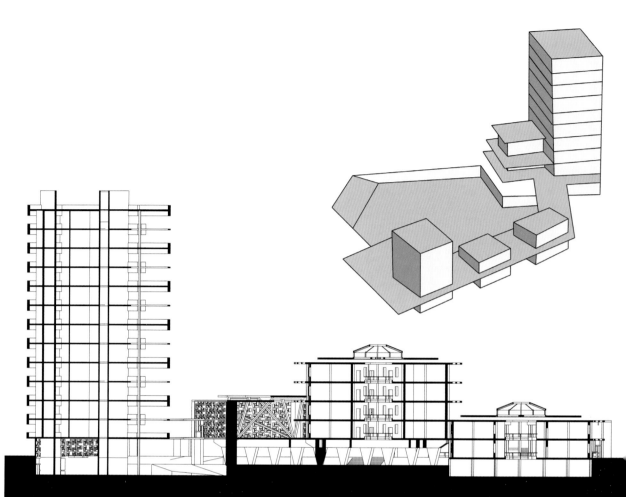

Image 39:

James D. Ford's Market Square intervention envisages the future transformation of Badheri as a potential magnet for urban migrants and as a segue setting for life in the city. It provides for trade-training opportunities and temporary accommodations for these displaced populations. Indian cities (including Chandigarh), have continually identified this need given the constant influx of urban migrants from surrounding rural areas to their fringes, but seldom endorsed any effective legislation towards mitigating this situation.

Badheri's new Market Square, positioned as a component of the Urban Edge group's action plan, would therefore catalyze the growth of the sector center. Given its mix of residential, retail, and institutional functions, private and public hierarchies, it would serve as a viable model towards Badheri's development. James D. Ford's octagonal commercial towers are, in effect, a provocative demonstration that Badheri may just be ready for strong urban change, especially at its center. While this would most certainly contrast with the Corbusier's city, it would also provoke change and replace legislative indifference with the re-invention of how a rural fabric should potentially transform.

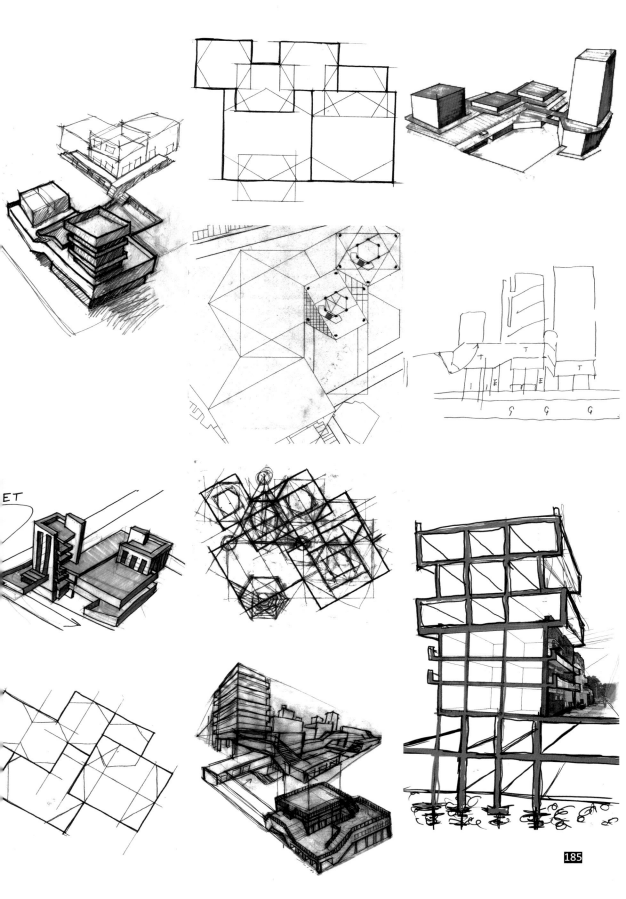

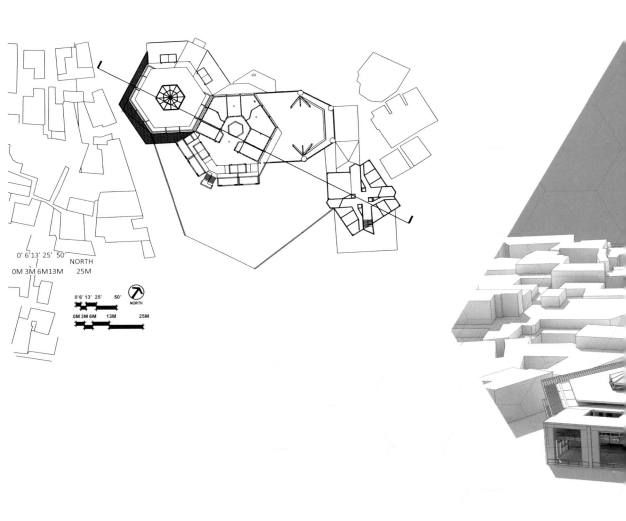

0' 6' 13' 25' 50'

0M 3M 6M13M   25M

NORTH

0' 6' 13' 25'   50'

0M 3M 6M   13M   25M

NORTH

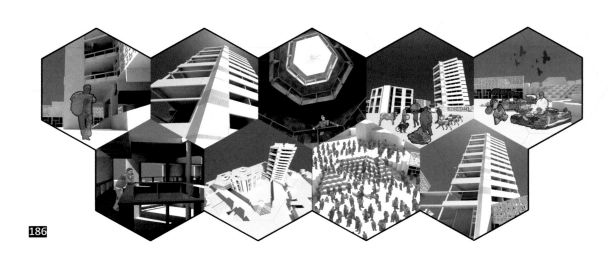

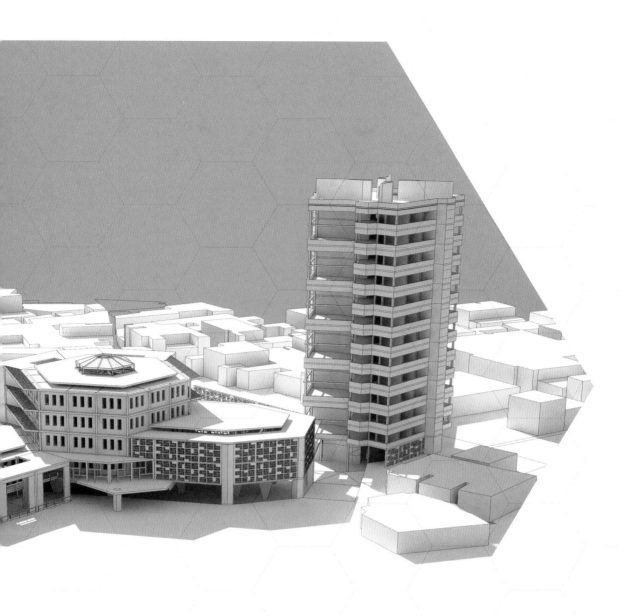

Image 40:

Ford's Market Square would provide Badheri with a real estate strategy in its metamorphosis from being an urban anomaly to becoming an active 'service sector' and urban catalyst within the city of Chandigarh. In its combination of public and private urban spaces, it would create a vantage for the hamal-canteen at street level, with relatively more private community spaces at the upper level, interspersed with shared apartments and dormitories.

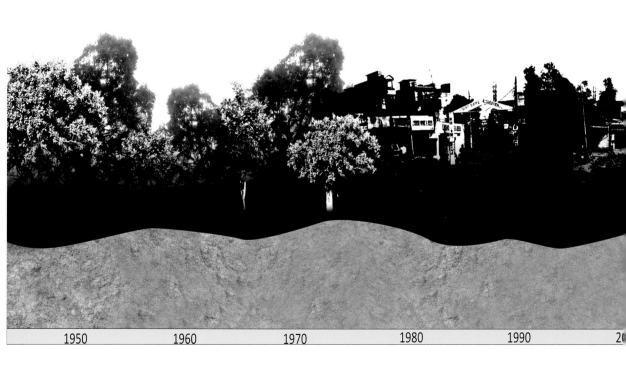

1950   1960   1970   1980   1990   2(

Image 41:

Elevational image of Badheri action area, with projects distributed along the time line. For the next several decades, Badheri would be a construction site of sorts, its adaptive and adapting buildings gradually enlarging to accommodate a myriad of social and urban functions.

| 2010 | 2020 | 2030 | 2050 | 2060 |

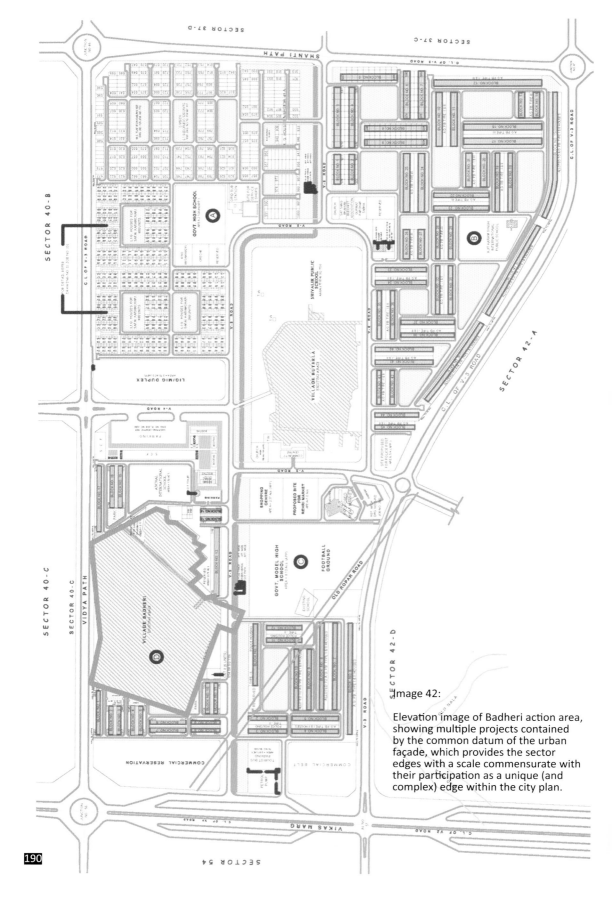

Image 42:

Elevation image of Badheri action area, showing multiple projects contained by the common datum of the urban façade, which provides the sector edges with a scale commensurate with their participation as a unique (and complex) edge within the city plan.

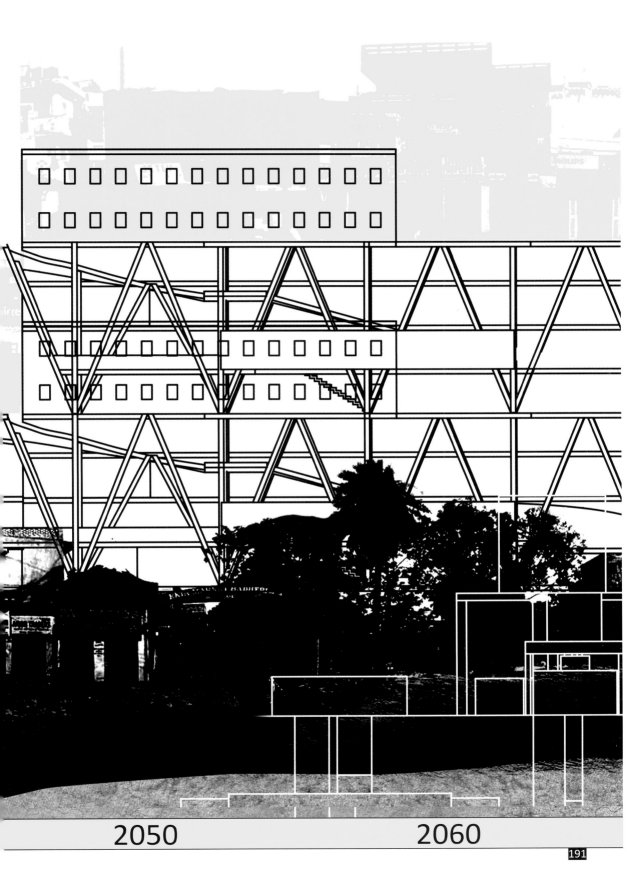

2050

2060

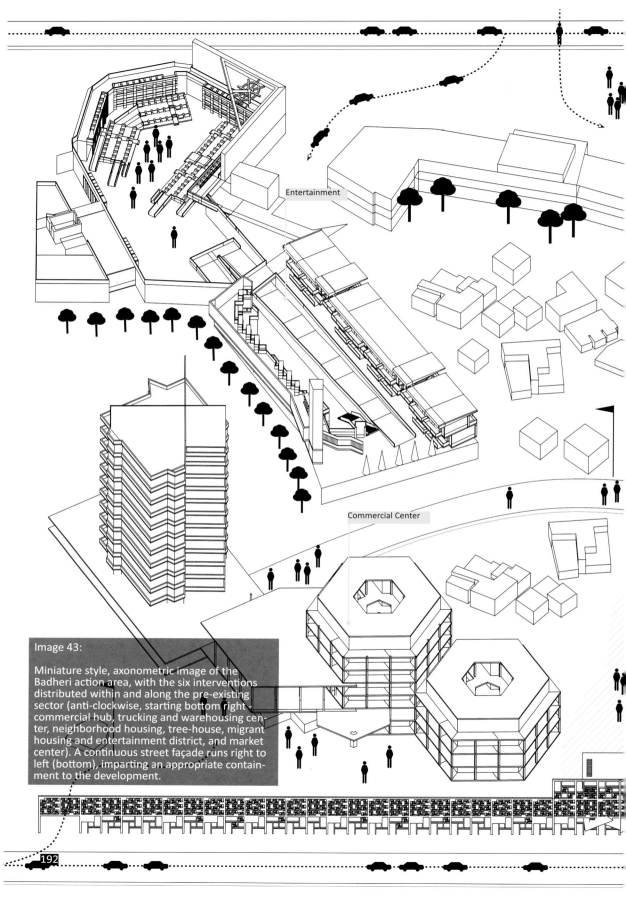

Entertainment

Commercial Center

Image 43:

Miniature style, axonometric image of the Badheri action area, with the six interventions distributed within and along the pre-existing sector (anti-clockwise, starting bottom right – commercial hub, trucking and warehousing center, neighborhood housing, tree-house, migrant housing and entertainment district, and market center). A continuous street façade runs right to left (bottom), imparting an appropriate containment to the development.

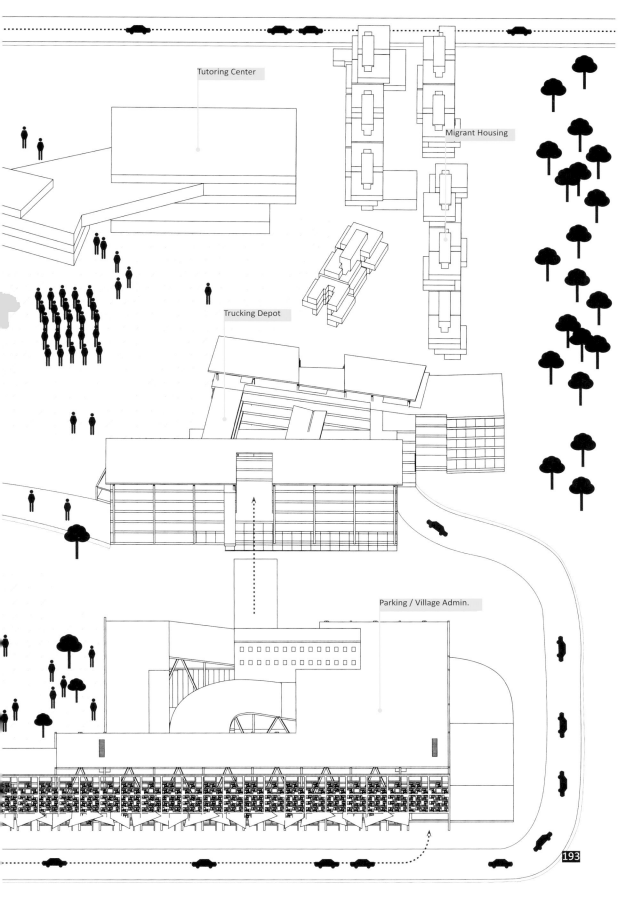

Tutoring Center

Migrant Housing

Trucking Depot

Parking / Village Admin.

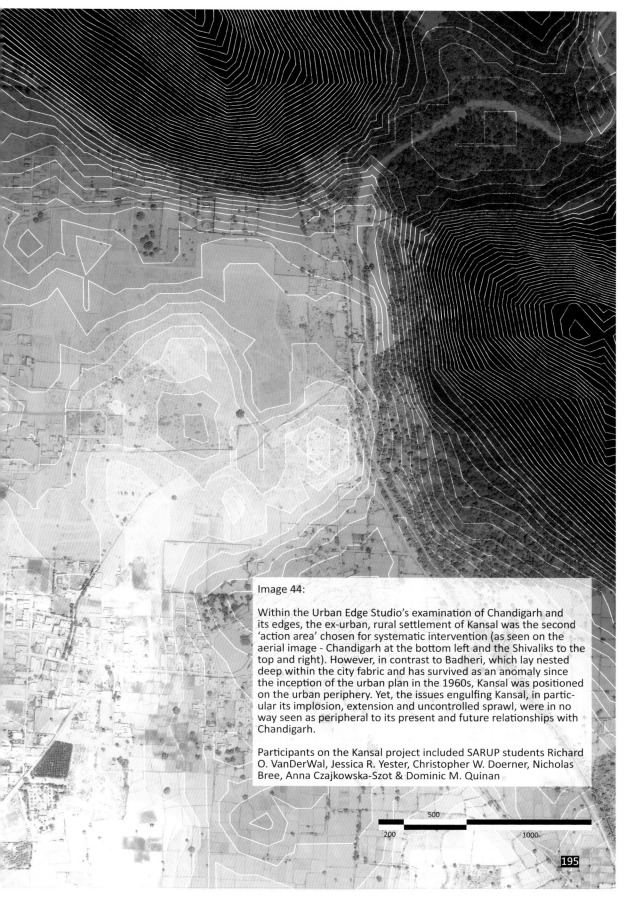

Image 44:

Within the Urban Edge Studio's examination of Chandigarh and its edges, the ex-urban, rural settlement of Kansal was the second 'action area' chosen for systematic intervention (as seen on the aerial image - Chandigarh at the bottom left and the Shivaliks to the top and right). However, in contrast to Badheri, which lay nested deep within the city fabric and has survived as an anomaly since the inception of the urban plan in the 1960s, Kansal was positioned on the urban periphery. Yet, the issues engulfing Kansal, in particular its implosion, extension and uncontrolled sprawl, were in no way seen as peripheral to its present and future relationships with Chandigarh.

Participants on the Kansal project included SARUP students Richard O. VanDerWal, Jessica R. Yester, Christopher W. Doerner, Nicholas Bree, Anna Czajkowska-Szot & Dominic M. Quinan

500

200   1000

Image 45:

Schematic drawing showing Hydrology and the associated Memory of land - situated northeast of the city of Chandigarh, Kansal is located within the historical alluvial plain of the Shivalik Hills. This once-agricultural plateau was fed by many seasonal waterways and river basins. Of these, some were carved in geological time by glacial recession from the end of the Pleistocene era (the most recent ice age) approximately 10,000 years ago. Others resulted from recent and present-day (continuing) Himalayan glacial melt, which has gradually eroded mountain rock and distributed mineral components along these water networks, indirectly fertilizing the land. The indelible marks of these large-scale acts still show on the landscap

mi
1/2   1   2

197

Red Soil, Admixture of Clay, Silt, and Sand with Kankar, Coarse, Gray Micaceous Sand, with Kankar Interbedded with Clay and Silt	Friable Gray Micaceous Sandstone, Brown, Red, and Purple Clay, and Conglomerate	Loose Gray Micaceous Sand and Pebbles Along Stream Courses	Blue Gray to Light Gray Micaceous Sand, Pebbles With Interband of Purple / Red Clay
Older Alluvium (Mid to Late Pleistocene)	Upper Siwalik Group (Late Pliocene to Early Pleistocene)	Newer Alluvium (Holocene)	

Image 46:

Schematic drawing showing Kansal's relationship with the Shivalik range - with Khuda Ali Sher situated to its west, and Kaimbwala to its east, the settlement of Kansal essentially stands atop alluvial deposits consisting of silt, clay, gravel, and frequently organic matter, creating a rich soil mix appropriate for plant growth. The early plan of Chandigarh retained this alluvial belt, effectively enhancing its 'lost waterways' by the addition of the Sukhna Lake and Leisure Valley. Furthermore, in 1963, the erstwhile Punjab Givernment acquired 259,842 ha of critical catchment area to consolidate this micro-ecosystem and thereby sustain life in the city. Today, the once 'sustainable' relationship of the rural Kansal settlement is lost owing to the haphazard allocation of the agricultural land pockets towards legislated and rampant sprawl development.

Image 47:

Left: Kansal's future development envisaged as a smart-village, wherein a network of 'cow-paths' would potentially enable renewable pasture lands to be integrated and interconnected via a series of 'lite-footprint' (yet relevant) interventions. The agricultural or rural core of Kansal would be consciously retained, also allowing the 'catchment areas' located to the north and northeast of Kansal (and Sukhna Lake) to be sustained.

Right: Kansal's fabric grain viewed in comparison with Chandigarh's large Capitol Complex buildings over the last two decades. Corbusier consciously separated the city and its rural setting by means of a peripheral road serving as a distinct, recessed landscape barrier - the so-called ha-ha wall, created by a brick revetment and an open culvert.

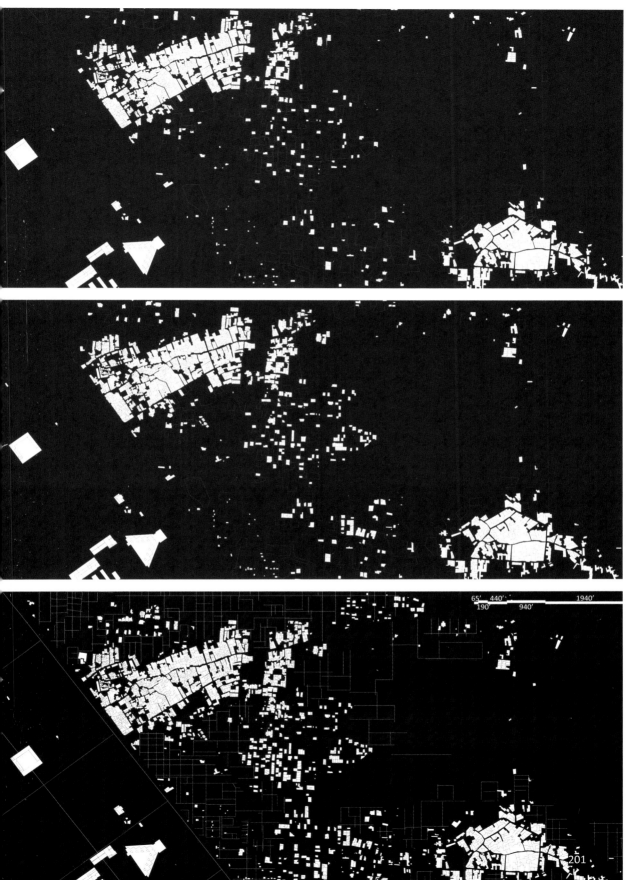

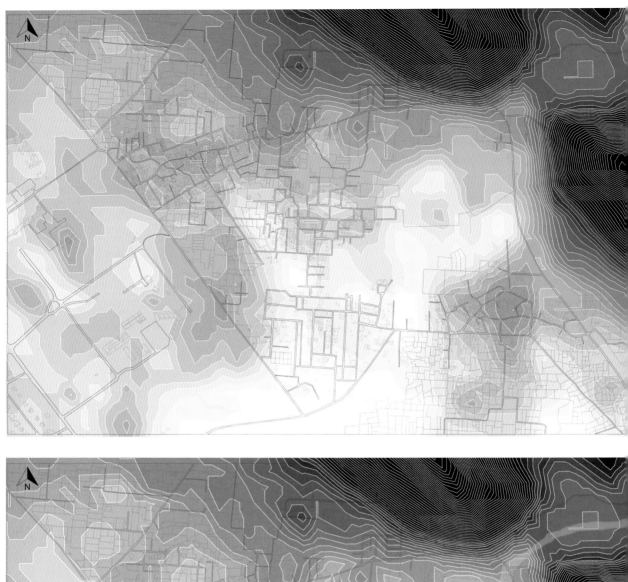

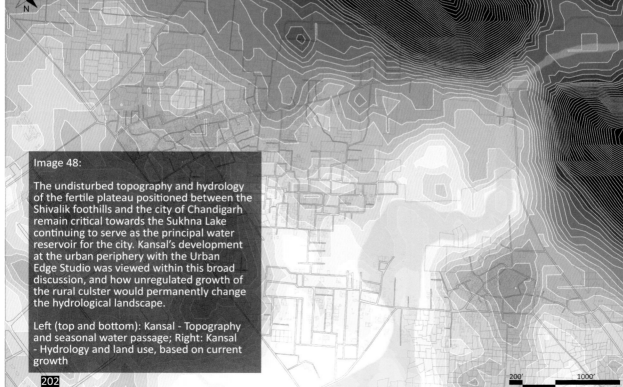

Image 48:

The undisturbed topography and hydrology of the fertile plateau positioned between the Shivalik foothills and the city of Chandigarh remain critical towards the Sukhna Lake continuing to serve as the principal water reservoir for the city. Kansal's development at the urban periphery with the Urban Edge Studio was viewed within this broad discussion, and how unregulated growth of the rural culster would permanently change the hydrological landscape.

Left (top and bottom): Kansal - Topography and seasonal water passage; Right: Kansal - Hydrology and land use, based on current growth

Legend
Reserved Forest
Leisure Valley
Capitol Complex
Present Water Body
Past River
Past Stream
V1 Road
V2 Road
V3 Road
Action Area

1/8 1/2 2
1/4 1
mi

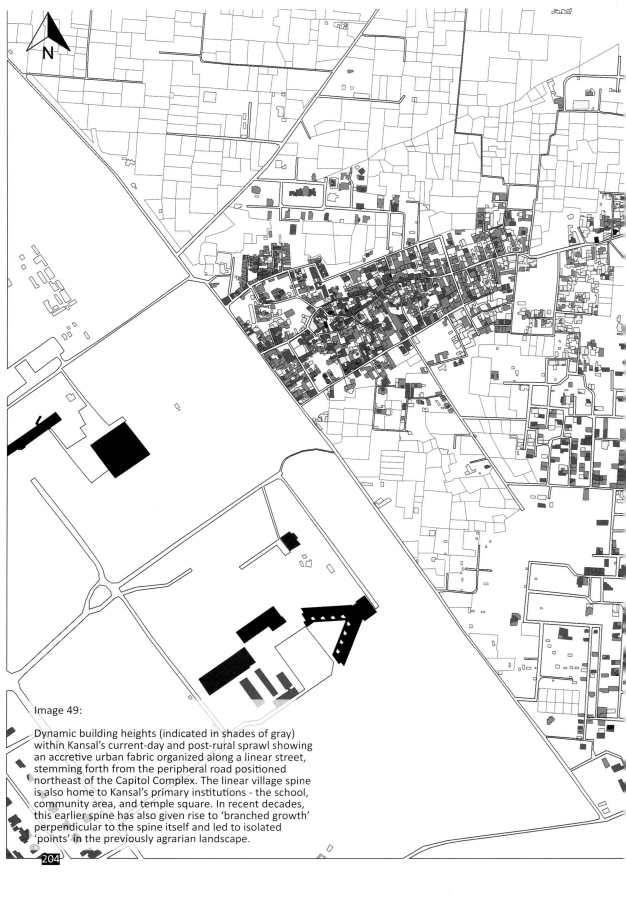

Image 49:

Dynamic building heights (indicated in shades of gray) within Kansal's current-day and post-rural sprawl showing an accretive urban fabric organized along a linear street, stemming forth from the peripheral road positioned northeast of the Capitol Complex. The linear village spine is also home to Kansal's primary institutions - the school, community area, and temple square. In recent decades, this earlier spine has also given rise to 'branched growth' perpendicular to the spine itself and led to isolated 'points' in the previously agrarian landscape.

200' 500' 1000'

Fabric Morphology and Sprawl Development

1

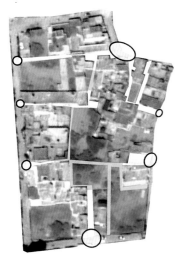

2

Entirely Recent Block

The overall block is defined by major linkages within the village following topographical lines of drainage and access to major nodes. Houses with ground retail start to build up the block's edges. Central green space is largely public with a few access points to private gardens and courtyards of the current occupants.

Mostly Recent Blocks in some Older Settlements

Block begins to densify with finer property grains along the main village corridors. Cental greenspace is divided up into medium-sized courtyards shared cooperatively by surrounding families. Access points into the heart of the block begin to develop at the edges.

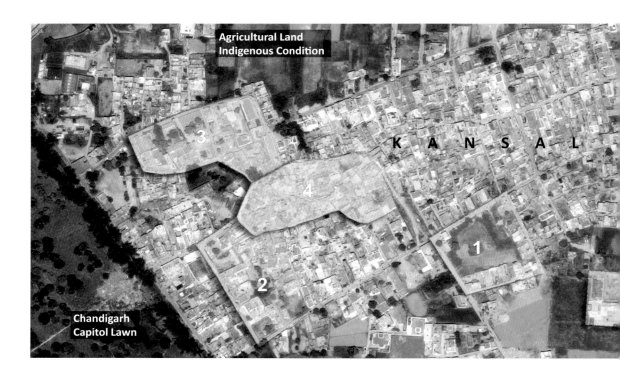

Agricultural Land
Indigenous Condition

K A N S A L

3

4

1

2

Chandigarh
Capitol Lawn

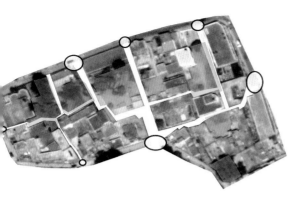
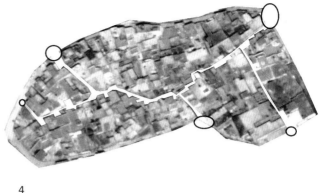

4

ft 50 ──── 100

Mix of Recent Development and Old Settlement

The edges of the block are now fully defined and access points are monitored by the social groups of families. The larger rectilinear order begins to break down as land ownership becomes saturated and the necessities of climate and drainage take precedent.

Almost Entirely Old Settlement Block

The block reaches its full urban saturation with all new developments progressing vertically. Shared courtyards are now much smaller with the majority of these acting only as lightwells. An internal network of pedestrian streets snap to nodes within the block.

Foreign Typology 'McMansion Block'

The cheaper cost of rural land, the lack of housing regulation, and the proximity of Kansal to Chandigarh has fueled the de-ruralization of the hinterland into residential sprawl. Large estates conform to a rectilinear division of land, now ignorant of topography and its constraints. Vehicular access dominates the entire linkage network.

ft 50 ──── 100

Stage 1 and Continuation

Image 50:

Analysis of the Kansal Village Block showing its Fabric Types and Morphologies - Kansal has grown over the years since Chandigarh's inception, developing 'sub-typologies' and 'pheno-typical hybrids' that combine earlier building types with the logistics of newer construction. The single-floor village home with a central courtyard has now effectively morphed into a built to edge dwelling, often 2-3 floors high, and often with no courtyards.

Shivalik Hills

PUNJAB

Agricultural Land

K   A

Rejendra Park

Capital Complex

C H A N D I G A R H

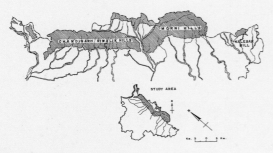

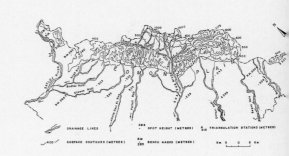

HARYANA

Agricultural Land

A   L

Lake Reserved Forests

Sukhna Lake

1000 Feet

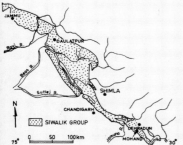

Image 51:

Site of Kansal as positioned within its proximity to landscape edges (human-made & natural). Bottom a), b) & c) - hydrological connection of Kansal to the Shivalik foothills.

Leisure Valley, Ridgeline Road, and River Memory

The *ha-ha* wall is located along the boundary line between Chandigarh and Kansal. It creates a vertical barrier while still preserving views.

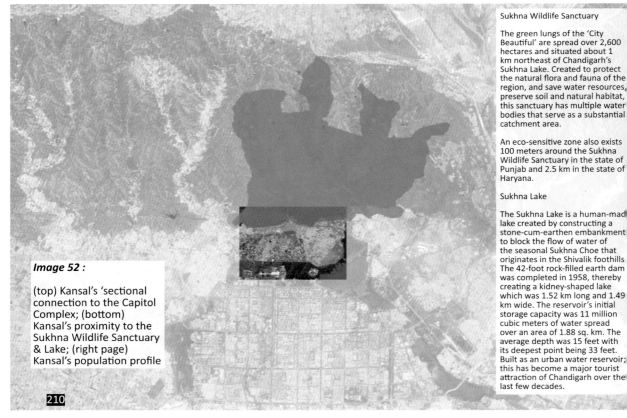

Image 52 :

(top) Kansal's 'sectional connection to the Capitol Complex; (bottom) Kansal's proximity to the Sukhna Wildlife Sanctuary & Lake; (right page) Kansal's population profile

Sukhna Wildlife Sanctuary

The green lungs of the 'City Beautiful' are spread over 2,600 hectares and situated about 1 km northeast of Chandigarh's Sukhna Lake. Created to protect the natural flora and fauna of the region, and save water resources, preserve soil and natural habitat, this sanctuary has multiple water bodies that serve as a substantial catchment area.

An eco-sensitive zone also exists 100 meters around the Sukhna Wildlife Sanctuary in the state of Punjab and 2.5 km in the state of Haryana.

Sukhna Lake

The Sukhna Lake is a human-made lake created by constructing a stone-cum-earthen embankment to block the flow of water of the seasonal Sukhna Choe that originates in the Shivalik foothills The 42-foot rock-filled earth dam was completed in 1958, thereby creating a kidney-shaped lake which was 1.52 km long and 1.49 km wide. The reservoir's initial storage capacity was 11 million cubic meters of water spread over an area of 1.88 sq. km. The average depth was 15 feet with its deepest point being 33 feet. Built as an urban water reservoir; this has become a major tourist attraction of Chandigarh over the last few decades.

Population in Kansal

Scale comparision

Total population of Kansal - 6452

3645   2807

CHANDIGARH population density
34 people per acre

KANSAL population density
54 people per acre

Incoming Migrants

As one among the fastest growing cities in India, Chandigarh attracts a large number of migrants who arrive at the city from its rural hinterlands. Among those who arrive, those who cannot afford to stay within the urban confines of the city search for cheaper accommodation options in the villages surrounding Chandigarh. Kansal, located on the city edge, is a suitable choice. These mentioned villages (including Kansal & Badheri) are the only areas available for extension, given their lax legislative codes.

Static Residents

The villages (such as Kansal and Badheri) existed well before the foundations of Chandigarh and many families who continue to reside there have lived there from generations. Given the physical transformations happening around them, these residents specifically continue to choose to stay in these quasi-rural environments. Is this given that these villages are ancestral homes, or is owing to convenient proximity to the city center?

Mobile population

Nested villages, such as Badheri, and peripheral villages such as Kansal, provide the viable options for easy job mobility at the city center, attracting those who seek to buy land outside of Chandigarh towards building their homes. In terms of investment, land prices in these villages still remain substantially lower than real estate within the city, though past decades have seen these jump.

Migrant population

While these villages offer a range of housing types within the limitations of their residents, they especially attract those looking for a temporary place to stay upon first arrival in Chandigarh. As a result, these rural settings have grown exponentially to accommodate cheap, and often unregulated rental spaces. Not all incoming migrants even stay in these urban villages. Several move on due to economic and social circumstances.

Image 53:

Plan of Kansal Land Parcels and Roads, showing the previously agricultural fabric transforming to valuable real estate, especially in proximity to the intermediate road connecting it to Chandigarh (see left of drawing, diagonally from top left to bottom center).

Kansal Parcels and Roads

200'   1000'

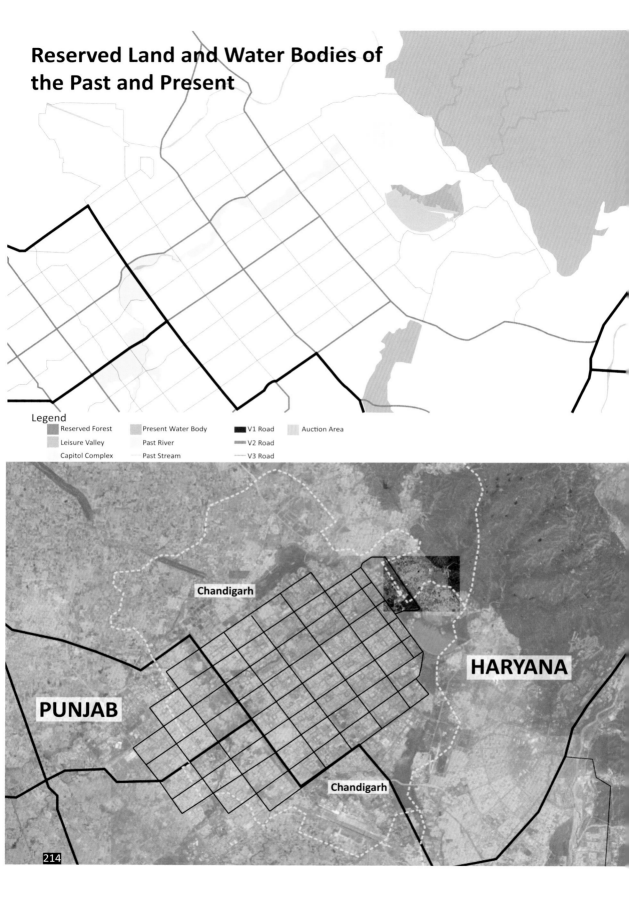

Reserved Land and Water Bodies of the Past and Present

Legend

Reserved Forest	Present Water Body	V1 Road	Auction Area
Leisure Valley	Past River	V2 Road	
Capitol Complex	Past Stream	V3 Road	

PUNJAB

HARYANA

Chandigarh

Chandigarh

Gray= Chandigarh(23.1%)   Brown = Agricultural(21.1%)   Dark Green = Foothills(17.9%)
Light Yellow = Light Urbanity(17.6%) Dark Yellow = Dense Urbanity(10.3%) Light Green = Ecological(10.0%)

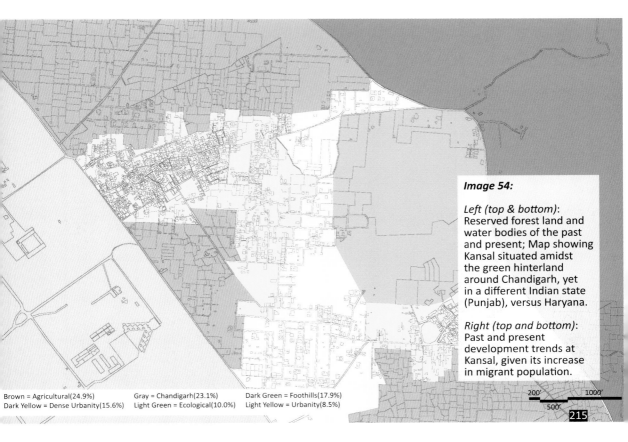

Image 54:

Left (top & bottom): Reserved forest land and water bodies of the past and present; Map showing Kansal situated amidst the green hinterland around Chandigarh, yet in a different Indian state (Punjab), versus Haryana.

Right (top and bottom): Past and present development trends at Kansal, given its increase in migrant population.

Brown = Agricultural(24.9%)   Gray = Chandigarh(23.1%)   Dark Green = Foothills(17.9%)
Dark Yellow = Dense Urbanity(15.6%) Light Green = Ecological(10.0%) Light Yellow = Urbanity(8.5%)

Image 55:

Kansal fabric superimposed on a Google map, showing the correlation of its development to the agrarian subdivisions of the past.

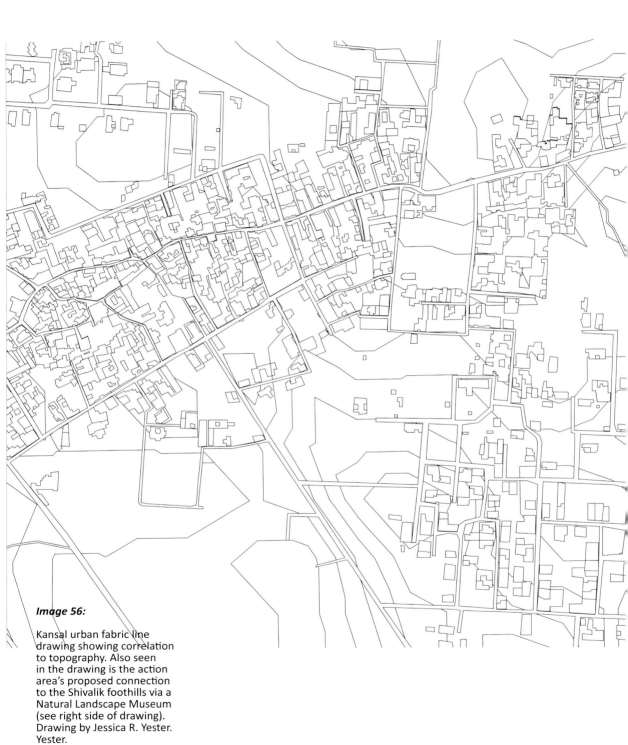

Image 56:

Kansal urban fabric line drawing showing correlation to topography. Also seen in the drawing is the action area's proposed connection to the Shivalik foothills via a Natural Landscape Museum (see right side of drawing). Drawing by Jessica R. Yester. Yester.

River Buffalo: Murrah Dairy Breed Systems Diagram

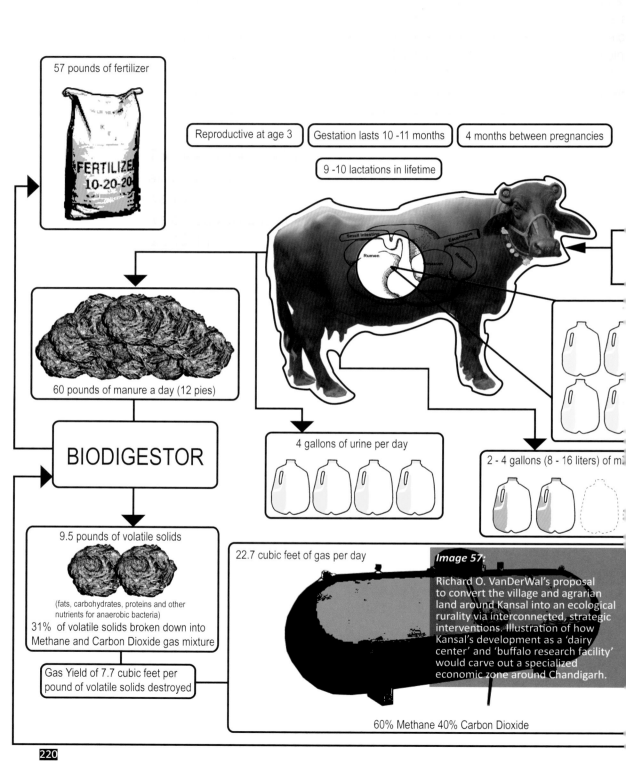

57 pounds of fertilizer

FERTILIZER 10-20-20

Reproductive at age 3

Gestation lasts 10 -11 months

4 months between pregnancies

9 -10 lactations in lifetime

Small Intestine

Esophagus

Rumen

60 pounds of manure a day (12 pies)

BIODIGESTOR

4 gallons of urine per day

2 - 4 gallons (8 - 16 liters) of m.

9.5 pounds of volatile solids

(fats, carbohydrates, proteins and other nutrients for anaerobic bacteria)

31% of volatile solids broken down into Methane and Carbon Dioxide gas mixture

Gas Yield of 7.7 cubic feet per pound of volatile solids destroyed

22.7 cubic feet of gas per day

Image 57:

Richard O. VanDerWal's proposal to convert the village and agrarian land around Kansal into an ecological rurality via interconnected, strategic interventions. Illustration of how Kansal's development as a 'dairy center' and 'buffalo research facility' would carve out a specialized economic zone around Chandigarh.

60% Methane 40% Carbon Dioxide

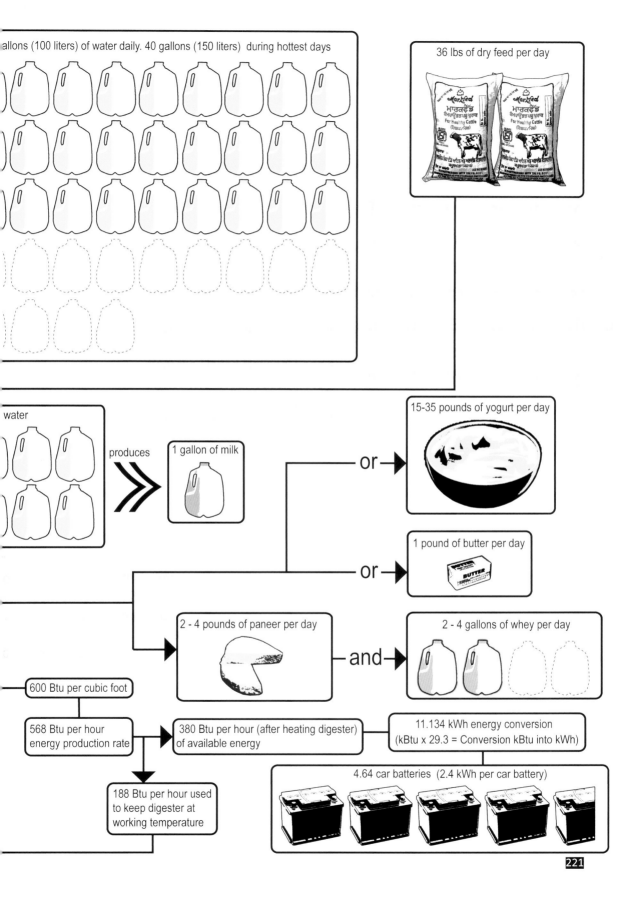

allons (100 liters) of water daily. 40 gallons (150 liters) during hottest days

36 lbs of dry feed per day

water

produces

1 gallon of milk

or → 15-35 pounds of yogurt per day

or → 1 pound of butter per day

2 - 4 pounds of paneer per day

and → 2 - 4 gallons of whey per day

600 Btu per cubic foot

568 Btu per hour energy production rate

380 Btu per hour (after heating digester) of available energy

11.134 kWh energy conversion (kBtu x 29.3 = Conversion kBtu into kWh)

188 Btu per hour used to keep digester at working temperature

4.64 car batteries (2.4 kWh per car battery)

Site Event Timeline

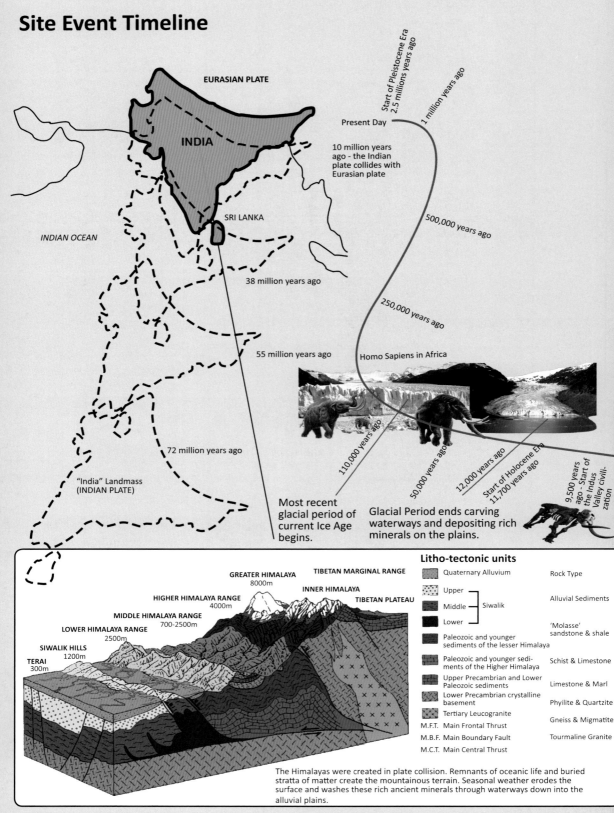

EURASIAN PLATE

INDIA

SRI LANKA

INDIAN OCEAN

"India" Landmass
(INDIAN PLATE)

72 million years ago

55 million years ago

38 million years ago

Present Day

10 million years ago - the Indian plate collides with Eurasian plate

Start of Pleistocene Era 2.5 millions years ago

1 million years ago

500,000 years ago

250,000 years ago

Homo Sapiens in Africa

110,000 years ago

50,000 years ago

12,000 years ago

Start of Holocene Era 11,700 years ago

9,500 years ago - Start of the Indus Valley civilization

Most recent glacial period of current Ice Age begins.

Glacial Period ends carving waterways and depositing rich minerals on the plains.

Litho-tectonic units

		Rock Type
Quaternary Alluvium		
Upper		Alluvial Sediments
Middle	Siwalik	
Lower		'Molasse' sandstone & shale
Paleozoic and younger sediments of the lesser Himalaya		
Paleozoic and younger sediments of the Higher Himalaya		Schist & Limestone
Upper Precambrian and Lower Paleozoic sediments		Limestone & Marl
Lower Precambrian crystalline basement		Phyilite & Quartzite
Tertiary Leucogranite		Gneiss & Migmatite
M.F.T. Main Frontal Thrust		
M.B.F. Main Boundary Fault		Tourmaline Granite
M.C.T. Main Central Thrust		

GREATER HIMALAYA 8000m

TIBETAN MARGINAL RANGE

INNER HIMALAYA

TIBETAN PLATEAU

HIGHER HIMALAYA RANGE 4000m

MIDDLE HIMALAYA RANGE 700-2500m

LOWER HIMALAYA RANGE 2500m

SIWALIK HILLS 1200m

TERAI 300m

The Himalayas were created in plate collision. Remnants of oceanic life and buried stratta of matter create the mountainous terrain. Seasonal weather erodes the surface and washes these rich ancient minerals through waterways down into the alluvial plains.

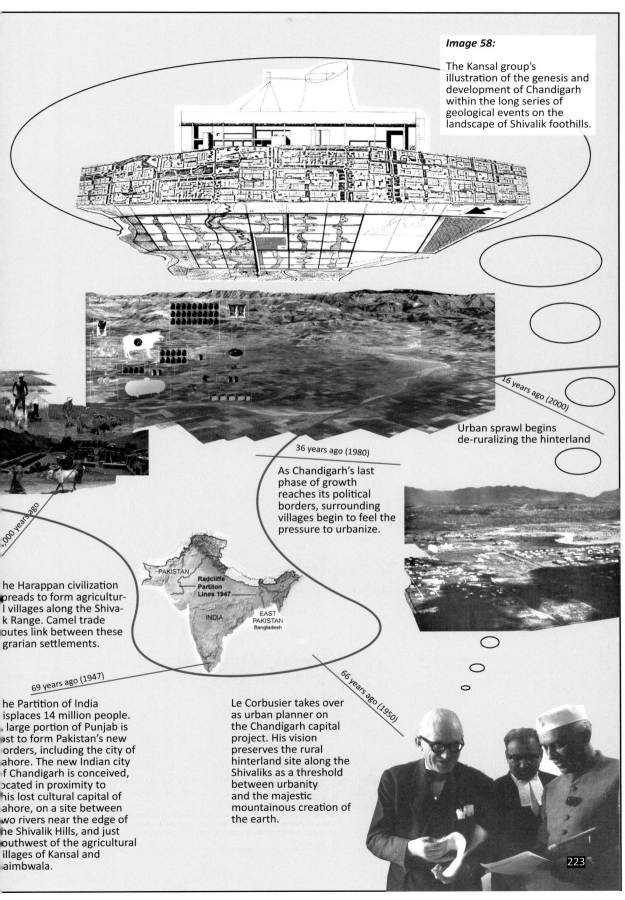

Image 58:

The Kansal group's illustration of the genesis and development of Chandigarh within the long series of geological events on the landscape of Shivalik foothills.

16 years ago (2000)

Urban sprawl begins de-ruralizing the hinterland

36 years ago (1980)

As Chandigarh's last phase of growth reaches its political borders, surrounding villages begin to feel the pressure to urbanize.

River Buffalo - Murrah Dairy Breed Systema De Breed

4,000 years ago

he Harappan civilization preads to form agricultur-l villages along the Shiva-k Range. Camel trade outes link between these grarian settlements.

PAKISTAN
Radcliffe Partiton Lines 1947
INDIA
EAST PAKISTAN
Bangladesh

69 years ago (1947)

he Partition of India isplaces 14 million people. large portion of Punjab is st to form Pakistan's new orders, including the city of ahore. The new Indian city f Chandigarh is conceived, ocated in proximity to his lost cultural capital of ahore, on a site between wo rivers near the edge of he Shivalik Hills, and just outhwest of the agricultural illages of Kansal and aimbwala.

66 years ago (1950)

Le Corbusier takes over as urban planner on the Chandigarh capital project. His vision preserves the rural hinterland site along the Shivaliks as a threshold between urbanity and the majestic mountainous creation of the earth.

223

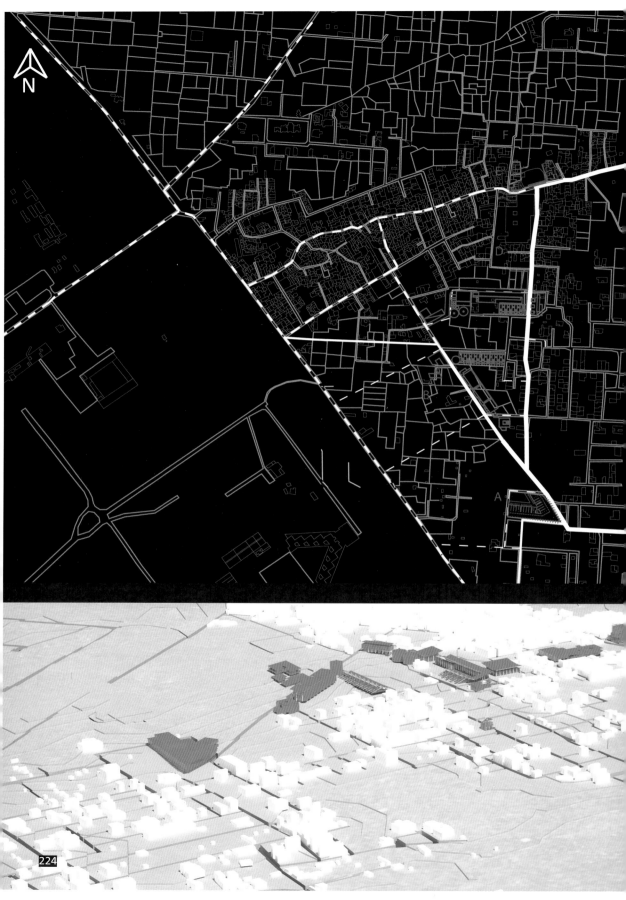

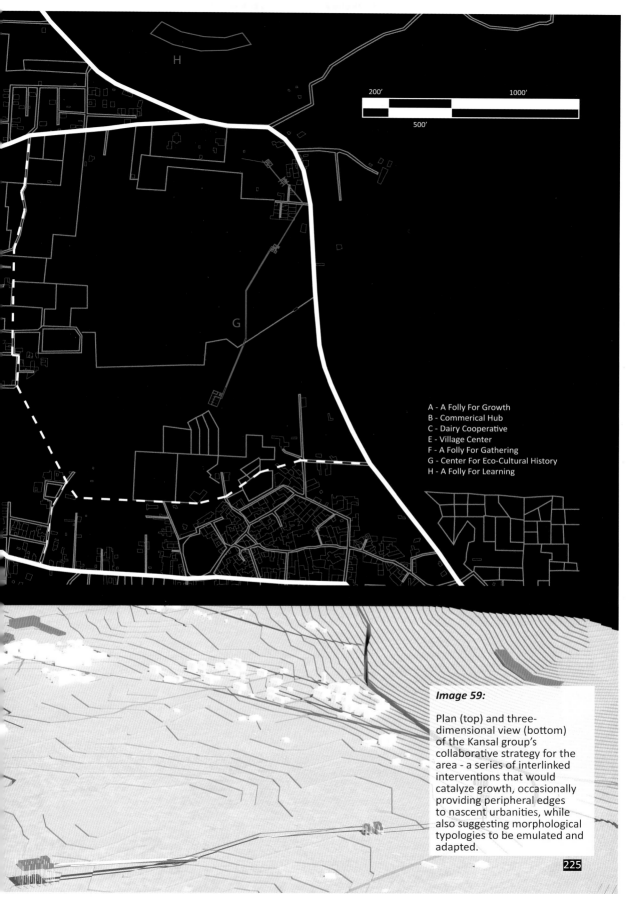

H

200'   1000'

500'

G

A - A Folly For Growth
B - Commerical Hub
C - Dairy Cooperative
E - Village Center
F - A Folly For Gathering
G - Center For Eco-Cultural History
H - A Folly For Learning

Image 59:

Plan (top) and three-dimensional view (bottom) of the Kansal group's collaborative strategy for the area - a series of interlinked interventions that would catalyze growth, occasionally providing peripheral edges to nascent urbanities, while also suggesting morphological typologies to be emulated and adapted.

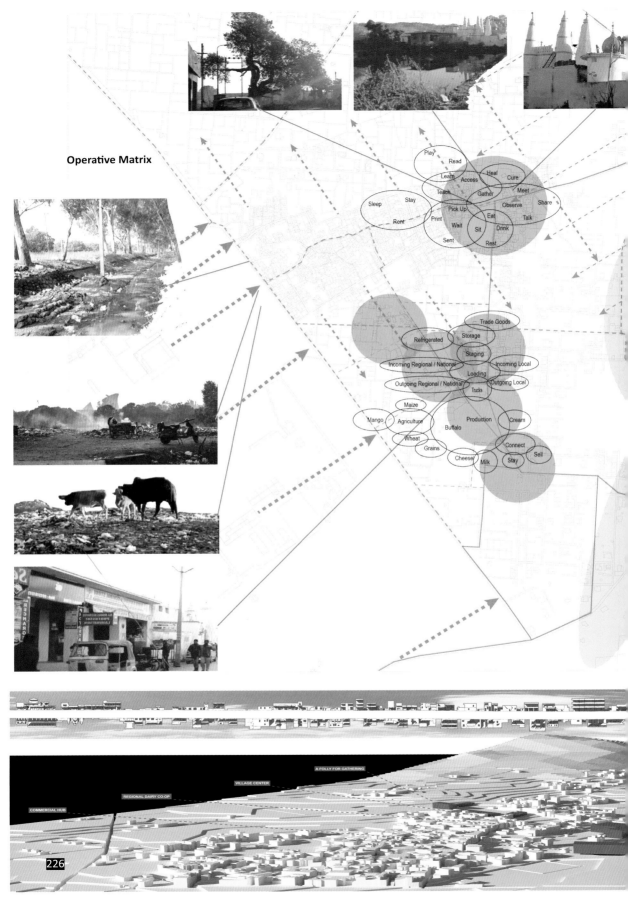

Operative Matrix

Play
Read
Learn
Access
Heal
Cure
Teach
Gather
Meet
Sleep
Stay
Observe
Share
Pick Up
Eat
Talk
Rent
Print
Wait
Sit
Drink
Sent
Rest

Trade Goods
Storage
Refrigerated
Staging
Incoming Regional / National
Incoming Local
Loading
Outgoing Regional / National
Outgoing Local
Trucks
Maize
Production
Cream
Mango
Agriculture
Buffalo
Wheat
Connect
Grains
Cheese
Milk
Stay
Sell

COMMERCIAL HUB
REGIONAL DAIRY CO-OP
VILLAGE CENTER
A FOLLY FOR GATHERING

226

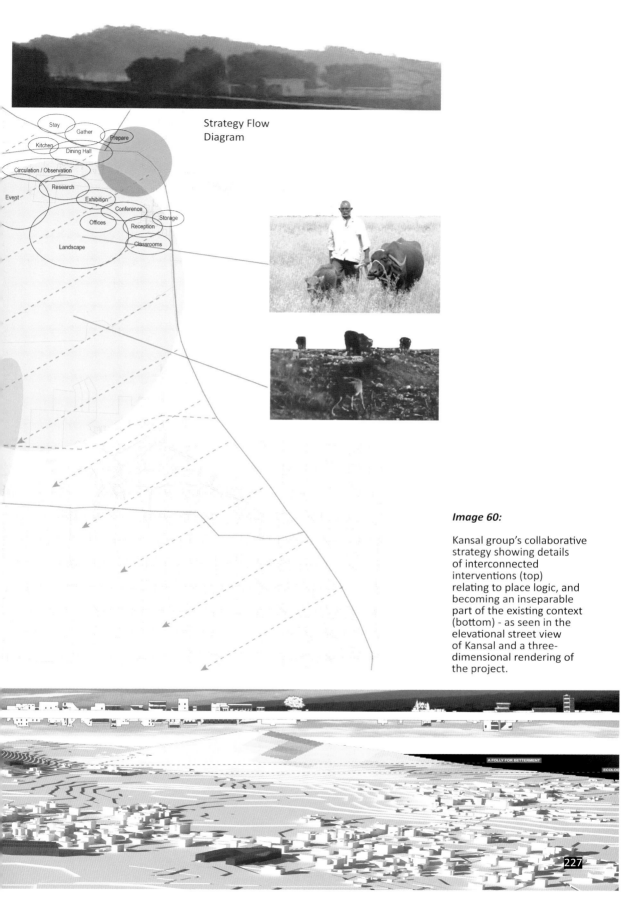

Strategy Flow
Diagram

Stay
Gather
Prepare
Kitchen
Dining Hall
Circulation / Observation
Research
Event
Exhibition
Conference
Offices
Storage
Reception
Landscape
Classrooms

Image 60:

Kansal group's collaborative
strategy showing details
of interconnected
interventions (top)
relating to place logic, and
becoming an inseparable
part of the existing context
(bottom) - as seen in the
elevational street view
of Kansal and a three-
dimensional rendering of
the project.

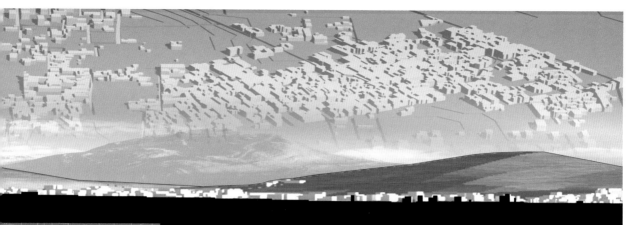

Image 61:

Kansal's landscape following interventions by Richard O. VanDerWal, Jessica R. Yester, Christopher W. Doerner, Nicholas Bree, Anna Czajkowska-Szot & Dominic M. Quinan (top), changing land-use as the the group visualizes the 'phased' addition of building interventions (bottom).

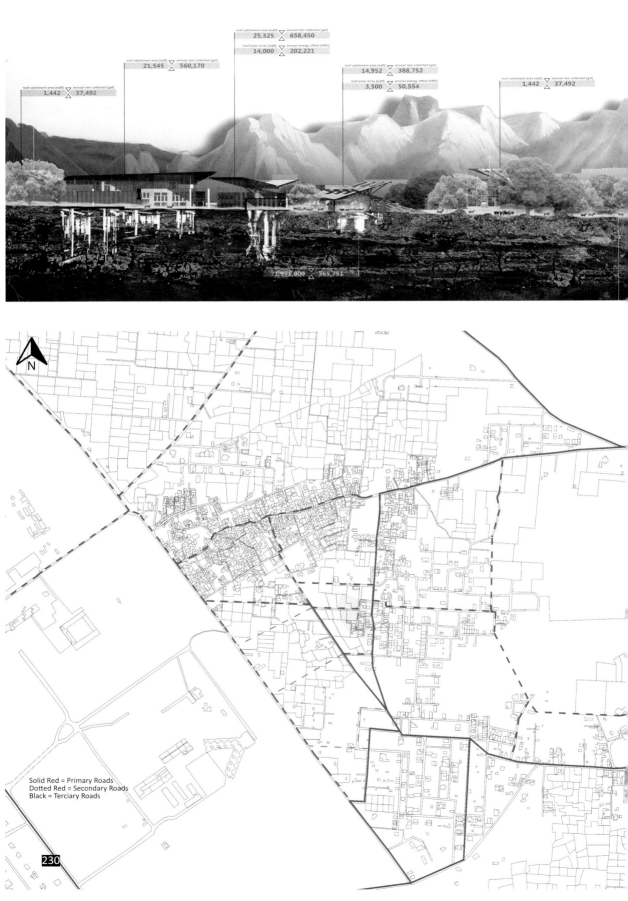

roof catchment area [sqft]
1,442   annual rain collected [gal] 37,492

roof catchment area [sqft]
21,545   annual rain collected [gal] 560,170

roof catchment area [sqft]
25,325   annual rain collected [gal] 658,450

roof solar array [sqft]
14,000   annual energy offset [kWh] 202,221

roof catchment area [sqft]
14,952   annual rain collected [gal] 388,752

roof solar array [sqft]
3,500   annual energy offset [kWh] 50,554

roof catchment area [sqft]
1,442   annual rain collected [gal] 37,492

1,971,000   365,751

Solid Red = Primary Roads
Dotted Red = Secondary Roads
Black = Terciary Roads

roof catchment area [sqft]   annual rain collected [gal]
  29,904   777,504

roof solar array [sqft]   annual energy offset [kWh]
  7,000   101,108

roof catchment area [sqft]   annual rain collected [gal]
  26,732   695,032

roof solar array [sqft]   annual energy offset [kWh]
  26,000   375,554

annual kwhare draw [tot]   annual energy offset [kWh]
3,942,000   751,502

Image 62:

Richard O. VanDerWal's dairy research and production center connected to Kansal's landscape via low, horizontal buildings that are flexible in plan, logical in their cumulative apparatus, and environmentally sustainable devices that encourage energy saving and water harvesting (top), and nodal points/linkages within the Kansal group's collective strategy (bottom).

200'   1000'
   500'

roof catchment area [sqft] ▽ annual rain collected [gal]
25,325 ✕ 658,450

roof solar array [sqft] ▽ annual energy offset [kWh]
14,000 ✕ 202,221

roof catchment area [sqft] ▽ annual rain collected [gal]
21,545 ✕ 560,170

roof catchment area [sqft] ▽ annual rain collected [gal]
1,442 ✕ 37,492

annual manure draw [lbs] ▽ annual ene
1,971,000 ✕ 365,

Image 63:

Richard O. VanDerWal's dairy research and production center is closely attached to Kansal's landscape, while also serving as an ideal site for the Murrah Dairy Breed buffalo. VanDerWal's project visualized the Murrah buffalo as critical to the village economy, as interwoven within the socio-cultural beliefs of the region, and examined a holistic network of places within and outside the settlement especially designed for the buffalo herds as they would move through its landscape at different times of the day and through the seasons.

chment area [sqft] annual rain collected [gal]
14,952 388,752

solar array [sqft] annual energy offset [kWh]
3,500 50,554

roof catchment area [sqft] annual rain collected [gal]
1,442 37,492

ground recharge area [sqft] annual rain collected [gal]
1,000,000 26,000,000

roof catchment area [sqft] ▽ annual rain collected [gal]
29,904 △ 777,504

roof solar array [sqft] ▽ annual energy offset [kWh]
7,000 △ 101,108

annual manure draw [lbs] ▽ annual energy offset [kWh]
3,942,000 △ 731,502

roof catchment area [sqft] ▽ annual rain collected [gal]
26,732 △ 695,032

roof solar array [sqft] ▽ annual energy offset [kWh]
26,000 △ 375,554

Image 64:

Richard O. VanDerWal's Dairy Research and Production Center and its public interface (right of drawing), effectively linking the agrarian environment to the urban world beyond - where the world of the village is no longer obscure, but rather a 'sustainable model' to be emulated by the growing city.

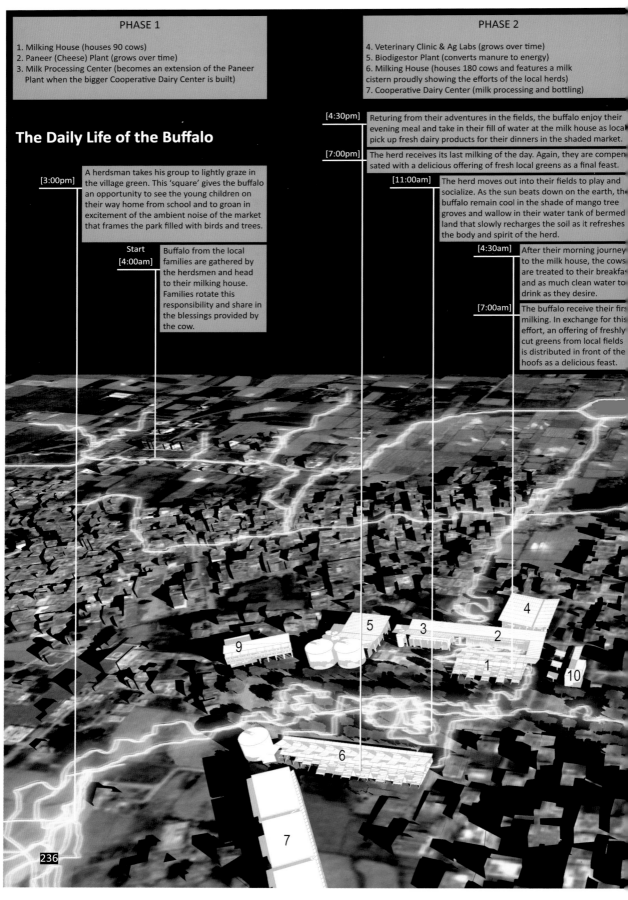

The Daily Life of the Buffalo

PHASE 1

1. Milking House (houses 90 cows)
2. Paneer (Cheese) Plant (grows over time)
3. Milk Processing Center (becomes an extension of the Paneer Plant when the bigger Cooperative Dairy Center is built)

PHASE 2

4. Veterinary Clinic & Ag Labs (grows over time)
5. Biodigestor Plant (converts manure to energy)
6. Milking House (houses 180 cows and features a milk cistern proudly showing the efforts of the local herds)
7. Cooperative Dairy Center (milk processing and bottling)

[3:00pm] A herdsman takes his group to lightly graze in the village green. This 'square' gives the buffalo an opportunity to see the young children on their way home from school and to groan in excitement of the ambient noise of the market that frames the park filled with birds and trees.

Start [4:00am] Buffalo from the local families are gathered by the herdsmen and head to their milking house. Families rotate this responsibility and share in the blessings provided by the cow.

[4:30pm] Returing from their adventures in the fields, the buffalo enjoy their evening meal and take in their fill of water at the milk house as local pick up fresh dairy products for their dinners in the shaded market.

[7:00pm] The herd receives its last milking of the day. Again, they are compensated with a delicious offering of fresh local greens as a final feast.

[11:00am] The herd moves out into their fields to play and socialize. As the sun beats down on the earth, the buffalo remain cool in the shade of mango tree groves and wallow in their water tank of bermed land that slowly recharges the soil as it refreshes the body and spirit of the herd.

[4:30am] After their morning journey to the milk house, the cows are treated to their breakfast and as much clean water to drink as they desire.

[7:00am] The buffalo receive their first milking. In exchange for this effort, an offering of freshly cut greens from local fields is distributed in front of the hoofs as a delicious feast.

7. Cooperative Dairy Center (artisan sweets and icecream
workshops with commercial space along street and worker
housing above)
8. Towers of Shadows (lookouts along the landscape towards Chandigath and the
Shivaliks)
9. Trucker Lodging (also provides room for storing lorries)
10. Bus Terminal (migrant worker / tourist arrival)
11. Temple (supplements existing religious cremation area)

[1:00pm] The buffalo now lie in the large shade of the mango groves and take a long afternoon nap. While his herd rests, the shepherd takes refuge from the hot midday sun in a tower of shadows that sits on the highest point of the pasture. He smokes his pipe and meditates on the beauty of the landscape and the strength of the herd. His apprentice plays the flute as they gaze upon the foothills of the Himalaya mountains and back to the beautiful city of Chandigarh.

End [8:00pm] The cows return to their families and bask in the appreciation that awaits them. Gratitude for their hard work and their humble mediation between man and the land.

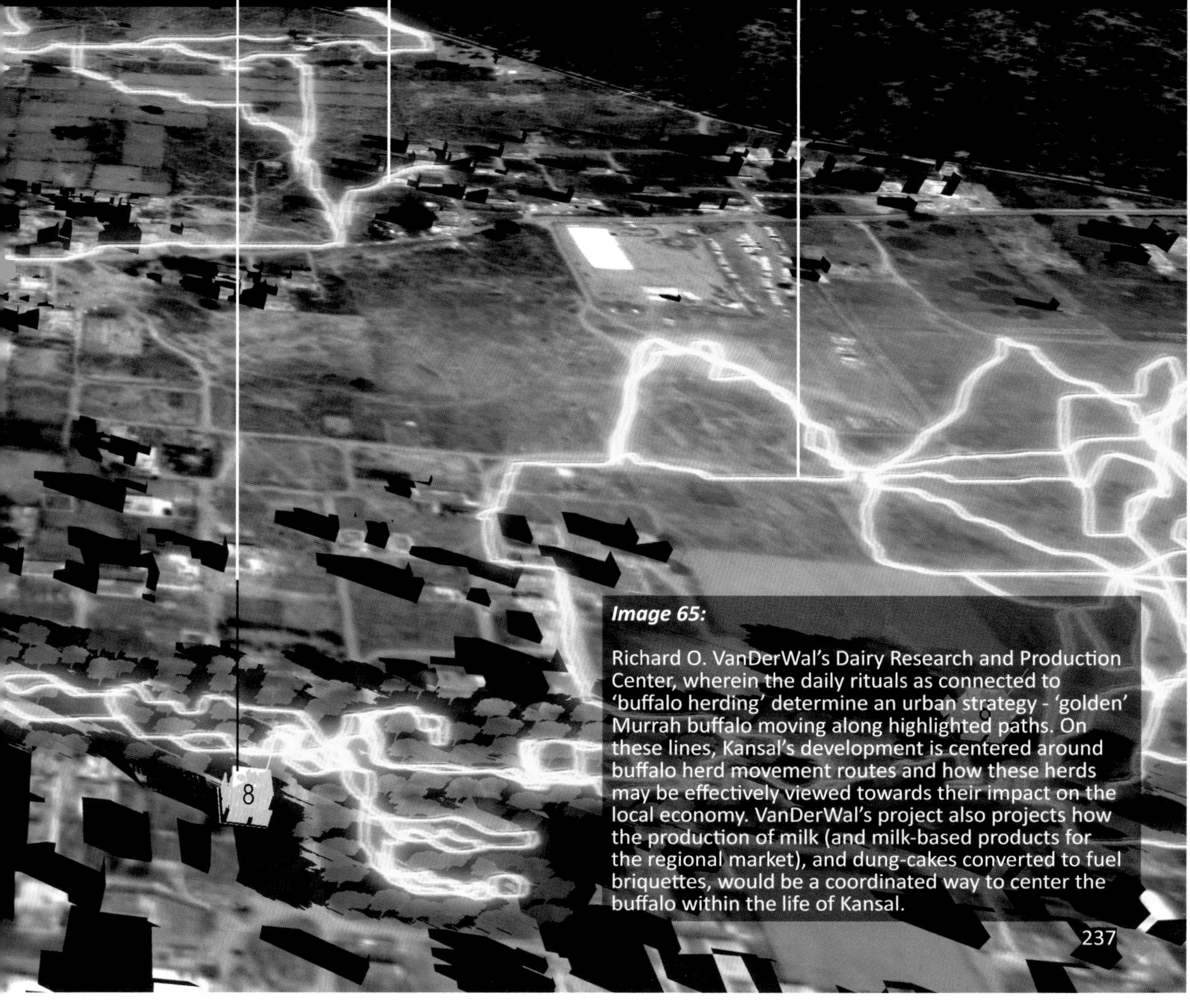

[3:00pm] As his colleague takes part of the herd to the village green, the herdsman follows his group as they head out onto the historical pasture land. Vibrant with life and soil, the land also features an eco-cultural hub perched over the memory of the seasonal river that used to meander through. The river has been restored as a series of silt ponds that slowly percolate rain into the water table while capturing precious minerals in their basins used for growing crops for both people and buffalo.

8

Image 65:

Richard O. VanDerWal's Dairy Research and Production Center, wherein the daily rituals as connected to 'buffalo herding' determine an urban strategy - 'golden' Murrah buffalo moving along highlighted paths. On these lines, Kansal's development is centered around buffalo herd movement routes and how these herds may be effectively viewed towards their impact on the local economy. VanDerWal's project also projects how the production of milk (and milk-based products for the regional market), and dung-cakes converted to fuel briquettes, would be a coordinated way to center the buffalo within the life of Kansal.

Image 66:

Richard O. VanDerWal's Dairy Research and Production Center seen along the the major, future linkage spine of Kansal.

Image 67:

Generous resting enclosures for Kansal's golden Murrah buffalo herds as they finally arrive at the Dairy Center after a day of choreographed 'herding' through the village settlement.

Image 68:

Enclosure sheds at Richard O. VanDerWal's 'Dairy Cooperative Center' at Kansal where the golden Murrah buffalos are kept - their 'participation' in the process of creating a 'sustainable' rural environment serving as a model for other villages in and around Chandigarh.

242

Image 69:

Anna Czajkowska-Szot's 'Village Center' at Kansal seeks the centrality of the existing Kansal village pond to create a site for itself. Situated at the edges of this water body, its modest architecture includes lighter 'filigree' and heavier 'mass' elements to create a public building that serves as one face of a larger urban space that extends around the water. The Village Center is sited with the goal that its extensions would validate this as the nodal site for a bigger, denser settlement in the future.

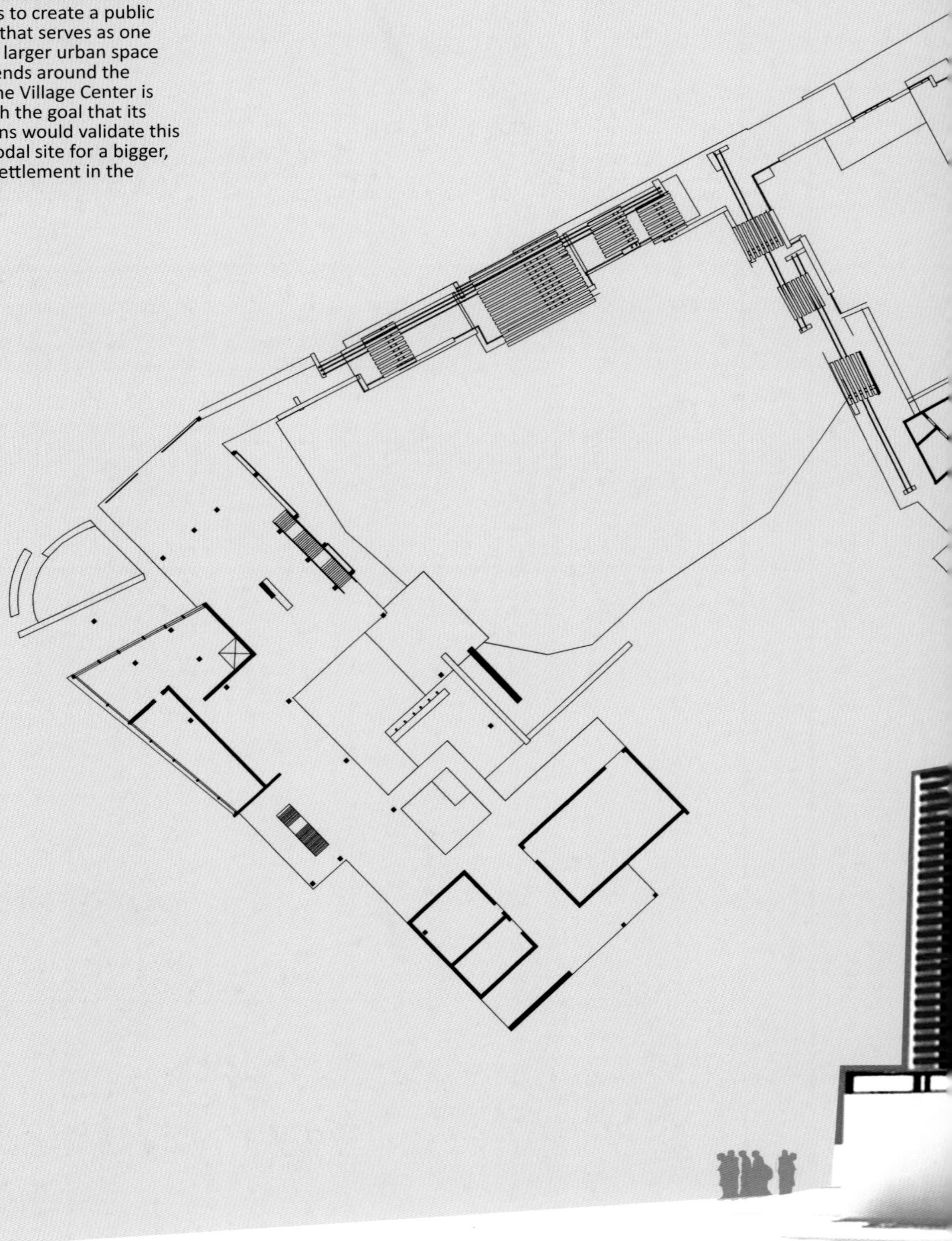

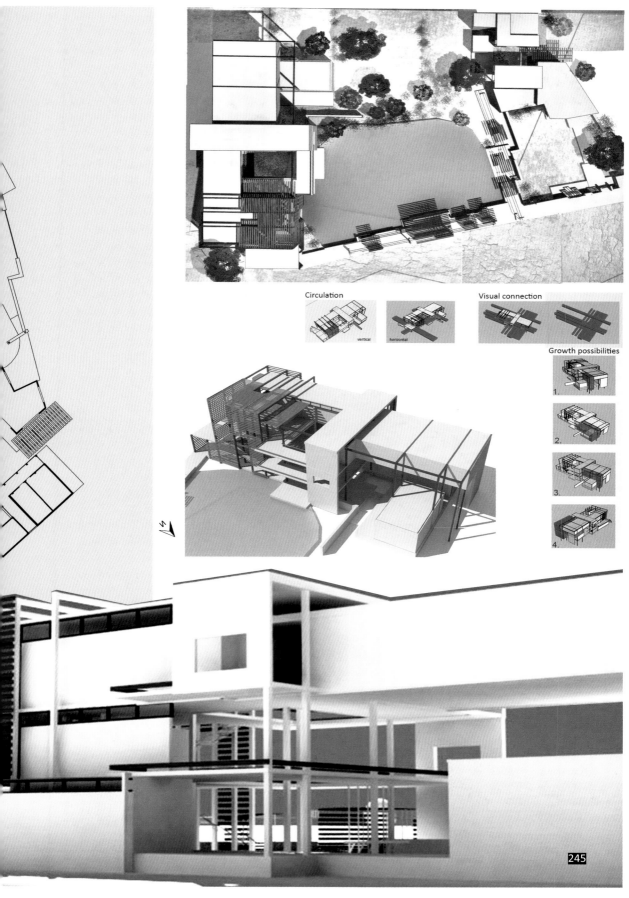

Circulation

vertical horizontal

Visual connection

Growth possibilities

1.

2.

3.

4.

Image 70:

The proximity of Szot's Village Center to the existing Kansal temple, sacred tree and mosque is important, since it helps create an agglomeration of public buildings and spaces at the end of Kansal's main street, oriented toward a large open space that may be used for public celebrations, the Shivalik foothills, and a path turning eastwards towards Kansal's now-dwindling agricultural land.

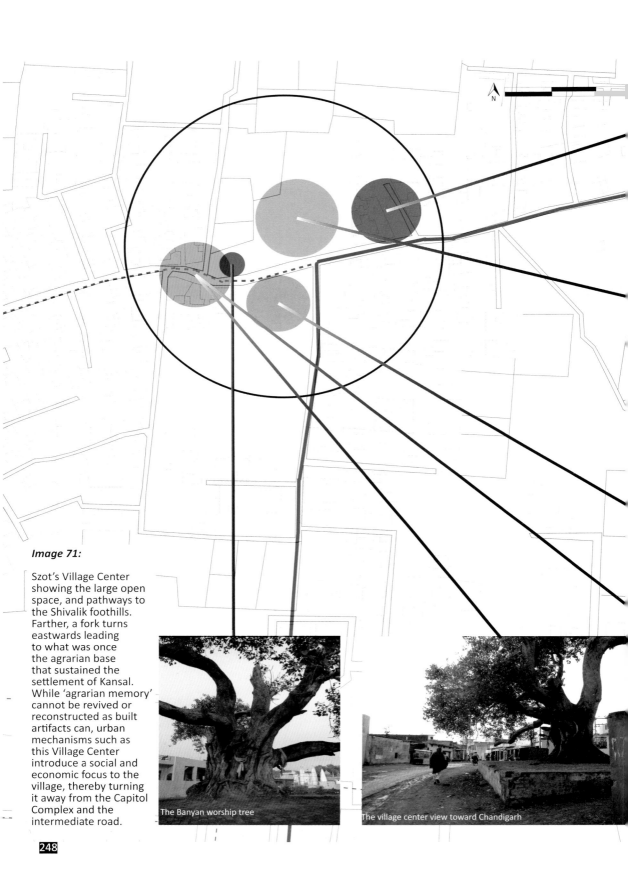

Image 71:

Szot's Village Center showing the large open space, and pathways to the Shivalik foothills. Farther, a fork turns eastwards leading to what was once the agrarian base that sustained the settlement of Kansal. While 'agrarian memory' cannot be revived or reconstructed as built artifacts can, urban mechanisms such as this Village Center introduce a social and economic focus to the village, thereby turning it away from the Capitol Complex and the intermediate road.

The Banyan worship tree

The village center view toward Chandigarh

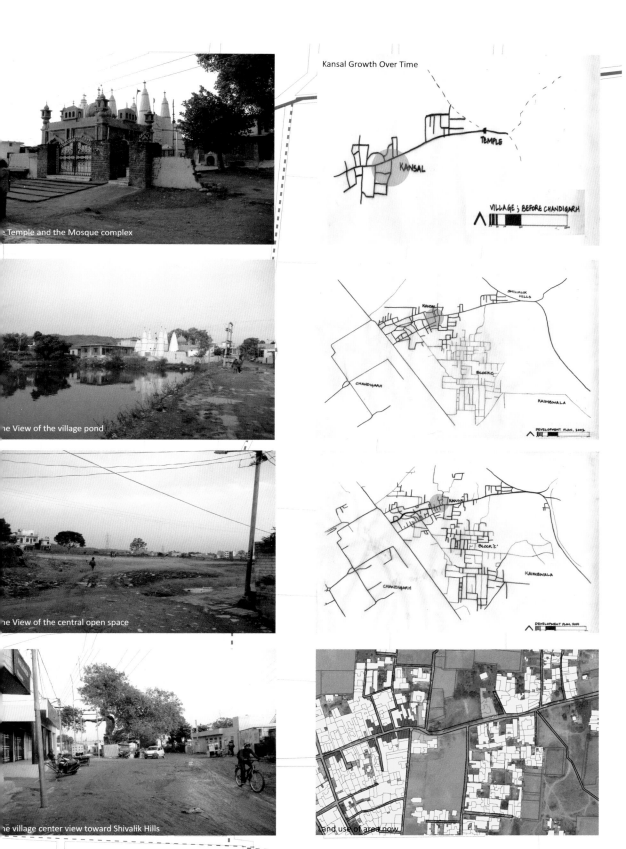

Temple and the Mosque complex

Kansal Growth Over Time

KANSAL

TEMPLE

VILLAGE ; BEFORE CHANDIGARH

View of the village pond

DEVELOPMENT PLAN, 2002

View of the central open space

DEVELOPMENT PLAN, 2004

village center view toward Shivalik Hills

Land use of area now

Place Description   249

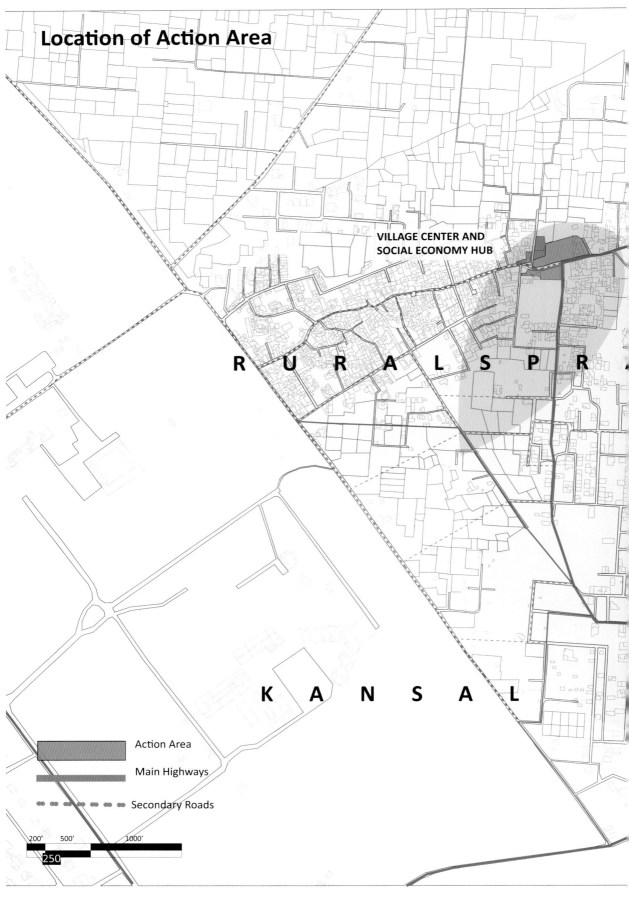

Location of Action Area

VILLAGE CENTER AND
SOCIAL ECONOMY HUB

R U R A L S P R A

K A N S A L

Action Area

Main Highways

Secondary Roads

200'   500'   1000'

250

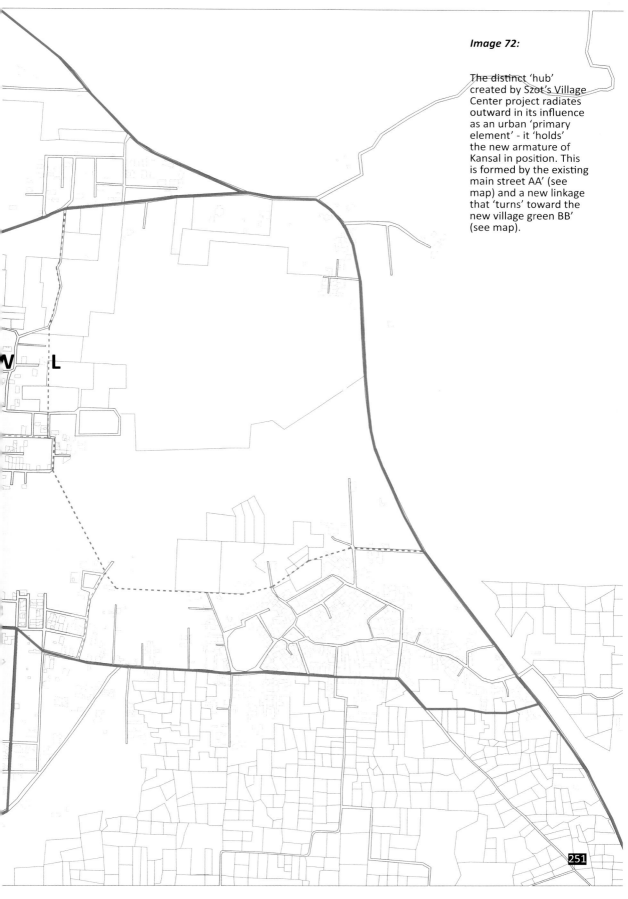

Image 72:

The distinct 'hub' created by Szot's Village Center project radiates outward in its influence as an urban 'primary element' - it 'holds' the new armature of Kansal in position. This is formed by the existing main street AA' (see map) and a new linkage that 'turns' toward the new village green BB' (see map).

W   L

Kansal: Folly Context Map

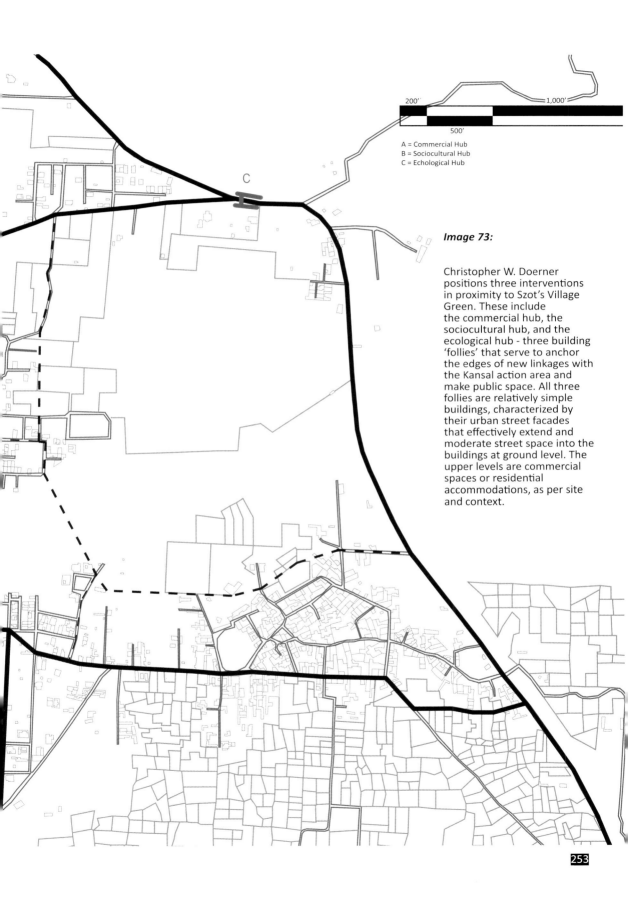

200'' 1,000'
500'

A = Commercial Hub
B = Sociocultural Hub
C = Echological Hub

C

Image 73:

Christopher W. Doerner
positions three interventions
in proximity to Szot's Village
Green. These include
the commercial hub, the
sociocultural hub, and the
ecological hub - three building
'follies' that serve to anchor
the edges of new linkages with
the Kansal action area and
make public space. All three
follies are relatively simple
buildings, characterized by
their urban street facades
that effectively extend and
moderate street space into the
buildings at ground level. The
upper levels are commercial
spaces or residential
accommodations, as per site
and context.

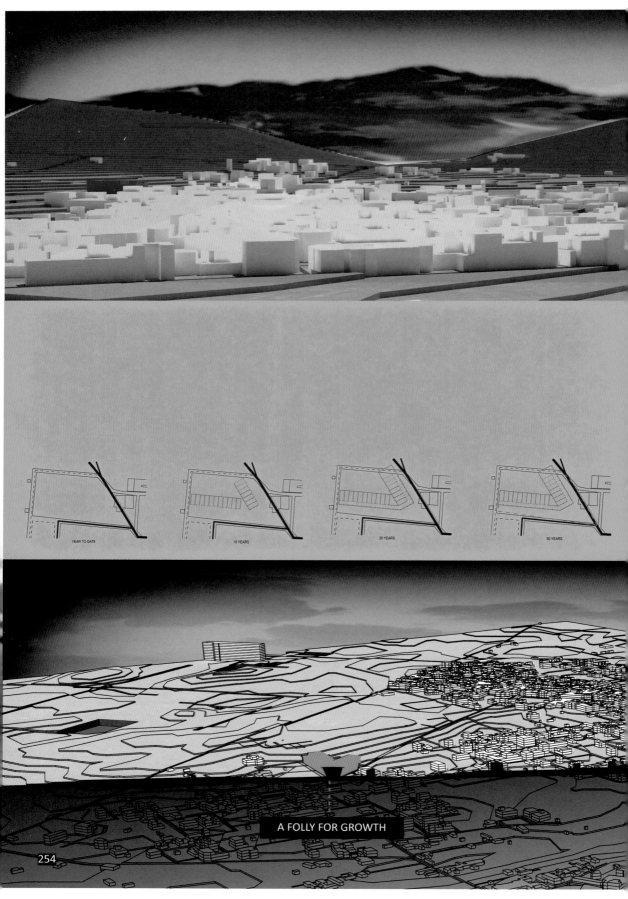

YEAR TO DATE   10 YEARS   20 YEARS   50 YEARS

A FOLLY FOR GROWTH

Image 74:

Christopher W. Doerner's three interventions are not mere ornamentations on the emerging streetscape at Kansal (as the term folly would imply). Instead, each of these emerge from the landscape, as a 'kit of parts' that adapts to the repositioning of the area. These follies also grow in time - the 'basic structure' covered with a skin as time progresses.

A FOLLY FOR GATHERING

A FOLLY FOR LEARNING

Commercial Hub:
A Folly for Growth

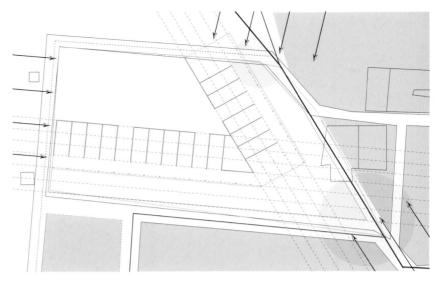

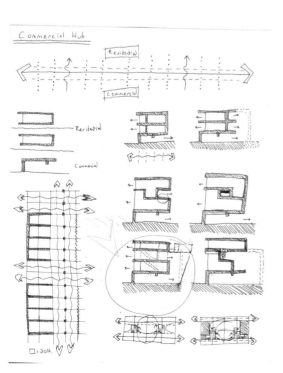

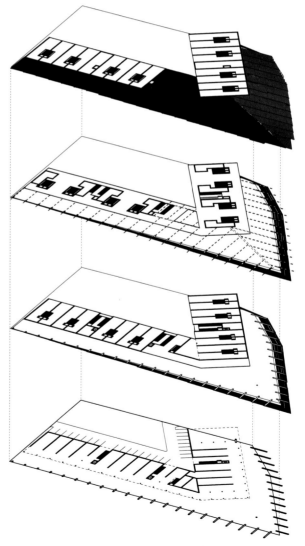

Image 75:

The 'Commercial Hub' folly envisaged change over time. It would begin as a housing (dorm) for the laborers and workers that would be constructing the various interventions. Once the large scale developments were complete, residential spaces would be moved to the first floor as the ground level spaces would supplement the commercial fabric of the hub. Over time, an additional floor of residences will be added, in addition to a shading device (screen and canopy) that would shield the mandi (market) from the hot summer.

With a view to layer functions, the project minimized non-billable spaces on the residential floors while embracing the densely -populated sidewalks within the relatively shaded spaces created beneath the cantilevered canopy. A fourth level was also conceived between the two residential levels. This level would act as the circulation space connecting all of the large residences. It would also provide for additional small residences and a series of neighborhood spaces where clusters of residences sharing an interior-exterior condition for both recreational and social use would interact.

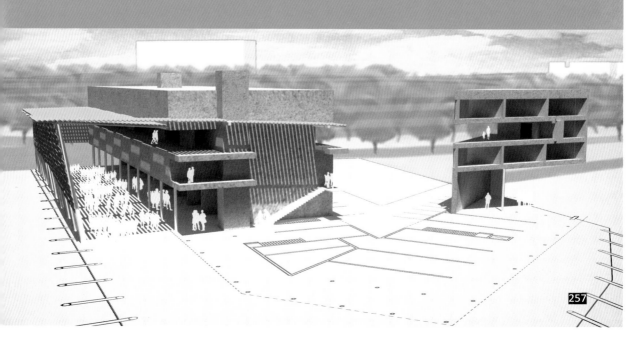

Kansal: Folly: Commercial Hub

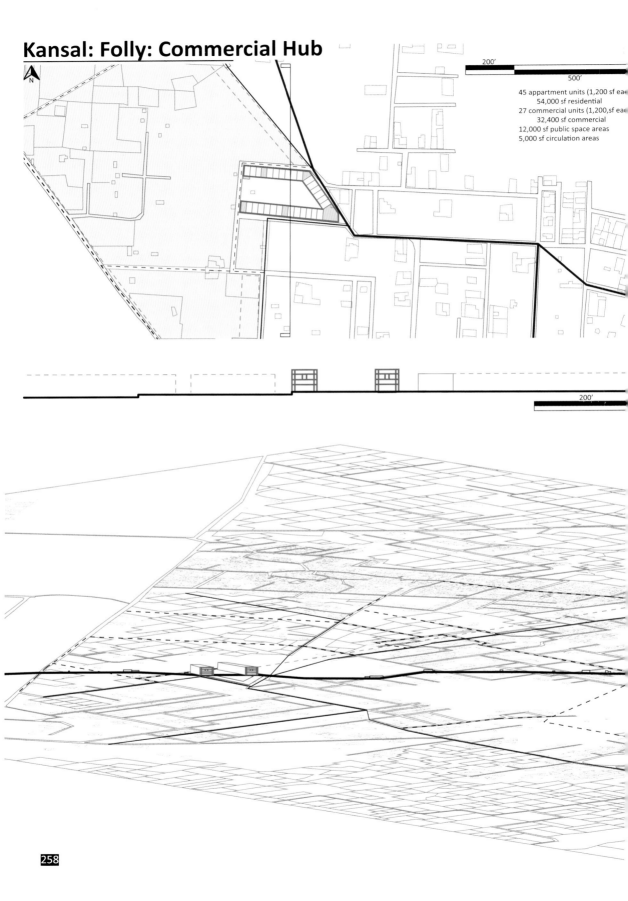

45 appartment units (1,200 sf ea
54,000 sf residential
27 commercial units (1,200,sf ea
32,400 sf commercial
12,000 sf public space areas
5,000 sf circulation areas

200'

500'

200'

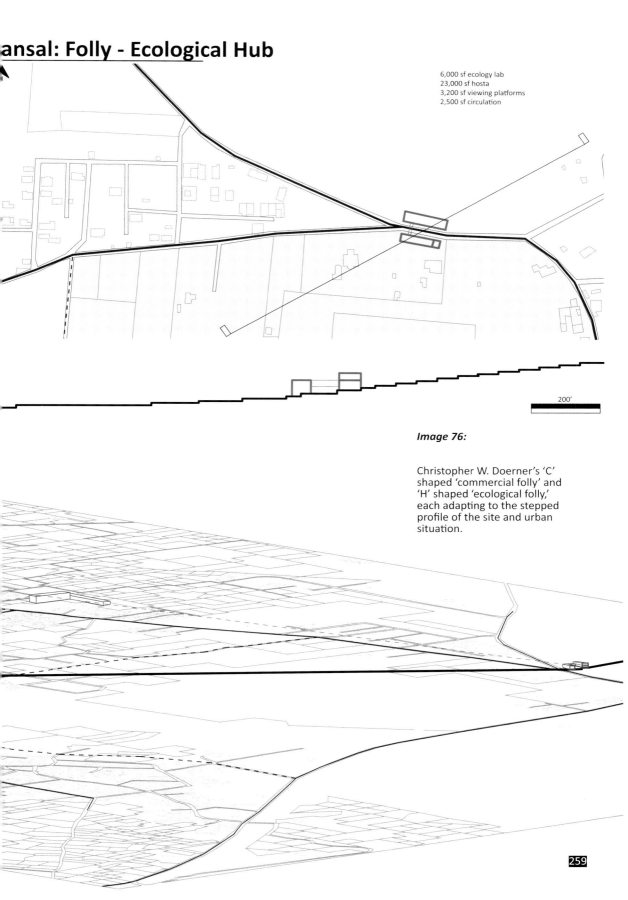

6,000 sf ecology lab
23,000 sf hosta
3,200 sf viewing platforms
2,500 sf circulation

200'

Image 76:

Christopher W. Doerner's 'C' shaped 'commercial folly' and 'H' shaped 'ecological folly,' each adapting to the stepped profile of the site and urban situation.

Image 77:

Left: Collaged view of the 'public space' that is accessible on the lower floor of the three Doerner follies
Right: Rendering to show scale of the facades of one of the follies and how these faces bias urban space at Kansal.

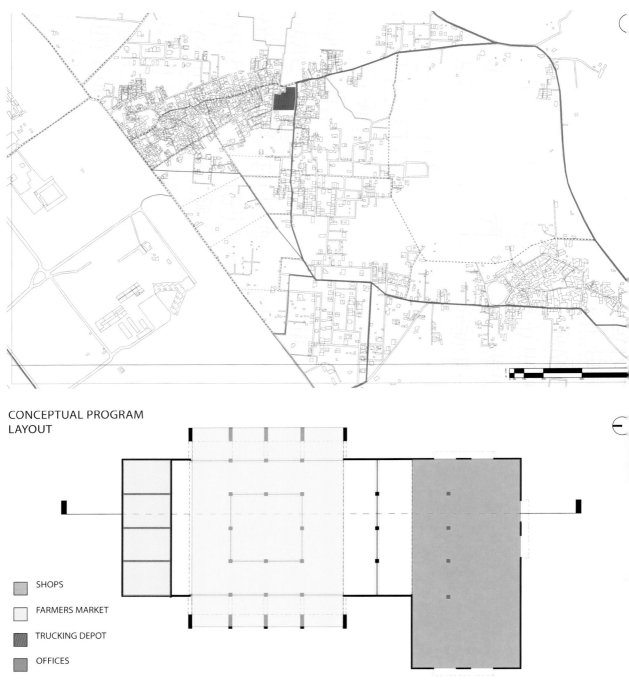

CONCEPTUAL PROGRAM LAYOUT

- SHOPS
- FARMERS MARKET
- TRUCKING DEPOT
- OFFICES

Image 78:

Dominic M. Quinan's centrally located 'Farmer's Market' at Kansal, in close proximity to Doerner's follies and opposite Szot's Village Center. Given that the Kansal action area is visualized as an agricultural hub for cash crops (fruits and vegetables for local area consumption), Quinan also adds a trucking depot to the Farmer's Market, in addition to an administrative center. In time, it is expected that this market would grow, both horizontally and vertically.

1"=16'

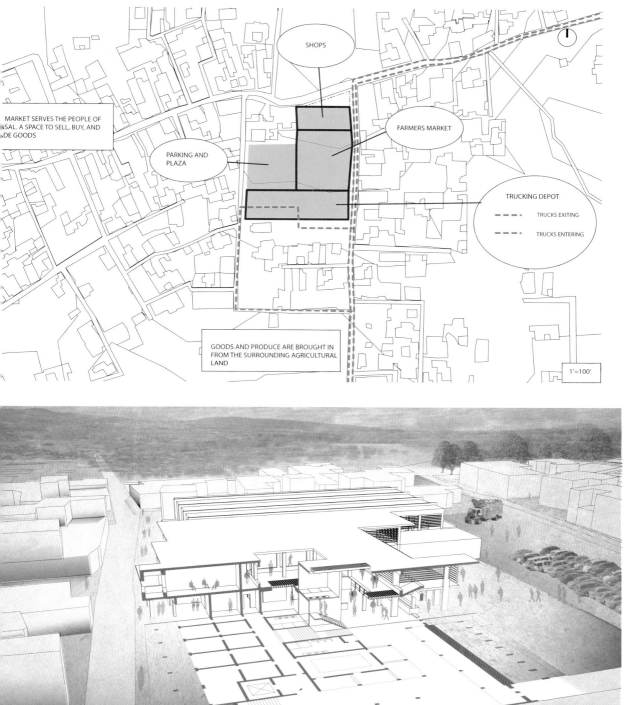

SHOPS

FARMERS MARKET

MARKET SERVES THE PEOPLE OF
SAL. A SPACE TO SELL, BUY, AND
DE GOODS

PARKING AND
PLAZA

TRUCKING DEPOT

- - - - TRUCKS EXITING

- - - - TRUCKS ENTERING

GOODS AND PRODUCE ARE BROUGHT IN
FROM THE SURROUNDING AGRICULTURAL
LAND

1'=100'

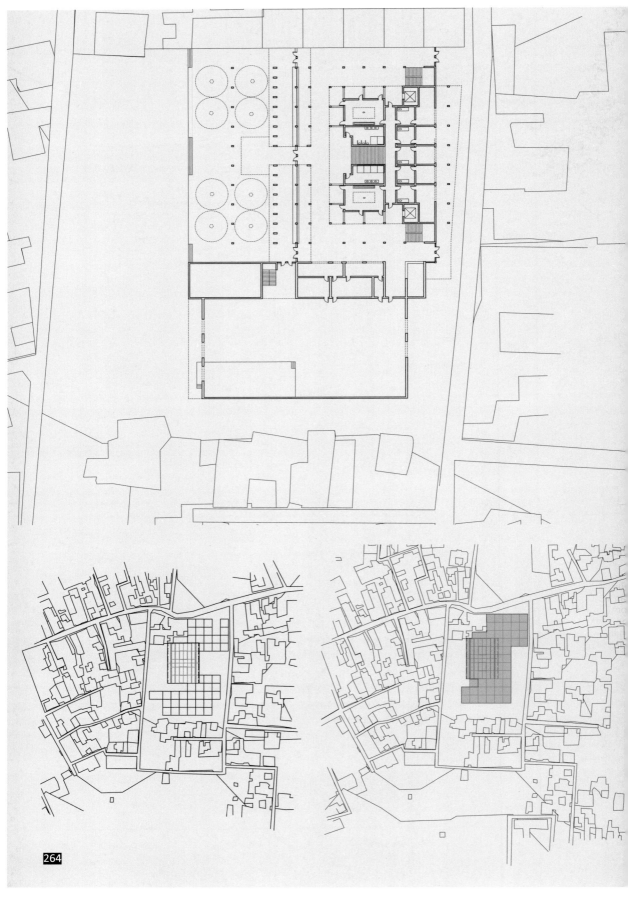

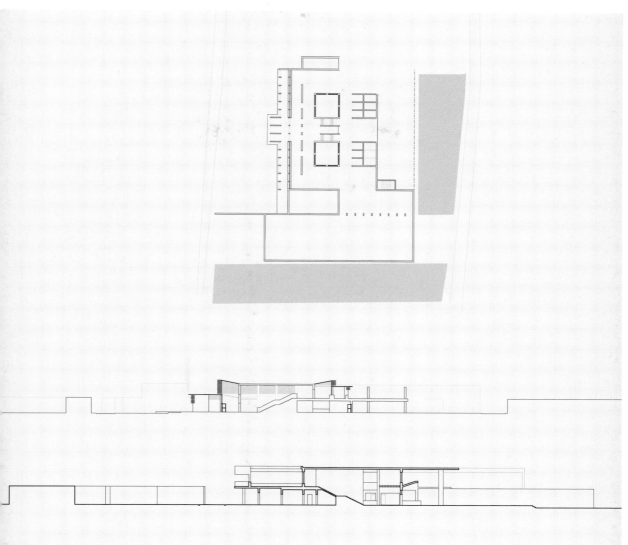

mage 79:

quinan's Farmer's Market at
ansal expanding horizontally,
ombining a formal building at
he core with informal additions
n its sides, while containing
ublic space in its interior.

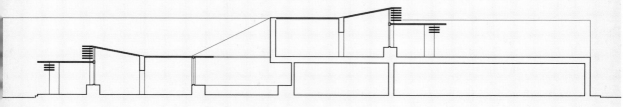

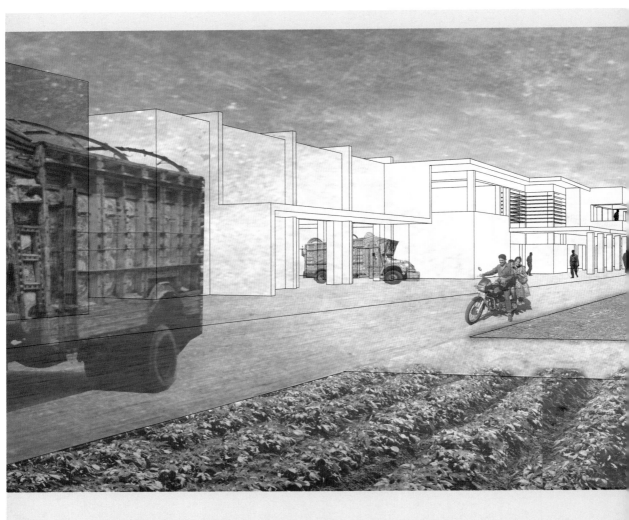

Image 80:

The urban atmosphere created by Quinan's Farmer's Market, Doerner's follies, and Szot's Village Center, exaggerated by the axis created by VanDerWal's Dairy Cooperative Center and Nick Bree's Commercial Center.

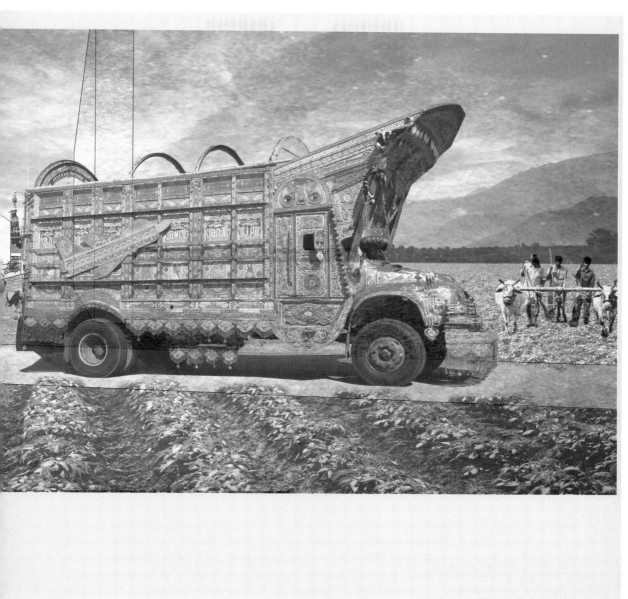

Creating a Commercial Corridor

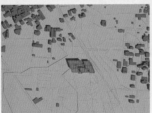

SITE CONTEXT PLAN

GROUND FLOOR SHOPS
(LARGE UNITS)

LEVEL 2 SHOPS
(MEDIUM UNITS)

LEVEL 3 SHOPS
(SMALL UNITS)

PATH OF THE MERCHANT

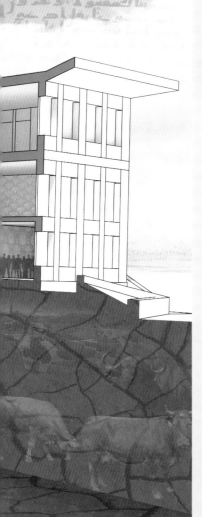

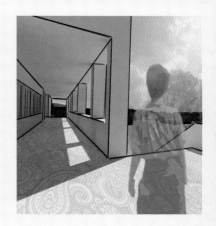

Image 81:

Nick Bree's Commercial Center conceived in close proximity to VanDerWal's Dairy Cooperative Center - an active urban environment resembling the streets and squares of the traditional Indian city, extendible vertically and horizontally. Bree also visualizes how this 'commercial center' belongs much to Kansal in its evocative spirit and language; it is simple placed on an elevated plinth in the midst of the paths of the golden Murrah buffalo herds.

Image 82:

Jessica R. Yester's Center For Eco-Cultural History captures the history of Kansal's past and future 'sites,' as positioned within the seasonal flood plain of the now disappeared river that emerged from the Shivaliks. Perched atop a light scaffold, it spans across the contours of the undulating landscape, creating multiple stopping moments that allow reflection on Kansal's changing history and identity.

GALLERY

EVENTS

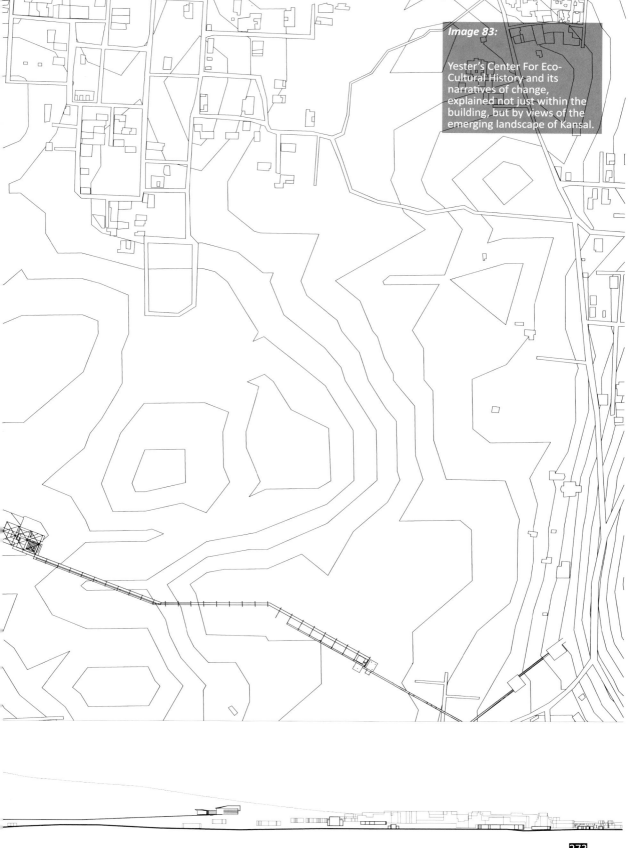

Image 83:

Yester's Center For Eco-Cultural History and its narratives of change, explained not just within the building, but by views of the emerging landscape of Kansal.

Image 84:

One of the stopping moments contained within the observation platform of Yester's Center For Eco-Cultural History.

Image 85:

Yester's Center For Eco-Cultural History and the re-visualization of riverine histories.

277

CONTRIBUTORS

SANGEETA BAGGA-MEHTA is an architect and urban designer with a special interest in the conservation of modern heritage ensembles. An alumnus of the Chandigarh College of Architecture-Chandigarh (CCA), and the School of Planning and Architecture-New Delhi, she received her PhD in Architecture from Punjab University-Chandigarh. She is currently Associate Professor at the CCA where she has conducted multiple collaborative student workshops with universities worldwide, including the Bezalel University of Art & Design (Israel), the Carnegie Mellon University, the University of Wisconsin-Milwaukee, and the Technical University at Delft (Netherlands). Her work and these collaborations are centered on the examination of urban landscapes, environmental design and social issues within Chandigarh. Her documentations of the rapid changes in Chandigarh's urbanity have been presented at international conferences both within India and globally. In recent years, she has worked with the Chandigarh Administration's Department of Tourism to develope Tourism Promotion Infrastructure, Facilitation, and Awareness Building projects vis-a-vis modern heritage ensembles in the city plan. She is also member of the Chandigarh Administration's Heritage Committee, a member of the INTACH, and ICOMOS - INDIA. Prof. Bagga-Mehta is consultant to the Official Dossier preparation of the Trans-national Serial Nomination of the Architectural Works of Le Corbusier to UNESCO proposing the buildings of Chandigarh's Capitol Complex for inscription.

VINAYAK BHARNE is a Los Angeles based urban design and city planning consultant. He is currently Adjunct Associate Professor of Urbanism at the Sol Price School of Public Policy at the University of Southern California (USC), Lecturer in Landscape Architecture and Heritage Conservation at the USC School of Architecture, and Associated Faculty at the USC Shinso Ito Center for Japanese Religions and Culture. His ongoing design and research work ranges from new towns, campuses, inner-city revitalization, resort-villages, and housing for corporate, private, and institutional clients; to urban regulations, policies, and strategic advising for government and non-government agencies in the United States, Canada, India, China, the United Arab Emirates, Panama, Kenya, and Mauritius. His books include *The Emerging Asian City: Concomitant Urbanities and Urbanisms* (Routledge, 2012), *Zen Spaces & Neon Places: Reflections on Japanese Architecture and Urbanism* (AR+D, 2013), and *Rediscovering the Hindu Temple* (Cambridge Scholars Publishing, 2012). A contributing editor of *Kyoto Journal* in Japan, contributing blogger for *Planetizen* in Los Angeles, and International Contributor to *My Liveable City* in India, he also serves on the Advisory Board of the international think-tank Global Urban Development and is on the Board of Directors of Pasadena Heritage, one of Southern California's oldest non-profit organizations.

ARPAN JOHARI is the founder and Principal Architect of AW Design, Ahmedabad, India. He has a B.Arch from School of Architecture – SCET, Surat, India and an MBA in Eco Business (Sustainability) from the University of Sheffield, UK. His PG dissertation featured a Green masterplan for Rolls Royce and was published by LSCM, Sheffield, UK, and was presented at NCHU Taiwan. Prior to setting up his firm, which has an international portfolio of projects, Johari worked with renowned global design practices like Building Design Partnership, Sheffield, UK, EPR Architects London - UK, and Burt Hill-USA (Ahmedabad Studio). He has keen interest in sustainability, transport design and Urbanism and regularly shares his thought process internationally through symposiums, lectures, and seminars. Cultivating sensitivity to urban landscape and social issues, his presentations are themed around thinking and rethinking of cities and he was invited by the South Asian Youth Council, Sri Lanka, to share views on Cities and Peace. He was also invited to speak at the 'Urban Edge Symposium' by UWM, USA. As a recognized professional and educator, his intervention as a jury and visiting faculty is sought by premier institutes like NID India and has been often involved in interaction with students on M.Arch and Construction management programs at CEPT, India. His practice distinguishes itself as being involved in a few of the first Indian Green Building Council (IGBC) certified buildings of Gujarat and has been advisor to the Bharuch Citizens Council for developing Bharuch-Ankleshwar as smart city on DMIC.

DONGSEI KIM is an architect, urbanist, and educator. He is Assistant Professor at the Department of Architecture at Korea University-Seoul (Korea). His current research focuses on understanding how nation-state borders influence bordering practices and spatial inclusion and exclusion across scales. His research on the Demilitarized Zone of Korea was recently exhibited in the Golden Lion Award winning Korean Pavilion at the 14th Venice Architecture Biennale. He has published articles in journals such as *Volume, Inflection*, and *Landscape Architecture Frontiers*, and in books such as *Crow's Eye View: The Korean Peninsula* and *The North Korean Atlas*. He has taught at Columbia University, Carleton University, RMIT University, Monash University, VUW, and Kyunghee University. He holds a Masters in Design Studies with highest distinction from Harvard University Graduate School of Design (GSD), and an MS in Architecture and Urban Design from Columbia University's Graduate School of Architecture, Planning and Preservation (GSAPP). Additionally, he holds a five-year professional B.Arch. (Hons) from the Victoria University of Wellington. He is currently completing his PhD at the University of Melbourne. He is a registered architect with the NZRAB and has been a full architect member of NZIA since 2007.

ARIJIT SEN is an architect and vernacular architecture historian who writes, teaches, and studies urban cultural landscapes. His research includes studies of South Asian immigrant landscapes in Northern California, New York, and Chicago. He has worked on post disaster reconstruction and community-based design in the Lower Ninth Ward, New Orleans and directed public history and cultural landscapes field schools in Milwaukee. Sen's academic and research background is in architectural history, social, cultural, and behavioral analysis of the built environment, and American cultural landscape studies. Currently an Associate Professor of Architecture at the University of Wisconsin-Milwaukee with an honorary appointment with the Department of Art History at the University of Wisconsin-Madison, Dr. Sen co-founded the multi campus Buildings-Landscapes-Cultures area of doctoral research. He has served as a fellow at various humanities centers such as the Center for 21st Century Studies, University of Wisconsin-Milwaukee, and the Center for Advanced Study, University of Minnesota. His grants include a Graham Foundation grant for a book project, a Research Grant Initiative award to study immigrant cultural landscapes, and two major Wisconsin Humanities Council grants for an architectural field school. In 2013, he received the American Association for State and Local History 2013 Award of Merit for that field school. Sen coedited *Landscapes of Mobility: Culture, Politics and Placemaking* (Ashgate Publishers, UK, 2013, Jennifer Johung coeditor) and *Making Place: Space and Embodiment in the City* (Indiana University Press, 2014, Lisa Silverman coeditor).

MANU P. SOBTI is currently Senior Lecturer at the School of Architecture, University of Queensland-Brisbane. He was Associate Professor in Buildings-Landscapes-Cultures (blc) at the School of Architecture & Urban Planning, UWM between 2006-16. His recent explorations have focused on the urban histories of early-medieval, Islamic cities along the Silk Road and the Indian Subcontinent, with specific reference to the complex, borderland geographies created by riverine landscapes. Within a trans-disciplinary examination of medieval Eurasian landscapes straddling the region's Amu Darya River, he is completing a manuscript entitled *The Sliver of the Oxus Borderland: Medieval Cultural Encounters between the Arabs and Persians* (expected completion Fall 2017). This unprecedented work on the historical, geo-politics of the Amu Darya, collates extensive fieldwork in libraries and repositories employing a host of Arabic, Persian, Russian, and Uzbek sources. The Oxus borderland is also the subject of his ongoing film documentary project entitled *Medieval Riverlogues* (90 minutes, intended for Public Television), which captures archival research with a re-drawn map series, state of the art computer-generated renderings and live footage on this Central Asian cultural crucible, suggesting provocative connections to our enduring questions on cultural 'indigeneities' and identities, sustainability and resources. Mapping and the spatial humanities also remain central to his work on Delhi, Chandigarh, Ahmedabad & Bhopal, documented in the completion of two forthcoming book manuscripts - the first titled *Space and Collective Identity in South Asia: Migration, Architecture and Urban Development* (under contract with I. B. Tauris Press, expected 2017); the second titled *Riverine Landscapes, Urbanity and Conflict: Narratives from East and West* (under contract with Ashgate Press, expected 2017).

Over Spring & Fall 2015, he was director of SARUP's prestigious Urban Edge Award and its related events. These included a Chandigarh Urban Design Studio (Spring 2015) - done collaboratively with the Chandigarh College of Architecture, two Urban Symposia in Spring & Fall 2015 that comprised 12 prolific urban thinkers, and an international Public-at-Large Seminar/Exhibition held at Chandigarh in Oct. 2015 - engaging urban legislators, media, and social thinkers.

STUDENT CONTRIBUTORS

Chandigarh City Center Studio - Hanna Rutkouskaya (2009-10) & Richard VanDerWal (2009-10), Chandigarh Urban Edge Studio 2015 - Badheri Group: Andreya S. Veintimilla, Michael J. Freund, James D. Ford, Sisco S. Hollard, Chao Thao & Hyrom Leon-Quartiez Stokes; Kansal Group: Richard O. VanDerWal, Jessica R. Yester, Christopher W. Doerner, Nicholas Bree, Anna Czajkowska-Szot & Dominic M. Quinan

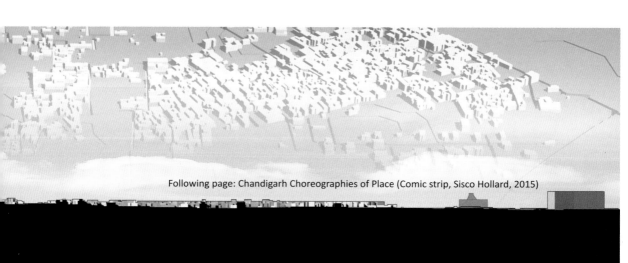

Following page: Chandigarh Choreographies of Place (Comic strip, Sisco Hollard, 2015)

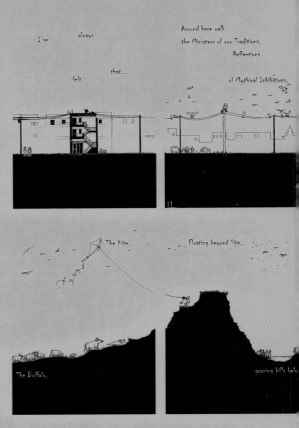

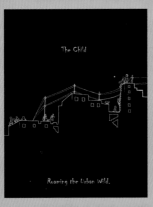